Covenants, Curses, and Courts:

A Manual of Freedom and

Self-Deliverance

Kerri Kidd Dill

Table Of Contents

Acknowledgements

I thank my wonderful husband Woody and my two beautiful children, Micah and Abby, for allowing me to spend countless hours in ministry and writing this book. Thank you to my wonderful parents Ron and Karen Kidd who brought me up to love Messiah Jesus and the Word of Yahweh God, and my sister and brother-in-law, Steve and Stephanie Moore for their love and support. Thank you to all my family and friends that have encouraged me, inspired me, and loved me on my kingdom journey: Alli Becker, Candy Bowling, Pat Byrum, Molly Clark, Vee Cooper, Beth Davis, Amy Denton, Marion Desien, Alicia Dill, Paige Finchum, Cathy Kotiadis, Lizzy Lopez, Jean Mabry, Beth McClure, Amy Milloway, Connie Mosser, Carrie Neal, Eric and Debra Orta, Shaynie Palisano, Janet Ratliff, Jamie Sanders, Brittany Springer, Melissa Stivers, Pam and Hannah Stott, Janel Tardy, Tina Thompson, Sarah Watkins, and Cheri Wright. I also want to thank my wonderful pastor Paul Dyar and his wife Kim along with all my church family at Alcoa Maryville Church of God for their love and support. Thank you, Abba Father, for all of your teaching and direction over the past 20 years of my life. Thank you to my Savior and Covenant Partner, Jesus the Messiah, who paid the price for my freedom and healing. May this book bring You glory and bring freedom to many who are searching for Your truth.

Blessings to the reader of this manual. May the Holy Spirit of Yahweh God open your eyes and heart to His Word and the truth and treasure that lies within it. May you receive freedom to walk in every purpose for which you were created, and may none of the words written in your book in heaven fall to the ground.

Shalom,

Kerri Dill

Introduction

You may be one of the many believers in the world today that cannot seem to be victorious in life. Although you have made a choice by faith to receive the free gift of salvation paid for by Messiah Jesus and have received eternal life, you cannot seem to find complete freedom here on the earth. You may have discovered one or more roadblocks in your path to victorious living. Some of the most common roadblocks are addiction, financial struggles, tormenting thoughts, continual problems and accidents, broken marriages and families, persistent feelings of rejection or confusion, or even broken communion with Yahweh God.

Have you spent much time in prayer, looking for answers; but, over time, your hope has begun to fade? Do you see anger, bitterness, strife, divorce, depression, poverty, sexual perversion, serious illness, and early death in your family line?

It's highly possible you are dealing with an unbroken curse that is still operating in your life. The curse may have come through dark covenants in the bloodline, and your personal sin has allowed the agreement the enemy needs to legally keep tormenting you. Whatever the cause, I have good news for you! Jesus the Messiah has made a way to freedom for us all! He came to defeat the works of darkness! He came to proclaim liberty to the captives!

> "The Spirit of the Lord God is upon Me, because the Lord has anointed Me to preach good tidings to the poor; He has sent Me to heal the brokenhearted, to proclaim liberty to the captives, and the opening of the prison to those who are bound; to proclaim the acceptable year of the Lord, and the day of vengeance of our God; to comfort all who mourn, to console those who mourn in Zion, to give them beauty for ashes, the oil of joy for mourning, the garment of praise for the spirit of heaviness; that they may be called trees of righteousness, the planting of the Lord, that He may be glorified." Isaiah 61:1-3

There is a scarlet thread that runs throughout the Bible painting pictures of the coming of Messiah as Deliverer. The stories are not only historical events, but also prophetic foretellings or shadows of things to come. Wisdom and treasures are hidden in these stories for those who would seek them.

One morning as I was writing this book, I had a vision during my prayer time. I could see the Israelites leaving Egypt on their journey to freedom. My spiritual eyes were being opened to the beautiful comparison of our lives as believers to the Israelite's journey to freedom found in the Biblical books of Exodus through Joshua. As I reread these books, so much became clearer. Follow along with me as we compare these two events.

In the book of Exodus, we see that Yahweh heard the cries of the Israelites who were in slavery in Egypt. He remembered His covenant with Abraham, Isaac, and Jacob. Yahweh God sent Moses as a savior and deliverer to the Israelites who were in slavery in Egypt, just like Messiah Jesus was sent to save us and deliver us from slavery to sin. Yahweh used His servant Moses to confront Pharoah, king of Egypt, to release His people so that they could go to the mountain and worship Him. Pharoah would not relent, so Yahweh brought ten plagues against the gods of Egypt to show His great power and might.

After almost a year of amazing wonders, it was finally time for the Israelites to be set free from slavery. On the night of the final plague, the death of the firstborn, Yahweh cut covenant with all who would choose to obey Him. Each family was told to choose a spotless lamb and sacrifice it on their threshold and apply the blood to the doorposts. The lamb's blood was the blood of the covenant that would save all in the home from death, and the lamb's flesh would restore them to health before their journey to the land of promise.

The next morning, those who chose to covenant with Yahweh left Egypt freed from slavery taking with them the wealth of the Egyptians. Shortly after that, the old life of slavery tried to take them back. Pharaoh hardened his heart and sent his army after the Israelites, but Yahweh made a path for them through the Red Sea, which was a form of baptism, that separated them from their enemies.

Once they were safely across the sea, Yahweh spoke to the people through his servant Moses in order to make a covenant with the entire nation. He gave them the choice to cut this covenant with Him after appearing to them on the mountain. Yahweh had promised Abraham that He would bless his children with a special land, a land of promise, flowing with milk and honey. Yahweh was now ready to fulfill that promise and wanted to make the children of Israel His holy set-apart people, to protect them and provide for them. In turn, they would promise to worship and obey Him alone. The Israelites agreed to this covenant. The Angel of the Lord was given to them to guide them through the wilderness to the land promised to Abraham many generations ago.

As I looked at this beautiful story of redemption, I could see the foreshadowing of Messiah Jesus as our Passover lamb whose body and blood would save us from slavery to sin. His blood is the blood of covenant that gives us access to communion with Yahweh God and rescues us from death. Through the stripes on His body, we are healed. We can become children of God through His sacrifice.

I compared the covenant at the mountain and the journey through the Red Sea to our choice as believers to promise to worship and obey God and be baptized in water as we are born again into his kingdom. I could also see the Holy Spirit given to us as a comforter and guide just like the Israelites were given the Angel of the Lord to guide them through the wilderness. Our own salvation was all so beautifully portrayed in the story of the exodus.

But what about the rest of the story? How do we get to the land of promise? The land of victory?

The promised land of Canaan was to be an inheritance to the children of Abraham. It would be a land flowing with milk and honey, the best of the best! This land would be allocated to each tribe by size and by lot, and the land would stay in the tribes forever. Twelve spies, one from each tribe, were sent into the land for 40 days to search it out and bring back a report. All twelve spies reported that it was indeed a land flowing with milk and honey, but it was also filled with giants! Ten of the spies were filled with fear of the land's inhabitants. They did not trust that Yahweh God was powerful enough to defeat the giants they saw there and were not willing to fight for it. Only two spies trusted that Yahweh could bring them victory. Because of this fear which circulated through the camp, an entire generation was not allowed into the land of promise, only the two who trusted in Yahweh.

The Israelites wandered in the wilderness for 40 years, one for each day the spies searched out the land. After all of the older generation died, it was time once again to enter the land. The Israelites would need to take possession of the land with Yahweh's help and drive out the giants that were living there.

They were given instructions in Numbers 33 to cross the Jordan River and destroy all the idols and high places, and expel all the people living in the land. In verse 55, Yahweh says:

> But if you do not drive out the inhabitants of the land from before you, then it shall be that those whom you let remain shall be irritants in your eyes and thorns in your sides, and they shall harass you in the land where you dwell.

If the inhabitants weren't driven out, they would torment and harass the Israelites. These peoples were not only idol-worshipers, but many were Nephilim, hybrids of humans and fallen angels. Yahweh promised to go with the tribes to possess the land. He said:

> 'This day I will begin to put the dread and fear of you upon the nations under the whole heaven, who shall hear the report of you, and shall tremble and be in anguish because of you.' Deuteronomy 2:25

> 'You must not fear them, for the Lord your God Himself fights for you.'
> Deuteronomy 3:22

Yahweh sent fear and dread ahead of the Israelite armies and agreed to fight on their behalf. He told the people not to fear. He would go before them as a consuming fire to destroy those inhabiting the land and bring them down!

> "Hear, O Israel: You are to cross over the Jordan today, and go in to dispossess nations greater and mightier than yourself, cities great and fortified up to heaven, a people great and tall, the descendants of the Anakim, whom you know, and of whom you heard it said, 'Who can stand before the descendants of Anak?' Therefore understand today that the Lord your God is He who goes over before you as a consuming fire. He will destroy them and bring them down before you; so you shall drive them out and destroy them quickly, as the Lord has said to you. Deuteronomy 9:1-3

The Israelite tribes were also commanded to work together to take the land until everyone had their portion. No one could go back to their own territory to settle down and raise their families, until every tribe had possessed their inheritance.

Our victory on this earth is like the possession of the land of promise. There are squatters living in the land of our inheritance. They are demonic forces that may look scary like the giants. They have gained access to the land through ancestral sins and covenants with darkness and our own sins have reinforced their boundaries. These evil spirits are not planning to leave on their own free will. If we do not drive them out, they will torment and harass us. We must go forward with the armies of heaven and possess the promised land!

Just like the twelve Israelite spies, ten out of twelve people may cower in fear of the demons in the land and continue to live in defeat. They will not enter the land of promise. But there is a small percentage that will hear the truth and trust Yahweh God for freedom. We cannot listen to the voice of fear that kept the Israelites wandering in the wilderness. Yahweh God has sent dread and fear ahead of us to make the demons tremble.

> You believe that there is one God. You do well. Even the demons believe—and tremble! James 2:19

We are ambassadors of the name of Jesus the Messiah! We have His seal and authority.

> Behold, I give you the authority to trample on serpents and scorpions, and over all the power of the enemy, and nothing shall by any means hurt you. Nevertheless, do not rejoice in this, that the spirits are subject to you, but rather rejoice because your names are written in heaven." Luke 10:19-20

We must trust that Yahweh wants us to inhabit the land of victory and that He will strengthen us to possess that land. We must join forces, put on our kingdom armor, and drive out the squatters. We must go in the powerful name of our covenant partner, Jesus the Messiah, name above every name. Through Him, the victory is ours!

This manual was created to help you possess your land of victory. You can work through it alone or find a prayer partner to go on the journey with you. Using Biblical principles, you will learn about covenants, curses, and legal rights and how to repent, renounce, and break the adversary's power to keep you in bondage. You can choose to agree with the work of Messiah Jesus in His death, burial, and resurrection and appropriate the atonement to your life through consecration and sanctification. Then you will be able to evict those evil squatters that are harassing and tormenting you. You can finally begin to walk in victory and fulfill Yahweh God's purpose for your life. He has an amazing plan for you, so let's get started!

Chapter 1:
Are You in Covenant?

We will start with covenant. What is a covenant? A covenant is a binding agreement between two parties that serves as a legal contract. It is usually accompanied by an oath, a ceremony, a sign, and witnesses like our modern-day wedding ceremony. The covenant agreement can be spoken or written designating the commitments and pledges of both parties. The problem is, many people don't take covenants seriously. They don't understand the legal ramifications involved and how making or breaking them can affect their lives.

In Bible times, a covenant always involved blood. The Hebrew phrase used for covenant is כרת ברית, (c'rat b'rit) which means to "cut covenant." This cutting referred to a sacrifice of the fattest, choice livestock. The sacrifice would be cut in two for those entering covenant to pass between the parts. In the story of the exodus, the Israelites cut covenant with Yahweh God at their thresholds and on the mountain. In God's eyes, covenants are everlasting, to be broken only by death. Covenant making is a serious decision.

Ancient Covenant

Let's look for a moment at the ancient covenant and its elements. There were ancient traditions of covenant making throughout most cultures, and they were all very similar. The ancient covenant is a picture of two becoming one. A covenant ceremony was called "a walk into death," because two separate individuals would die to themselves and become one. These ceremonies usually involved many trades and were sworn to the death. If the covenant was broken, there were severe circumstances and curses expected for the covenant breaker.

Many covenants were cut at the threshold of the home. The threshold was not only a door to a man's house, but a door to his life. The threshold was considered the family altar and was usually at the door over or near the cornerstone of the house. Many times, a door would hold the image or name of the family god. Sometimes lights and wreaths would be placed at the door to honor gods. Sacrifices of blood, food, and drink would be offered there. The sacrificial animal for the covenant was killed over a bowl or basin built into the threshold which caught the blood and allowed it to run into a groove the full distance of the threshold itself.

During the ceremony, the man becoming a 'blood brother' would be invited to cross over this threshold of blood at the door and become a member of the family. If the man stepped over the blood and into the home, he would accept and come into the covenant. If he rejected the covenant, he would step on the blood to show disrespect.

If the ceremony took place outdoors, the men would use the blood sacrifice to create a 'door' and a 'threshold.' The door was created by cutting the covenantal sacrifices in two and laying them out across from each other forming a sacred path between them. Then the life blood was poured across the path creating a 'threshold.' The men would walk across the blood between the pieces and join right hands.

They would then begin to make several trades which each signified the two becoming one. They traded robes and said... "I am putting on you, and you are putting on me. We are one." They traded their belts and said... "When you are weak, I will be your strength. We are one." They traded weapons and said... "Your enemies are mine. We are one." They traded rings and said... "My riches are yours. We are one." They traded names and said... "I am now you, and you are now me. We are one."

Each man would make a cut on his palm or wrist and the two men mingled their blood while they spoke an oath... "May God do so to me and worse if I break this covenant." This penalty referred to the animal sacrificed and cut in two. Oaths typically included not only the man present, but all his seed or future generations. This could mean blessings or curses for everyone included. Keeping the covenant would provide protection for children and future generations, even if the covenant partner died. Breaking the covenant could end in a curse or even death for all attached to the oath breaker. The scar from this blood pact would be a constant reminder of the covenant. Sometimes the covenant was written down, rolled up, and kept next to each man's heart.

Finally, the men would sit down and have a meal together where they would feed each other bread and wine representing their own body and blood entering each other. After the meal, they would build a monument or plant a tree as an outward remembrance of the covenant. Each time the men or others would see the memorial, the covenant would be remembered.

Covenants of Yahweh Elohim in the Bible

Because our God is a God of covenant, there are many examples of covenant in the Bible. As we look at some of them, you will see elements of the ancient covenant. I can only include part of these stories here, but please read them in their entirety in the Bible for a deeper understanding.

The creator God of the universe, Yahweh Elohim, made a covenant with Noah and all the living creatures on the Earth after the flood in Genesis 9:14-16:

> "Whenever I bring clouds over the earth and the rainbow appears in the clouds, I will remember my covenant between me and you and all living creatures of every kind.

Never again will the waters become a flood to destroy all life. Whenever the rainbow appears in the clouds, I will see it and remember the everlasting covenant between God and all living creatures of every kind on the earth."

The rainbow was a sign for this covenant, a reminder to God and all creation that He would never again flood the earth and destroy all life. Noah made a blood sacrifice of clean animals before God:

Then Noah built an altar to the Lord, and, taking some of all the clean animals and clean birds, he sacrificed burnt offerings on it. Genesis 8:20

You will notice as we go that each Biblical covenant was built upon the previous ones rather than replacing them. Yahweh God also made a covenant with Abram (Abraham). God chose Abram to be the father of His chosen people.

Now the Lord had said to Abram: "Get out of your country, from your family and from your father's house, to a land that I will show you. I will make you a great nation; I will bless you and make your name great; and you shall be a blessing. I will bless those who bless you, and I will curse him who curses you; and in you all the families of the earth shall be blessed." Genesis 12:1-3

They cut covenant in Genesis 15:7-21:

Then He said to him, "I am the Lord, who brought you out of Ur of the Chaldeans, to give you this land to inherit it." And he said, "Lord God, how shall I know that I will inherit it?" So, He said to him, "Bring Me a three-year-old heifer, a three-year-old female goat, a three-year-old ram, a turtledove, and a young pigeon." Then he brought all these to Him and cut them in two, down the middle, and placed each piece opposite the other; but he did not cut the birds in two. And when the vultures came down on the carcasses, Abram drove them away. Now when the sun was going down, a deep sleep fell upon Abram; and behold, horror and great darkness fell upon him. Then He said to Abram: "Know certainly that your descendants will be strangers in a land that is not theirs, and will serve them, and they will afflict them four hundred years. And also, the nation whom they serve I will judge; afterward they shall come out with great possessions. Now as for you, you shall go to your fathers in peace; you shall be buried at a good old age. But in the fourth generation they shall return here, for the iniquity of the Amorites is not yet complete."

And it came to pass, when the sun went down and it was dark, that behold, there appeared a smoking oven and a burning torch that passed between those pieces. On the same day the Lord made a covenant with Abram, saying: "To your descendants I have given this land, from the river of Egypt to the great river, the River Euphrates— the Kenites, the Kenezzites, the Kadmonites, the Hittites, the Perizzites, the Rephaim, the Amorites, the Canaanites, the Girgashites, and the Jebusites."

We can see that the door and threshold were created, but only God Himself walked between the pieces as a smoking oven and a burning torch. After this covenant was made, they each took a part of the other's name.

> When Abram was ninety-nine years old, the Lord appeared to Abram and said to him, "I am Almighty God; walk before Me and be blameless. And I will make My covenant between Me and you, and will multiply you exceedingly." Then Abram fell on his face, and God talked with him, saying: "As for Me, behold, My covenant is with you, and you shall be a father of many nations. No longer shall your name be called Abram, but your name shall be Abraham; for I have made you a father of many nations. I will make you exceedingly fruitful; and I will make nations of you, and kings shall come from you. And I will establish My covenant between Me and you and your descendants after you in their generations, for an everlasting covenant, to be God to you and your descendants after you. Also, I give to you and your descendants after you the land in which you are a stranger, all the land of Canaan, as an everlasting possession; and I will be their God."
>
> And God said to Abraham: "As for you, you shall keep My covenant, you and your descendants after you throughout their generations. This is My covenant which you shall keep, between Me and you and your descendants after you: Every male child among you shall be circumcised; and you shall be circumcised in the flesh of your foreskins, and it shall be a sign of the covenant between Me and you." Genesis 17:1-11

Abram became Abraham. A letter ה from Yahweh's name (יהוה) was placed in Abram's name changing the meaning from "exalted father" to "father of many." Yahweh God the creator became known as the "God of Abraham."

We also see the terms of the covenant on Abraham's end were to walk before Yahweh blameless and to keep the covenant sign of circumcision in all his generations. This same covenant was renewed by both Isaac and Jacob, so that Yahweh God became known as the God of Abraham, Isaac, and Jacob.

A third example of covenant was the covenant with the Israelites through Moses. We talked about this in the introduction. We see Yahweh God making a threshold covenant with the people before the tenth plague was released. He gave Israel directions through Moses:

> Then Moses called for all the elders of Israel and said to them, "Pick out and take lambs for yourselves according to your families, and kill the Passover lamb. And you shall take a bunch of hyssop, dip it in the blood that is in the basin, and strike the lintel and the two doorposts with the blood that is in the basin. And none of you shall go out of the door of his house until morning. For the Lord will pass through to strike the Egyptians; and when He sees the blood on the lintel and on the two doorposts, the Lord will pass over the door and not allow the destroyer to come into your houses to strike you. And you shall observe this thing as an ordinance for you and your sons forever.
> Exodus 12:21-24

Each family could choose to obey and covenant with Yahweh by sacrificing the Passover lamb at the threshold to make a bloodline for Him to cross over. This covenant prevented the destroyer from coming into the home. Three months after the exodus, the God of Abraham, Isaac, and Jacob (Israel) met the children of Israel who were camped in the Wilderness of Sinai and cut a covenant with them as a people. He used Moses as a mediator of the covenant.

> And Moses went up to God, and the Lord called to him from the mountain, saying, "Thus you shall say to the house of Jacob, and tell the children of Israel: 'You have seen what I did to the Egyptians, and how I bore you on eagles' wings and brought you to Myself. Now therefore, if you will indeed obey My voice and keep My covenant, then you shall be a special treasure to Me above all people; for all the earth is Mine. And you shall be to Me a kingdom of priests and a holy nation.' These are the words which you shall speak to the children of Israel."
>
> So, Moses came and called for the elders of the people, and laid before them all these words which the Lord commanded him. Then all the people answered together and said, "All that the Lord has spoken we will do." So, Moses brought back the words of the people to the Lord. Exodus 19:3-8

This covenant required the people to follow God's commands and obey Him. God gave His commands to Moses who brought them to the people. Because the covenant brought the two parties together in a 'Oneness," Yahweh God was revealing Himself to His people through His commands. We can see His "Covenant of Love" in the Ten words or Commandments He gave to them on the stone tablets. All the other commandments fall under these.

Covenant in the Ten Commandments

The Ten commandments are a written covenant of love. They are a picture of the merging of the Israelites with their God...the two becoming one. They are called the "tables of the covenant" and kept in the "ark of the covenant." When the people agreed to the covenant, they and the tables were sprinkled with the blood. Yahweh God spoke His part of the covenant in Exodus 19:5-6:

> "Now therefore, if you will indeed obey My voice and keep My covenant, then you shall be a special treasure to Me above all people; for all the earth is Mine. And you shall be to Me a kingdom of priests and a holy nation.' These are the words which you shall speak to the children of Israel."

The first four commandments focused on the Israelites relationship to Yahweh, and the last six focused on their relationship with each other.

1. I am the Lord your God, who brought you out of the land of Egypt, out of the house of bondage. You shall have no other gods before Me. (Exodus 20:2-3)

Only one God was chosen in this covenant. A divided heart cannot make a covenant of love. No other God should separate these covenant partners.

2. You shall not make for yourself a carved image—any likeness of anything that is in heaven above, or that is in the earth beneath, or that is in the water under the earth; you shall not bow down to them nor serve them. For I, the Lord your God, am a jealous God, visiting the iniquity of the fathers upon the children to the third and fourth generations of those who hate Me, but showing mercy to thousands, to those who love Me and keep My commandments. (vs.4-6)

God wanted to be worshiped in spirit because He is spirit. No image could represent Him and would be a hindrance to worship. Only by spirit could they connect as one.

3. You shall not take the name of the Lord your God in vain, for the Lord will not hold him guiltless who takes His name in vain. (vs. 7)

Carrying God's name was a show of intimacy and union with Him. As a representative of this union, the people were expected to be ambassadors of God's name and uphold His reputation. Privilege equals responsibility. They were not to use it lightly or insincerely. It was to always be honored as if it were their own.

4. Remember the Sabbath day, to keep it holy. Six days you shall labor and do all your work, but the seventh day is the Sabbath of the Lord your God. In it you shall do no work: you, nor your son, nor your daughter, nor your male servant, nor your female servant, nor your cattle, nor your stranger who is within your gates. For in six days the Lord made the heavens and the earth, the sea, and all that is in them, and rested the seventh day. Therefore the Lord blessed the Sabbath day and hallowed it. (vs. 8-11)

The Sabbath day was a sign to remember the covenant...an appointed time to be with Yahweh, their covenant partner, and rest in Him. A time to set aside normal activity and focus on intimacy.

5. Honor your father and your mother, that your days may be long upon the land which the Lord your God is giving you. (vs.12)

God established authority (even His own) to be honored as put in place by Him. This command is not limited to parents, but includes superiors and leaders appointed by and given power by God. To honor the authority is to honor God Himself.

6. You shall not murder. (vs. 13)

Life belongs to God. It is to be sacredly guarded. Only God must decide when it would end. The life is in the blood.

7. You shall not commit adultery. (vs.14)

God established marriage and the family and it was to be honored by all. One man and one woman equals one flesh. Marriage is also a covenant of love.

8. You shall not steal. (vs. 15)

God established property rights and sanctioned it. He set up boundaries of tribal division and strict justice for moving property lines.

9. You shall not bear false witness against your neighbor. (vs. 16)

Just as God cares for his own reputation, he cares for that of His children. No one is to slander or use careless speech toward God's children. He has made covenant with them all.

10. You shall not covet your neighbor's house; you shall not covet your neighbor's wife, nor his male servant, nor his female servant, nor his ox, nor his donkey, nor anything that is your neighbor's. (vs. 17)

Don't compare yourselves with others. Be content with what God has given you and has planned for your life...your assignment, sphere, influence, etc. Your Father knows your calling and your purpose. Lovingly devote your life to Him.

All ten of these commandments were exposing God's heart and character to the people. By agreeing to the covenant, the people chose to become one with Yahweh by taking on His characteristics. They were to be consecrated and set apart from the rest of humankind. The commandments weren't so much rules to follow as a new way of life. The Israelites would die to their old way of life and become new. Union with Yahweh is spiritual and sincere. One must be willing to completely surrender to a merger of holy love. Love is the fulfillment of the law!

Once the people were given Yahweh God's commands, they were to observe them and teach them to their future generations. Following these commands would merge them with their God and set them apart from the other nations. They were to hear and obey and remember these commands every day, talking about them, putting them into their hearts.

Now this is the commandment, and these are the statutes and judgments which the Lord your God has commanded to teach you, that you may observe them in the land which you are crossing over to possess, that you may fear the Lord your God, to keep all His statutes and His commandments which I command you, you and your son and your grandson, all the days of your life, and that your days may be prolonged. Therefore hear, O Israel, and be careful to observe it, that it may be well with you, and that you may multiply greatly as the Lord God of your fathers has promised you— 'a land flowing with milk and honey.'

"Hear, O Israel: The Lord our God, the Lord is one! You shall love the Lord your God with all your heart, with all your soul, and with all your strength.

"And these words which I command you today shall be in your heart. You shall teach them diligently to your children, and shall talk of them when you sit in your house, when you walk by the way, when you lie down, and when you rise up. You shall bind them as a sign on your hand, and they shall be as frontlets between your eyes. You shall write them on the doorposts of your house and on your gates." Deuteronomy 6:1-9

The Israelites were also given a list of blessings that would follow them if they obeyed God, and a list of curses that would follow them if they did not. You can read about these in Deuteronomy 28. The curses could operate for 3-4 generations, but the blessings would operate for 1000 generations.

Know therefore that the Lord your God is God, the faithful God who keeps covenant and steadfast love with those who love him and keep his commandments, to a thousand generations. Deuteronomy 7:9

A New Covenant

In the Bible, we read about the many times the Israelites broke their covenant with Yahweh God. Although this covenant with Yahweh was good, the evil hearts of the people were drawn away from it. Because of this, Yahweh spoke of a time when He would make a new covenant with His people. This time, He would write His words on their hearts instead of tablets of stone. He would take out their stony hearts of rebellion and give them a heart of flesh. Then He would put His own Spirit inside them to make them walk in His ways.

"Behold, the days are coming, says the Lord, when I will make a new covenant with the house of Israel and with the house of Judah— not according to the covenant that I made with their fathers in the day that I took them by the hand to lead them out of the land of Egypt, My covenant which they broke, though I was a husband to them, says the Lord. But this is the covenant that I will make with the house of Israel after those days, says the Lord: I will put My law in their minds, and write it on their hearts; and I will be their God, and they shall be My people. Jeremiah 31:31-33

For I will take you from among the nations, gather you out of all countries, and bring you into your own land. Then I will sprinkle clean water on you, and you shall be clean; I will cleanse you from all your filthiness and from all your idols. I will give you a new heart and put a new spirit within you; I will take the heart of stone out of your flesh and give you a heart of flesh. I will put My Spirit within you and cause you to walk in My statutes, and you will keep My judgments and do them. Then you shall dwell in the land that I gave to your fathers; you shall be My people, and I will be your God. Ezekiel 36:24-28

He would do this through His servant, the Messiah. This Messiah would pay the penalty for the sins of the people once and for all and redeem them from the darkness to which they had been enslaved. His own blood would be the blood sacrifice that would atone for the people's sins.

> Surely, He has borne our griefs and carried our sorrows; yet we esteemed Him stricken, smitten by God, and afflicted. But He was wounded for our transgressions, He was bruised for our iniquities; the chastisement for our peace was upon Him, and by His stripes we are healed. All we like sheep have gone astray; We have turned, every one, to his own way; and the Lord has laid on Him the iniquity of us all. Isaiah 53:4-6

Messiah, who was God made flesh, would trade his sinless life for the corrupt lives of the people Yahweh loved so much. He would take on their sin and give them His righteousness. He would trade their poverty for His riches. He would trade His strength for their weakness. He would trade their death for His eternal life. He would be provider and protector to His own.

Messiah Yeshua, Jesus of Nazareth, came and did just that. His blood became the blood of the covenant that would be a door for us to the Father. Jesus would become a curse for us in trade for the blessing. Though God's original covenant was with Abraham and His generations, even gentiles were granted access to this covenant through faith in Jesus. You and I can be grafted into the tree of Israel through this covenant and can become heirs to the promise of Abraham. We will cover this covenant in more detail in Chapter 2.

Covenants between men in the Bible

Most covenants we read about in the Bible are between God and man, but some are made between two men such as the covenant between Abraham and Abimelech, king of Gerar. Abimelech approached Abraham to make a covenant after seeing God's favor on him. After some decisions over a well, they made the covenant in Genesis 21:27-34:

> So, Abraham took sheep and oxen and gave them to Abimelech, and the two of them made a covenant. And Abraham set seven ewe lambs of the flock by themselves. Then Abimelech asked Abraham, "What is the meaning of these seven ewe lambs which you have set by themselves?" And he said, "You will take these seven ewe lambs from my hand, that they may be my witness that I have dug this well." Therefore, he called that place Beersheba, because the two of them swore an oath there.

> Thus, they made a covenant at Beersheba. So, Abimelech rose with Phichol, the commander of his army, and they returned to the land of the Philistines. Then Abraham planted a tamarisk tree in Beersheba, and there called on the name of the Lord, the Everlasting God. And Abraham stayed in the land of the Philistines many days.

The men made trades and commitments, then Abraham planted a tamarisk tree in honor of the covenant. Another covenant between men is seen in the book of 1 Samuel between David and Jonathan.

> Now when he had finished speaking to Saul, the soul of Jonathan was knit to the soul of David, and Jonathan loved him as his own soul. Saul took him that day, and would not let him go home to his father's house anymore. Then Jonathan and David made a covenant, because he loved him as his own soul. And Jonathan took off the robe that was on him

and gave it to David, with his armor, even to his sword and his bow and his belt.
1 Samuel 18:1-4

We see the two men making trades; and, throughout the next two chapters, we can see the dedication of the two men to each other and their families. Jonathan's father, King Saul, made many attempts to kill David, but Jonathan did all in his power to save his covenant brother.

> And Jonathan said to David, "Come, let us go out into the field." So, both of them went out into the field. Then Jonathan said to David: "The Lord God of Israel is witness! When I have sounded out my father sometime tomorrow, or the third day, and indeed there is good toward David, and I do not send to you and tell you, may the Lord do so and much more to Jonathan. But if it pleases my father to do you evil, then I will report it to you and send you away, that you may go in safety. And the Lord be with you as He has been with my father. And you shall not only show me the kindness of the Lord while I still live, that I may not die; but you shall not cut off your kindness from my house forever, no, not when the Lord has cut off every one of the enemies of David from the face of the earth." So, Jonathan made a covenant with the house of David, saying, "Let the Lord require it at the hand of David's enemies." Now Jonathan again caused David to vow, because he loved him; for he loved him as he loved his own soul.   1 Samuel 21:11-17

Jonathan and David renewed their covenant which included future generations. With God as witness, they vowed to care for each other's families in the case that one or the other should die. David kept this covenant by caring for Jonathan's son Mephibosheth years after Jonathan was dead. Our great God Yahweh has also extended His covenant to our future generations:

> But the mercy of the Lord is from everlasting to everlasting on those who fear Him, and His righteousness to children's children, to such as keep His covenant, and to those who remember His commandments to do them.   Psalm 103:17-18

Other Covenants

Now that we can see that our God is a God of covenant and how covenants operate, I hope it will be beneficial to you to recognize covenant practice in other areas of your life. God takes covenant seriously even when we do not know the importance of what we are doing.

We can make covenants with God and man in a holy way, but it is also possible to make a covenant with darkness or evil men. You might not even be aware that you made a covenant with darkness through some ritual acts or through an oath or vow, but the adversary doesn't care if you understand what you did. He is a legalist and will still claim his legal rights. He has the evidence to prove it, as everything we say and do is recorded in books in heaven. Just like an enemy will dig into the past of a governmental candidate before an election, our enemy, the adversary or satan, will go back into our past and our bloodline to find legal rights he can use to deny us our blessings or victory in our daily lives.

Thankfully we have the Holy Spirit who can expose these secret or hidden contracts. He leads us into truth. He can reveal these dark covenants to us. If you or your ancestors have made covenants in your lives with evil men or with other gods, these covenants need to be renounced, and you need to repent for making dark covenants or any covenants that could not be kept.

This could include oaths or pledges made during your life that might seem insignificant, such as, blood pacts with children in a secret club; vows to sororities / fraternities or school clubs; secret societies of any kind, inner vows, etc.

> Do not be unequally yoked together with unbelievers. For what fellowship has righteousness with lawlessness? And what communion has light with darkness? And what accord has Christ with Belial? Or what part has a believer with an unbeliever? And what agreement has the temple of God with idols? For you are the temple of the living God. 2 Corinthians 6:14-16

"Why is this so important?" you might ask. "That was so long ago, and I don't even see those people anymore." The next chapter will better explain legal rights and how they give the enemy access to our lives.

Chapter 2:
Curses, Legal Rights, and the Courts of Heaven

You might be wondering, "How does the enemy have any legal rights to me, and why are curses operating in my life?" Let's look for a moment at the lives of the Israelites and how they came under a curse.

God's people broke His covenant

In many instances in the Bible, we see the people of God breaking covenant with Him by choosing to worship the false gods of other lands. Yahweh calls this idolatry, which is spiritual adultery, and it is addressed in the first two commandments:

> "I am the Lord your God, who brought you out of the land of Egypt, out of the house of bondage. "You shall have no other gods before Me. "You shall not make for yourself a carved image—any likeness of anything that is in heaven above, or that is in the earth beneath, or that is in the water under the earth; you shall not bow down to them nor serve them. For I, the Lord your God, am a jealous God, visiting the iniquity of the fathers upon the children to the third and fourth generations of those who hate Me, but showing mercy to thousands, to those who love Me and keep My commandments. Exodus 20:2-6

Because Yahweh was sending the Israelites into the land of promise to possess the land, He warned them of the temptation to take part in the worship of pagan gods or demon gods.

> "When the Lord your God cuts off from before you the nations which you go to dispossess, and you displace them and dwell in their land, take heed to yourself that you are not ensnared to follow them, after they are destroyed from before you, and that you do not inquire after their gods, saying, 'How did these nations serve their gods? I also will do likewise.' You shall not worship the Lord your God in that way; for every abomination to the Lord which He hates they have done to their gods; for they burn even their sons and daughters in the fire to their gods. "Whatever I command you, be careful to observe it; you shall not add to it nor take away from it. Deuteronomy 12:29-32

Yahweh did not want his people to learn the ways the pagan nations worshiped their gods. For these abominations, He was driving the pagan nations out of the land. His covenant people were to be holy and set apart. They were to obey the commands He had set forth. To obey God was to worship Him. Their nation was to reflect His character.

> "When you come into the land which the Lord your God is giving you, you shall not learn to follow the abominations of those nations. There shall not be found among you anyone who makes his son or his daughter pass through the fire, or one who practices witchcraft, or a soothsayer, or one who interprets omens, or a sorcerer, or one who conjures spells, or a medium, or a spiritist, or one who calls up the dead. For all who do these things are an abomination to the Lord, and because of these abominations the Lord your God drives them out from before you. You shall be blameless before the Lord your God. For these nations which you will dispossess listened to soothsayers and diviners; but as for you, the Lord your God has not appointed such for you."
> Deuteronomy 18:9-14

Rejection of knowledge brings destruction and a curse

Some of the consequences of breaking covenant with God were very severe. Many serious sins were punishable by death. We wonder how the Israelites ever got to a place where they broke covenant as an entire nation. Compromise, in all reality, usually comes slowly and deceptively, just like the serpent in the Garden of Eden, that asked, "Did God really say...?"

In Hosea 4:1-6 God's people, Israel, had once again broken covenant with Him as a nation. This time they had come to a place where they had forgotten His laws to the point that there was no truth, mercy, or knowledge in the land.

> Hear the word of the Lord, you children of Israel, for the Lord brings a charge against the inhabitants of the land: "There is no truth or mercy or knowledge of God in the land. By swearing and lying, killing and stealing and committing adultery, they break all restraint, with bloodshed upon bloodshed. Therefore, the land will mourn; and everyone who dwells there will waste away with the beasts of the field and the birds of the air; even the fish of the sea will be taken away. "Now let no man contend, or rebuke another; for your people are like those who contend with the priest. Therefore, you shall stumble in the day; the prophet also shall stumble with you in the night; and I will destroy your mother. My people are destroyed for lack of knowledge. Because you have rejected knowledge, I also will reject you from being priest for Me; because you have forgotten the law of your God, I also will forget your children."

Without knowledge of Yahweh's holy commands, the sins of the people and even the priests increased to a point that a curse was over the land. They were sinning against God and each other. By rejecting the knowledge of Yahweh God and their covenant with Him, the people were being rejected and forgotten by God.

Compromise and deception in the life of a believer

In many ways, believers today have reached a place of compromise and deception. In many of our churches, faith in the God of Abraham, Isaac, and Jacob has been mixed with the ways of pagan religion or the world. This is called syncretism, a joining of two or more religions. The church has come to a point where it is being destroyed because of lack of knowledge. Many have rejected God's commands or chosen only those parts of scripture which seem good to them. The serpent is hissing in the ears of God's people, "Did God really say this? Did God really mean that? That verse doesn't mean that to me. I interpret it this way...." Many are paving their own walks of faith, creating their own theology, and not heeding the warning in Proverbs 14:12:

> There is a way that seems right to a man, but its end is the way of death.

This rejection of God's truth is the beginning of folly. Rejection of Yahweh God and His holy way of living, along with turning to idolatry, can give legal rights for a curse to operate. Idolatry is spiritual adultery in the eyes of Yahweh God. We are told as followers of Jesus, to flee from idolatry.

> Therefore, my beloved, flee from idolatry!..You cannot drink the cup of the Lord and the cup of demons; you cannot partake of the Lord's table and of the table of demons. Or do we provoke the Lord to jealousy? Are we stronger than He? 1 Corinthians 10:14, 21-22

Idolatry in our own lives or the lives of our ancestors is cause for a curse. Some believers do not choose this compromise or the curse that follows on their own, but are like sheep led astray by family tradition or charismatic leaders that are rejecting truth. They wonder why their lives are so full of frustration, torment, sorrow and pain. Some blame God. Others recognize the attack of darkness, but don't understand why God is allowing it. All of them can get to a place of hopelessness and despair.

How can I break free from a curse?

Now that we see how a curse can come into operation through rejecting God and His covenant, how can we be free from it?

Remember Messiah Jesus came to free us from the curse. We read in Isaiah 53 that He took on Himself the punishment for our sins and iniquities.

> Surely, He has borne our griefs and carried our sorrows; yet we esteemed Him stricken, smitten by God, and afflicted. But He was wounded for our transgressions, He was bruised for our iniquities; the chastisement for our peace was upon Him, and by His stripes we are healed. All we like sheep have gone astray; We have turned, every one, to his own way; and the Lord has laid on Him the iniquity of us all. Isaiah 53:4-6

He made a trade with us and bought us peace with God and healing. He also redeemed us from the curse according to Galatians 3:13-14

Christ has redeemed us from the curse of the law, having become a curse for us (for it is written, "Cursed is everyone who hangs on a tree"), that the blessing of Abraham might come upon the Gentiles in Christ Jesus, that we might receive the promise of the Spirit through faith.

Because He did this for us, we can be free from slavery to sin and death and any dark covenants to which we are bound. We must first receive what He has done for us by faith and choose to come into covenant with Him. There are several Biblical steps to cutting this covenant:

1. Hear the message of redemption and believe with your heart. Count the cost, and choose to cut the covenant. Jesus said that He was the door. We can only come to the Father, through Him. His blood is the blood of the covenant. It speaks on your behalf. The covenant mark is on His wrists, His ankles, and His side.

2. Repent for your sins and iniquities (the bloodline sins or sins of our ancestors) that bring about the wages of death. Jesus paid the death penalty for your sins and iniquities. He traded His life for yours. He traded His righteousness for your filthy rags. He traded His strength for your weakness and His wealth for your poverty. Jesus took on your enemies and became victorious over them.

3. Renounce any specific covenants or agreements with the kingdom of darkness made by yourself or your ancestors. Yahweh God requires that He is your only God. There is no room for idolatry or compromise.

4. Pledge life and loyalty to Yahweh God and His kingdom.

5. Die to the old man along with Messiah in the waters of baptism and rise up to new life through His resurrection. Become one with Yahweh God.

6. Invite Yahweh's Holy Spirit to fill and baptize you with power. This is the covenant seal and sign. All things are made new as you are born again of the Spirit.

7. At this point, your body becomes a temple of God. He places His mark on your forehead. Any dark spirits that have had residence in your body or bloodlines have lost their legal claims and should be cast out and evicted. No longer are you the same man or bloodline that cut covenant with darkness. That man has died and you are new. Death is the end of a covenant pledge.

8. Once this covenant is made, read the love letter from your covenant partner (the Bible.) It will help you to understand Who He is. You are one with Him and should begin to take on His characteristics and thoughts. Spend times of intimacy with Him. He will never leave you or break the covenant.

9. Take the covenant meal now and at regular intervals including the Passover Seder. Remember your covenant with Him when you bless the bread and the wine that represent his body and blood.

10. Know that you are not your own. You have been cleansed and set apart for His kingdom. You have been adopted into His family. You are a son of God.

Wow!!! Does all this sound familiar? Is your heart flooded with love as you remember the time you made your covenant with Jesus and Yahweh God? I pray that you are already born again and filled with the Spirit of the Living God, the God of Abraham, Isaac, and Jacob. I pray you have a beautiful, intimate relationship with Him. But if this does not sound familiar, choosing this covenant is your first step to freedom. Please consider the seriousness and permanency of this covenant. It is a lifetime commitment and a choice to die to your old self and become one with Jesus. Once you decide to make this decision, I have included a covenant declaration you can pray aloud. Even if you have chosen to follow Jesus in the past, you may want to renew that commitment by praying the declaration. Read over your commitment first and count the cost before declaring it aloud.

Covenant Declaration

I _____ on this day _____ choose as an act of my will on my own faith to covenant with Yahweh God (יהוה), Creator of the universe, the God of Abraham, Isaac, and Jacob and His Son, the Messiah, Jesus of Nazareth. I renounce and break covenant with all other gods. I repent of sinning against God and walking my own way. I ask for forgiveness and cleansing to walk in holiness obeying God's commands. I believe Jesus was God made flesh, born of a virgin, and lived a sinless life on earth. I believe He willingly died for the sins of the world, was buried, and rose from the grave after three days victorious over sin and death. I believe and receive the atonement for my sins that was made when Jesus traded His life for mine. He died in my place, an innocent substitutionary sacrifice. As I stand upon the covenant blood of the Sacrifice Lamb, Jesus the Messiah, I pledge my life and loyalty to Yahweh God and His kingdom. I choose to lay my life down and die to the old man in death with Messiah, and rise up to new life through His resurrection. I am a new creation and choose to invite Yahweh's Holy Spirit to fill me and baptize me with power. I renounce all dark covenants, trades, dedications, sacrifices, offerings, and worship of other gods made by myself or my ancestors. As I cancel these covenants, I return to the enemy anything that is his that I have received by trades with darkness. I repent of any ways I have worshiped or participated with the enemies of God. His enemies are now my enemies. I choose to walk in the Spirit and not in the flesh. I choose to study the word of God and let it fill my mouth and heart and renew my mind.

As I take the communion elements of bread and wine, I remember the sacrifice of His body and blood on my behalf and the covenant we have made, we are one. As I take upon myself the robe of righteousness, he has taken my filthy garments of sin. As I see the scars in His hands, I see the covenant sign and remember the blood of the covenant. I receive the inheritance Jesus has earned for me: forgiveness of sin, iniquity, and curses; peace with God; healing in my body, soul, and spirit; entrance into the kingdom of heaven; eternal life; a new name; sonship; freedom from sin and death; release of all heavenly blessings; return of all that the thief has stolen; and a relationship and fellowship with the Father.

As I choose this covenant, I realize that it is eternal and pledge to be loyal to it even unto death. The blood of this covenant is my overcoming testimony. I will covenant with no other gods. I *will not be ashamed of my covenant with Yahweh God and will confess Him before men. He is my King and Lord. Amen.*

If you have already chosen to follow Jesus, but haven't completed His instructions, that will be your next step. All parts of this covenant have great value. Being baptized in water and the Holy Spirit are vital for your victory here on the earth. Please talk with your pastor or a trusted friend who is a believer about these baptisms and make them a priority.

If you have never repented deeply of your sins or the sins of your ancestors, there is direction and help provided in the next few chapters. You will also be renouncing those sins and any covenants with darkness. When you are finished with the manual, please seek out a trusted friend or deliverance ministry that can agree with you and assist you with casting out all the darkness that has lost its legal rights to you through the process.

Curses cannot operate without a cause

Proverbs 26:2 tells us that operating curses require legal rights.

> Like a flitting sparrow, like a flying swallow, So a curse without cause shall not alight.

Unfortunately, most of us have not completed all these steps of covenant after choosing to follow Jesus. Different denominations have separated themselves from part of these steps over hundreds of years, saying that they weren't all necessary for salvation. This is truly the work of the enemy to keep us from walking in victory. The truth is that the spiritual principles in these steps of covenant with God are all of importance. Maybe your salvation doesn't depend on completing all these steps, but your victory on earth does. God had a reason for commanding us to follow His plan for coming into His kingdom.

If you haven't spent time in deep repentance and renunciation, there is a good chance that the enemy is claiming legal rights to torment and frustrate your life through a curse. He is called the accuser of the brethren and accuses us day and night according to Revelation 12:10. One day, he will be cast down, but right now he is still accusing us. He digs into our past looking for areas of sin and iniquity that haven't been dealt with properly.

Cleansing the temple

After renouncing the occult, it is important to cleanse the temple, which is your body.

> Or do you not know that your body is the temple of the Holy Spirit who is in you, whom you have from God, and you are not your own? For you were bought at a price; therefore, glorify God in your body and in your spirit, which are God's.
> 1 Corinthians 6:19-20

This is especially important where there is evidence of occult practice of self-sacrifice and blood-sacrifice through piercings, tattoos, cuttings, marks, burnings, brandings, self-mutilation, insertion of objects under the skin, ingestion of objects, etc. These practices were used by pagan nations in worship, but Yahweh God does not want to be worshiped in that way. His Word is clear on the matter.

> You shall not make any cuttings in your flesh for the dead, nor tattoo any marks on you: I am the Lord. Leviticus 19:28

These marks can be used as touch points or points of contact by the dark kingdom. They are portals that can be used to track and oppress you. Anoint yourself with oil where any piercings, tattoos, cuttings, marks, burnings, etc. have had a place in your physical body from any occult involvement.

Yahweh is the Great Judge of All the Earth

Our Yahweh God is not only a wonderful, loving Father, but He is also the Great Judge. We can see a picture of Him, The Ancient of Days, seated on His judgment throne in Daniel 7: 9-10:

> "I watched till thrones were put in place, and the Ancient of Days was seated; His garment was white as snow, and the hair of His head was like pure wool. His throne was a fiery flame, its wheels a burning fire; a fiery stream issued and came forth from before Him. A thousand thousands ministered to Him; ten thousand times ten thousand stood before Him. The court was seated, and the books were opened."

He is just and must rule from a place of justice. If we have unrepentant sin in our lives, the enemy can bring a case before the courts of heaven to bring forth that evidence to convict us. Let me show you an example in the Parable of the Unforgiving Servant found in Matthew 18:21-35. Peter comes to Jesus with a question about forgiveness:

> Then Peter came to Him and said, "Lord, how often shall my brother sin against me, and I forgive him? Up to seven times?" Jesus said to him, "I do not say to you, up to seven times, but up to seventy times seven. Therefore, the kingdom of heaven is like a certain king who wanted to settle accounts with his servants. And when he had begun to settle accounts, one was brought to him who owed him ten thousand talents. But as he was not able to pay, his master commanded that he be sold, with his wife and children and all that he had, and that payment be made. The servant therefore fell down before him, saying, 'Master, have patience with me, and I will pay you all.' Then the master of that servant was moved with compassion, released him, and forgave him the debt.

> "But that servant went out and found one of his fellow servants who owed him a hundred denarii; and he laid hands on him and took him by the throat, saying, 'Pay me what you owe!' So, his fellow servant fell down at his feet and begged him, saying, 'Have patience with me, and I will pay you all.' And he would not, but went and threw him into prison till he should pay the debt. So, when his fellow servants saw what had been done, they were very grieved, and came and told their master all that had been done. Then his master, after he had called him, said to him, 'You wicked servant! I forgave you all that debt because you begged me. Should you not also have had

compassion on your fellow servant, just as I had pity on you?' And his master was angry, and delivered him to the torturers until he should pay all that was due to him. "So, My heavenly Father also will do to you if each of you, from his heart, does not forgive his brother his trespasses."

Do you see that last sentence! It says that, just like the unforgiving servant, you will be turned over to the tormentors if you do not forgive your brother from your heart! This is an example of how the enemy can have legal rights to torment you if you do not forgive like you have been forgiven.

You will see in chapter 10 of this manual, one way you can pursue freedom is to forgive and release your bitterness. To be free of sin and come back into right standing with God, you need to repent of your sins and agree with your adversary's evidence against you.

> Agree with your adversary quickly, while you are on the way with him, lest your adversary deliver you to the judge, the judge hand you over to the officer, and you be thrown into prison. Assuredly, I say to you, you will by no means get out of there till you have paid the last penny. Matthew 5:25-26

Remember your adversary is keeping notes on your actions and words. He is ready to accuse you when you disobey God. God is light, and you must choose to walk in the light and obey Him. By disobeying God and going your own way, you are choosing to walk in the darkness. But, when you choose to return to God and repent for your sins, He is full of mercy and will forgive you and cleanse you.

> This is the message which we have heard from Him and declare to you, that God is light and in Him is no darkness at all. If we say that we have fellowship with Him, and walk in darkness, we lie and do not practice the truth. But if we walk in the light as He is in the light, we have fellowship with one another, and the blood of Jesus Christ His Son cleanses us from all sin. If we say that we have no sin, we deceive ourselves, and the truth is not in us. If we confess our sins, He is faithful and just to forgive us our sins and to cleanse us from all unrighteousness. If we say that we have not sinned, we make Him a liar, and His word is not in us. 1 John 1:5-10

When you confess your sin and repent by turning away from it and walking toward God, you will be forgiven and cleansed. You can have fellowship with Him through Jesus. Your fellowship with other believers can also be restored.

Once the legal rights of the adversary are removed, his case against you is nullified. The Great Judge will then hear the other voices speaking for you in the heavenly courts. The Blood of Jesus speaks for you, He is your covenant partner and will stand for you. The Holy Spirit is your advocate and your helper. The books in heaven give record of your covenant and your citizenship in heaven. There are also records of your offerings, service, and all other times you have repented. The Great Judge of All can then rule on your behalf for freedom from the torment and curses that have been frustrating your life. He can place a holy restraining order on the kingdom of darkness where the curse is concerned. He can also release any blessings held back from your bloodline.

As you begin to remove the enemy's legal rights to torment your life, you must also repent for the sins of your fathers to cleanse your bloodline of iniquities and the curses that follow them. We will cover this more in the next chapter.

Chapter 3:
Ancestral Sins and Curses

Throughout the Word of God, we see examples of Godly men repenting for their sins and the sins of their fathers or ancestors. Though this type of repentance is not talked about much in our churches today, it was a common occurrence during Bible times. Ancestral sin brought iniquities into the bloodline which opened the door for curses to operate for many generations.

We can see this curse in Exodus 20 where the Ten Commandments or Ten Words of Yahweh God were recorded by Moses:

> And God spoke all these words, saying: "I am the Lord your God, who brought you out of the land of Egypt, out of the house of bondage. "You shall have no other gods before Me. "You shall not make for yourself a carved image—any likeness of anything that is in heaven above, or that is in the earth beneath, or that is in the water under the earth; you shall not bow down to them nor serve them. For I, the Lord your God, am a jealous God, visiting the iniquity of the fathers upon the children to the third and fourth generations of those who hate Me, but showing mercy to thousands, to those who love Me and keep My commandments. Exodus 20:1-6

This curse of the father's iniquities passing along to their children is found in many other places in the Bible. It is mostly found in context with the sin of idolatry or worshiping other gods. This was considered spiritual adultery and breaking covenant with Yahweh God.

Although breaking covenant is a serious offense, it is also clear that Yahweh is a God of mercy and grace. He is willing to forgive our sins when we confess them and repent, return to Him, and keep covenant with Him by loving Him and obeying His commands

> 'The Lord is longsuffering and abundant in mercy, forgiving iniquity and transgression; but He by no means clears the guilty, visiting the iniquity of the fathers on the children to the third and fourth generation.' Numbers 14:18

We see examples of repentance for the sins of the fathers in the prayers and stories of Ezra, Nehemiah, Daniel, and Josiah. Ezra repented for his sins and the sins of his ancestors in Ezra chapters 9-10 when he found that the remnant had married women from other nations against Yahweh's instructions. Nehemiah repented for his father's sins and brought God into remembrance of His covenant of mercy:

> On hearing that Jerusalem was in ruins and the remnant left there distressed, Nehemiah fasted, prayed, and cried out to Yahweh God to forgive the sins of Israel including the father's sins: So, it was, when I heard these words, that I sat down and wept, and mourned for many days; I was fasting and praying before the God of heaven. And I said: "I pray, Lord God of heaven, O great and awesome God, You who keep Your covenant and mercy with those who love You and observe Your commandments, please let Your ear be attentive and Your eyes open, that You may hear the prayer of Your servant which I pray before You now, day and night, for the children of Israel Your servants, and confess the sins of the children of Israel which we have sinned against You. Both my father's house and I have sinned. We have acted very corruptly against You, and have not kept the commandments, the statutes, nor the ordinances which You commanded Your servant Moses. Remember, I pray, the word that You commanded Your servant Moses, saying, 'If you are unfaithful, I will scatter you among the nations; but if you return to Me, and keep My commandments and do them, though some of you were cast out to the farthest part of the heavens, yet I will gather them from there, and bring them to the place which I have chosen as a dwelling for My name.' Now these are Your servants and Your people, whom You have redeemed by Your great power, and by Your strong hand. O Lord, I pray, please let Your ear be attentive to the prayer of Your servant, and to the prayer of Your servants who desire to fear Your name; and let Your servant prosper this day, I pray, and grant him mercy in the sight of this man." For I was the king's cupbearer. Nehemiah 1:4-11

Daniel repented and confessed the sins of his ancestors:

> And I prayed to the Lord my God, and made confession, and said, "O Lord, great and awesome God, who keeps His covenant and mercy with those who love Him, and with those who keep His commandments, we have sinned and committed iniquity, we have done wickedly and rebelled, even by departing from Your precepts and Your judgments. "O Lord, to us belongs shame of face, to our kings, our princes, and our fathers, because we have sinned against You. To the Lord our God belong mercy and forgiveness, though we have rebelled against Him. Yes, all Israel has transgressed Your law, and has departed so as not to obey Your voice; therefore, the curse and the oath written in the Law of Moses the servant of God have been poured out on us, because we have sinned against Him. "As it is written in the Law of Moses, all this disaster has come upon us; yet we have not made our prayer before the Lord our God, that we might turn from our iniquities and understand Your truth.
>
> And now, O Lord our God, who brought Your people out of the land of Egypt with a mighty hand, and made Yourself a name, as it is this day—we have sinned, we have done

wickedly! "O Lord, according to all Your righteousness, I pray, let Your anger and Your fury be turned away from Your city Jerusalem, Your holy mountain; because for our sins, and for the iniquities of our fathers, Jerusalem and Your people are a reproach to all those around us. O my God, incline Your ear and hear; open Your eyes and see our desolations, and the city which is called by Your name; for we do not present our supplications before You because of our righteous deeds, but because of Your great mercies. O Lord, hear! O Lord, forgive! O Lord, listen and act! Do not delay for Your own sake, my God, for Your city and Your people are called by Your name." Daniel 9:4-5, 8-9, 11, 13, 15-16, 18-19

When Josiah became king of Judah, he began to reform the broken idolatrous kingdom. As the temple of Yahweh God was being restored, the Torah scroll was found.

Now it happened, when the king heard the words of the Book of the Law, that he tore his clothes. Then the king commanded Hilkiah the priest, Ahikam the son of Shaphan, Achbor the son of Michaiah, Shaphan the scribe, and Asaiah a servant of the king, saying, "Go, inquire of the Lord for me, for the people and for all Judah, concerning the words of this book that has been found; for great is the wrath of the Lord that is aroused against us, because our fathers have not obeyed the words of this book, to do according to all that is written concerning us."

Now the king sent them to gather all the elders of Judah and Jerusalem to him. The king went up to the house of the Lord with all the men of Judah, and with him all the inhabitants of Jerusalem—the priests and the prophets and all the people, both small and great. And he read in their hearing all the words of the Book of the Covenant which had been found in the house of the Lord. Then the king stood by a pillar and made a covenant before the Lord, to follow the Lord and to keep His commandments and His testimonies and His statutes, with all his heart and all his soul, to perform the words of this covenant that were written in this book. And all the people took a stand for the covenant. 2 Kings 22:11-13; 23:1-3

King Josiah recognized the sins of his fathers and chose to make covenant with Yahweh God. He then cleansed the land of all idolatry and initiated the feasts again to worship the God of Abraham, Isaac and Jacob.

King Soloman, when dedicating the Temple of God during a time of peace, prayed asking Yahweh to forgive the future generations when they sinned and returned to Him.

"When Your people Israel are defeated before an enemy because they have sinned against You, and when they turn back to You and confess Your name, and pray and make supplication to You in this temple, then hear in heaven, and forgive the sin of Your people Israel, and bring them back to the land which You gave to their fathers.

"When they sin against You (for there is no one who does not sin), and You become angry with them and deliver them to the enemy, and they take them captive to the land of the enemy, far or near; yet when they come to themselves in the land where they were carried captive, and repent, and make supplication to You in the land of those who took them captive, saying, 'We have sinned and done wrong, we have committed wickedness'; and when they return to You with all their heart and with all their soul in the land of their enemies who led them away captive, and pray to You toward their land which You gave to their fathers, the city which You have chosen and the temple which I have built for Your name: then hear in heaven Your dwelling place their prayer and their supplication, and maintain their cause, and forgive Your people who have sinned against You, and all their transgressions which they have transgressed against You; and grant them compassion before those who took them captive, that they may have compassion on them (for they are Your people and Your inheritance, whom You brought out of Egypt, out of the iron furnace) 1 Kings 8:33-34, 46-51

Deuteronomy 26 portrays the blessings that will come on Yahweh's people when they follow His Torah and keep their covenant with Him. It also reveals the curses that will come against the people when they forget their God and break covenant by rejecting His teaching and commands. We see in verses 39 and following, what will happen when they return to Yahweh and repent for their sins and the sins of their ancestors:

And those of you who are left shall waste away in their iniquity in your enemies' lands; also in their fathers' iniquities, which are with them, they shall waste away. 'But if they confess their iniquity and the iniquity of their fathers, with their unfaithfulness in which they were unfaithful to Me, and that they also have walked contrary to Me, and that I also have walked contrary to them and have brought them into the land of their enemies; if their uncircumcised hearts are humbled, and they accept their guilt—then I will remember My covenant with Jacob, and My covenant with Isaac and My covenant with Abraham I will remember; I will remember the land. Leviticus 26:39-42

"So, what does this mean for me?" You might be asking. Could one of these curses be operating in my life?

Like a flitting sparrow, like a flying swallow, so a curse without cause shall not alight. Proverbs 26:2

Some signs of a generational curse could be abuse, victimization/violence, poverty, fear/anxiety, sickness/disease, mental illness, marital problems, infertility, early death and accidents, hopelessness, sexual perversion, rejection/abandonment, separation from God, addiction, bitterness, suicide, failure, and other negative elements that you might see following your generational line.

If you are seeing signs of a curse in your life, you should repent of your own personal sins and generational sins that could be providing the enemy with legal rights to allow a curse to operate. Then choose to follow Yahweh with your entire being.

So, let's get started with the steps to freedom in this manual. In Deuteronomy 7, Moses told the Israelites not to be afraid to possess the promised land because Yahweh God is great and awesome. He would drive the nations out little by little until they were destroyed.

> You shall not be terrified of them; for the Lord your God, the great and awesome God, is among you. And the Lord your God will drive out those nations before you little by little; you will be unable to destroy them at once, lest the beasts of the field become too numerous for you. But the Lord your God will deliver them over to you, and will inflict defeat upon them until they are destroyed. And He will deliver their kings into your hand, and you will destroy their name from under heaven; no one shall be able to stand against you until you have destroyed them. Deuteronomy 7:21-24

In the next chapters, you will go little by little, step by step taking ground back from the enemy. Yahweh God will go before you and deliver these evil spirits into your hands. The kings or strongmen will not be able to stand against you with Yahweh as your covenant partner.

As you read through each subject, you will encounter areas of your life where you have never dealt with sin. Some of these sins may have been hidden from your remembrance. Some sins may be lingering over your life bringing guilt and shame. When you recognize how you have sinned against Yahweh, Godly sorrow will arise in you, but it has a purpose. Paul's letter to the congregation in Corinth, brought about this Godly sorrow for sin:

> For even if I made you sorry with my letter, I do not regret it; though I did regret it. For I perceive that the same epistle made you sorry, though only for a while. Now I rejoice, not that you were made sorry, but that your sorrow led to repentance. For you were made sorry in a godly manner, that you might suffer loss from us in nothing. For godly sorrow produces repentance leading to salvation, not to be regretted; but the sorrow of the world produces death. For observe this very thing, that you sorrowed in a godly manner: What diligence it produced in you, what clearing of yourselves, what indignation, what fear, what vehement desire, what zeal, what vindication! In all things you proved yourselves to be clear in this matter. 2 Corinthians 7:8-11

This sorrow does not bring guilt, shame, or death. Godly sorrow leads us to repentance, repentance leads to confession of sin, which leads to forgiveness and cleansing. Paul also says that it will produce diligence to clear our conscience of sin with desire and zeal which leads to vindication. When we are cleared of the charges of sin, we can find freedom.

In the following chapters, you will start with repenting and renouncing demon gods worshiped by your ancestors and any occult practices involved in their lives or in your own past. This is an important beginning step to remove any legal rights from idolatry and dark covenants in your life. Remember our God does not share His glory with another. Please invite and allow the Holy Spirit to expose any darkness that has been a part of your life or bloodline. As you look through the list of occult activities, you may be surprised at what you find. You may have participated in some activity without knowing what you were doing as many people try to "Christianize" or redeem occult activities. You may also see activities that you have learned through family tradition. Please resist the urge to defend your past choice and allow Yahweh to open your eyes to the truth behind these activities. Choose to be free from all darkness. Trust the Holy Spirit to lead you to everything you should renounce. When you renounce it, you choose to turn away from it and cut it out of your life for good. May Yahweh God give you boldness to make those choices!!!!!

You may also have the Holy Spirit bring something to mind that is not on the list or that seems trivial. Just trust His leading and obey Him. He knows everything about you and your bloodline. He is trustworthy and wants you to be free!

Let's start with an opening prayer as we come into the courts of heaven before the throne of mercy and grace to make a petition today for your freedom. Please read through the prayer first to make sure you are ready to surrender all of yourself to Yahweh God and make this petition. Then read it out loud. You will speak every declaration and prayer in this manual aloud. Your words are powerful! It is important that heaven and earth both hear your words of repentance, renunciation, petition, and declaration. They will be your witnesses for this court session. This is a legal matter and will be recorded in the courts of heaven. If you need to work through this manual over the span of several days, you can pick back up where you left off. As you enter back into the heavenly courts, just ask that the records be opened from the previous session.

Opening prayer and petition:

Father in heaven, I come boldly before Your throne of mercy and grace today, in the mighty name of Messiah Jesus, knowing You are the Great Judge of All. I come seeking complete freedom for me and my bloodline from the forces of darkness. I also petition today to receive all the blessings that were paid for on my behalf by Jesus the Messiah in the atonement. I come to hear the accusations speaking against me in Your heavenly courts, so I can repent and bring my case before You. I come with my Advocate, Jesus, the Lamb of God, and with the testimony of His blood and righteousness as my covering. I am in Him. I also come with the Holy Spirit as my counselor, witness, and truth.

I come in repentance for myself and my family line, both father and mother's sides, for all the sins committed against You, including the dark covenants, dedications, trades, sacrifices, and worship of other gods, including self. I also repent of all sins committed against my body, and all other sins unknown to me. I repent for all idle words, and words of death or curse spoken by me or my family members.

(If married): I also come in repentance in the same way for my husband's sins and those of his ancestors, as I have married into his bloodline and have taken his name. I am one with him.

As I go through the process of repentance and renouncing, please expose all darkness and forgive my transgressions and iniquities and cleanse my bloodline with the blood of Jesus. Please bring to my remembrance any information that I need to know for complete and total freedom and wholeness of my entire being.

I ask that You would open the record books before your courts, and that all previous records of repentance by me, (my husband,) and my (our) ancestors be opened and used as evidence.

I ask that the records of my citizenship in heaven be opened and the records of our tithes, offerings, sacrifices, and service to Your kingdom be opened.

I ask You to remember the blood that was shed on my behalf by Your Son, Yeshua haMaschiach, Jesus the Messiah, and the testimony it speaks for me. I ask You to remember the records of my dedication to You and the covenant that has been made between us which includes my future generations.

I ask that You would remember the book in heaven that has Your plans for my life and my bloodline. I agree with those plans and choose to walk in Your plans and destiny and complete the tasks You have for me on this earth.

I ask You to remember the prayers of all the saints and the voices of the great cloud of witnesses in heaven that have gone up before You as a sweet-smelling fragrance on my behalf.

As I seek to know the accusations formed against us in order to repent, I ask that You make a clear path for freedom by binding the adversary and his power over me. I know that no one compares to You. You are greater than my adversary. May Your powerful hosts surround me and my family as I seek freedom today, and in the days following. May the blood of Jesus seal off the holy ground of this courtroom from external warfare and send confusion into the enemy's camp.

I ask that You subpoena, arrest, and isolate all demonic forces that need to appear before You for this case today. I ask You to close off their entrances and exits and bring them all under Your obedience with only those forces present that have legal rights to be in this court session. May all communication with outer darkness, calls for reinforcements, and strategic warfare of the enemy be prohibited during this time. I ask that You forbid violent manifestations, blocking maneuvers, and torment. I ask You to render all of their weapons ineffective in this court session and cause them to testify truthfully under oath.

I petition that Your great Sword of the Spirit that is living and powerful separate me today from any forces of darkness that have attached to me through the bloodline, my own sins, or the sins of others. I petition that any demons being judged today would be arrested and taken away by Your heavenly host and be forbidden to transfer to anyone present or to return to me or anyone else in my bloodline from now to eternity. I also petition that no backlash will take place in the future concerning this court case. May the fire of the Holy Spirit cleanse and purge this holy ground and my body, soul, and spirit throughout this process to remove all defilement, deposits, and attachments of darkness as the legal rights are removed.

I petition that every power of darkness and their touchpoints over me be broken and rendered ineffective today in the name of Jesus, including all curses, hexes, vexes, spells, attachments, assignments, seals, programming, triggering, nets, webs, grids, hooks, pulleys, snares, shackles, chains, radars, targets, marks, brands, evil cycles or time clocks, bonds, defilement, bounties, satellites, chips, evil technologies, trackers, tattoos, bondage, captivity, death, destruction, torment, and any other deposit of darkness or points of contact.

I submit my will and life to You now, Yahweh God. I command every part of myself to submit to You. I command the demons at work in my life to submit to You. Please hear my cry from heaven and set me and my bloodline free, in Jesus' name.

Chapter 4:
Renouncing Ancestral Demon Worship and Covenants

Because all of our ancestors go back to Noah, we know that somewhere along the line, some of them have worshiped other gods. You will begin by renouncing those demon gods from your ancestral backgrounds. You may choose to renounce each bloodline below or choose those that apply to your known genealogy. If you do not see your specific heritage listed below, it is easy to find a list of gods worshiped by any ancestry through a quick internet search. Just insert them in the renunciation prayer.

Pray the following aloud:

Father in heaven, I choose today to repent for and renounce the sins of idolatry in my generational bloodline. I respect my ancestors and my ancestry, but I renounce any sinful practices within their culture-groups which are in conflict with the Word of God including festivals and rituals of protection, provision, birth, coming of age, marriage, initiations, funerals, and death. Please separate me and my bloodline from the influence of and slavery to these evil spirits as I renounce them today.

I specifically renounce the following demons and dark entities worshiped in my ancestral lines, as well as, certain rituals and superstitions connected to them:

Gods of Babylon, Canaan, and Freemasonry- Nimrod, Semiramis, Tammuz, Ishtar (Inanna), Nabu, Apshu, Shamash, Ea, Tiamat, Nergal, Marduk, Adad, An, Enlil, Enki, Ninhursag, Utu, El, Asherah, Ba'al, Anat, Molech, Chemosh, Hadad, Bel, Dagon, Milcom, Yam, Yarikh, Astarte, Mot, Great Architect of the Universe (GAOTU), Lucifer, Hiram Abiff, Baphomet, Jezebel, Abaddon, Apollyon (also the Egyptian gods Osiris, Isis, Horus, Set, and Ra) and all other false gods.

*I did not have space here to include a sufficient prayer for the renunciation of freemasonry and all its occultic levels and degrees. If your ancestors have been involved in freemasonry or another secret society, there is a deeper prayer of renunciation from Selwyn Stevens of Jubilee Resources included at the end of this manual. It is vital to your freedom, that you complete this prayer.

Nordic and German Ancestry- Odin (Woden), Thor, Loki, Fenrir, and Freyja/Freya/Frigg, Balder, Vidar, Vale, Hel, Brage, Heimdall, Ty, Njord, Froy, Ull, Forsete, Ymir, Mimir, Týr (Tiw), Bragi, Baldr, Heimdallr, Ullr, Víðarr, Váli, Sif, Forseti, Njörðr, Höðr, Hœnir, Hermóðr, Dellingr, Óðr, Máni, and all other Norse and Germanic gods; Vikings, Valhalla, pillaging, murder, barbarics, looting, raiding, raping, kidnapping, drunkenness, trolls, Dovregubben (troll king), jotners, nissers, giants, goblins, dwarves, and other mythical creatures.

Celtic Ancestry- Aine, Adsullata, Arawn, Bel, Brigit, Ebhlinne, Inghean Bhuidhe, Crobh Dearg. Lassair, Latiaran, Rosmerta, Sul, Lady of the Lake, and all other Celtic gods; eight seasonal festivals, two solstices, two equinoxes and the four fire festivals, male and female druidic hierarchies, mind-control, cauldron worship, 13 councils, satan, lucifer, father of light, grandmaster, the star, the giver of pain, the anti-Christ, four elements, witchcraft, and neolithic shamanism.

Scottish Ancestry- renounce Celtic gods, feuding, border reivers, and curse of Gavin Dunbar.

Egyptian Ancestry- Nine chief deities - Ra, Shu and Tefnut, Geb and Nut, Osiris and Isis, Set and Nephthys (four sets of twins); Three secondary deities - Hathor, Horus and Anubis; others: Amun, Bastet, Thoth, Ptah, Sobek, Bes, Ma'at, Khnum, Khepri, Khonsu, Atum, Aten, Neith, Heka, and all other Egyptian gods; religious jewelry, amulets, scarab beetle, the ren or secret name, temples, pyramids, book of death, sixth and seventh books of Moses, and magical books.

Indian Ancestry:

Hinduism: false Trinity: Brahma, Vishnu, and Shiva; Shakti, Kali, Rama, Ganesh, Krishna, Budsha, Kalkin, Prana, Shesha, and all other Hindu gods; upanishads, vedas, puranas, bhagavad gita, brahmanas, reincarnation, karma and past-lives, yoga, samskara superstitions, suttee, maya, dharma, moksha, puja rituals -flowers, food, and drink offered to the gods, aarti candle lighting, tilaka mark on the forehead or third eye, tree worship, kirtan chanting, vrata vows, yatra pilgrimage, and festivals to gods.

Buddhism: Siddhartha Gautama Buddha, "eight great bodhisattvas": Ksitigarbha, Vajrapani, Akasagarbha, Avalokitesvara, Maitreya, Amitabha, Sarvanivāraṇaviṣkambhin, Samantabhadra and Manjushri; 2 branches of Buddhism (Theraveda and Mahayana), the Noble Eightfold Path to reach nirvana, achieving my own salvation and becoming a god, soul-ties with Lamas (priests), pagodas, sacred items, wheel of dharma, eye of wisdom (third eye); Three jewels: Buddha, Dharma, and Sangha, the big bell of witness; burning incense, chanting, and bowing in shrines; priestly robes, beggar's bowl, white elephant, sacred sound, "Aum", glorified lightbody, ascension flame, opening of 21 chakras, codes from the keys of Enoch, the ungodly "I Am" presence, and ascended master.

Asian Ancestry:

Chinese: Buddhism, Taoism, Confucianism, Tudi Gong (elemental spirits), Kuei-shen (nature spirits), eight Immortals of Holy Taoism, Nuwa, Fuxi, P'an Ku, the dragon Yinglong, the dragon

Hongshen, yin and yang energies, Chinese zodiac, Shangti, Jade Emperor, Xihua, Mugong, Guanyin, Lord Yama, Caishen, Chang'e, Zao-shen, Niu Lang & Zhi Nu, guei (dead human spirits), ancestral worship, menschen guardians of the door; feng shui, traditional Chinese medicine, acupuncture, tai chi, vital energy chi or ki, torii gateways, maneki-neko, the character Fu for good luck, fortune cookies, and Chinese knots to ward off evil spirits.

Japanese: Shinto, kamis, shamanism, Buddhism, Confucianism, ancestor worship, Izanami, Izanagi, deity of fire, Amaterasa, Tsukuyomi, god of force (impetuous male), Susanoo, mazoku, Futsunushi, and all other Japanese gods; ninja warfare, samurai warfare, jujutsu, judo, kendo, aikido, karate, kiai, luck, fate and superstition, and jinja shrines.

Korean: Buddhism, Confucianism, shamanism, ancestral worship, dragons, gumiho (nine-tailed fox), beads of power, Dokkaebi (goblins), gods and goddesses from Korean folklore, tigers as guardian spirits and protectors, Hwanung, Seokga, Dalnim, Haenim, Haemosu, Koenegitto, Yeomna, Samsin halmeoni, Hwanin, Jacheongbi, Sanshin, and Yongwang, and all other Korean gods.

Russian (Slavic) Ancestry- Perun, Veles, Mokosh, Dažbog, Chernobog, Belobog, Svarog, Stribog, Jarilo, Marzanna, Lada, Svetovid, Triglav, Rod, Khors, Radegast, Simargl, Devana, Dodola and Perperuna, Baba Yaga, Kikimora, Zorya, Kupala Night, Porevit, Leshy, Morena, Veles, Dazhbog, Svarozhits, Dola, Mat Zemlya, Rozhanitsy, Sudenitsy, Narechnitsy, Zvezda, Utrenica, Danica, Yarovit, Zhiva, Prove, Prone, Proue, Rugievit, Porenut, Podaga, and all other Slavic gods; superstitious customs involving life cycles and festivals including the following: Święto Godowe (Zimowy Staniasłońc, winter solstice), tree of life ceremony, luck rituals, tryzny; Jare Święto (śmigus Dyngus, rebirth of nature), drowning of the Marzana doll, decorating and using eggs as talismans for curing sickness, spells, removing evil spirits with catkins, water purification; Kupalnocka, celebration of fire and water, fertility rites, ritual washing after three months without bathing, making flower wreaths to float in the water to find lovers, leaping over the fire, fortune telling with flowers and herbs; Święto Plonów (harvest holiday for Świętowit, the god of war and fertility), huge wreaths and cakes baked in his honor, rituals connected to the forefathers, feeding the Dzaidy (dead ancestors) as they visited, grumadki (pieces of wood) used to point the dead back to Nawia (heaven), Zaduszki, Rekawka holiday; Birth superstitions- red ribbons tied on cradles to scare away demons, sharp tools under the bed, garlic, thorny-plants, fire, and faking the death of babies, babies dedicated to Rod, leaving food out for the three deities who mark babies foreheads after birth, Rod and the Rodzanice were invited to mark the baby's forehead by setting out food and drink offerings, the baby's real name was hidden until he was 12 years old to protect him from demons; Family superstitions- ax over the threshold at marriage and under the bed on the wedding night for a boy to be conceived; Death superstitions- dead carried out a broken window, ax placed at the threshold to keep the dead spirit from returning, burying jars of ashes under the threshold to protect it, Dziady rituals to feed dead ancestors, and reincarnation with the help of magical creatures (wyrag and rarog).

Hispanic/Latino ancestry-

Spain -Iberian gods: Nabia, Epona, Trebaruna, Endovelicus, Bandua, Reo, Sucellus, Taranis, Borvo, Ogmios, Sugaar, Bandi, Arentia, Cariocecus, Arentius, Consus, Duberdicus, Toutatis, Urtzi, Indalo, Cossus, Durius, Runesocesius, Ilurbeda; Basque gods: Mari, Basajaun, Tartalo, Akerbeltz, Jentil, Olentzero, Gaueko, Iratxoak, Sorginak, Amalur, Egoi, Herensuge, Aatxe, Odei, Mairu, San Martin, Txiki, Lamia, Eate, Inguma, Galtzagorri, Eki, Aide, Eguzkilore, and Aker (also renounce Celtic gods)

Central and South America-red ribbons around babies wrist for protection, animal and human blood sacrifices and offerings, blood-letting, shamanism, santeria, espiritsmo, goddess Maria Lionza, holy pilgrimages, festivals and life-cycle rituals, weather and fertility rituals, idolatry and ancestor worship, carnivale, divination, voo-doo, witchcraft, witch doctors, casting spells and curses, augury, astrology, patron deities, maize beads, Aztec gods: Ometeotl, Quetzalcoatl, Chicomecoatl, Tlaloc, Tezcatlipoca, Huitzilopochtli, Xipe Totec, Xochiquetzal, Mixcoatl, Metztli, Chalchiuhtlicue, Xolotl, Xōchipilli, Centeōtl, Ōmeteōtl, Patecatl, Tlaltecuhtli, Xiuhtecuhtli, and all other Aztec gods, Mayan gods: Itzamna, Kinich Ahau, Chaac, Bolon Dzacab, Bacab, Ixchel, Ixtab, Ek Chuah, Kukulcan, Vucub Caquix, Tlaloqueh, Camazotz, Hunab Ku, Ah Puch, Ek Chuaj, Yum Kaax, Camazotz, Huracan, Ah-Muzen-Cab, Cabrakan, Gucumatz, K'awiil, Acan, aluxob, codical gods A-Z, the deified Hero Twins, and all other Mayan gods.

African Ancestry- Loas, Oshun, Ogun, Anansi, Yemoja, Oya, Shango, Yemmaya, Nana Buluku, Adroa, Obatala, Olorun, Eshu, Olokun, Mami Wata, Papa Legba, Asase Ya, Ngai, Kibuka, Inkosazana, Mawu, Mbaba Mwana Waresa, Amadioha, Mbombo, Babalú-Ayé, Orunmila, Oduduwa, Bumba, Babalú Ayé, Eshu, Python, Leviathan, Baron Samedi, Gran Brijit, Queen of the Coast, Ghede,and all other African gods, the demon of death, marine spirits, snakes, village altars, family idols, blood sacrifice of animals and humans, voodoo, charms, spells, rituals, drinking blood, ritual baths, kingdom under the sea, spirit husbands and wives, seeking help from witch doctors, naturalists, herbalists, village healers, shamans, and sangomas.

Arabic ancestry- Allah (moon god), "House of Idols" called the "Kaaba," hajj ritual, Quraysh, Sun goddess, three goddesses (Al-lat, Al-uzza and Manat), crescent moon, Ramadan, Mohammed, Sharia, Jizya tax, Jihad, anger, rage, hatred, murder, brutality, rape, abuse, intimidation, domination, superiority, mind control, death, suicide, Qur'an, reciting the Shahada, prayer toward Mecca, dhimma pact, slavery, oppression, rejection, and fear.

Greek Ancestry- Zeus, Poseidon, Hera, Hestia and Demeter, Hades, and later on Apollo, Artemis, Hermes, Athena, Hephaestus, Aphrodite and Ares, Dionysus, and all other Greek gods; Mount Olympus, rituals and blood sacrifice, humanism, philosophy, sororities and fraternities, Greek clubs, complaining, arguing, pride, addiction, gossip, sexual perversion, and laziness.

Jewish Ancestry- kabbalah, occult mysticism, evil eye, hamsa hand, occult gematria, rejection of Messiah Jesus, curse of the blood of Jesus, pride, idolatry, following tradition without worshiping Yahweh, superstition, and religion (also renounce worship of gods of Babylon, Canaan, and Egypt)

Italian ancestry- Jupiter, Minerva, Ceres, Aphrodite, Vesta, Venus, Neptune, Dionysus, Mars, Diana, Jove, Juno, Mercury, Cybele, Fortuna, Luna, Faunus, Pax, Flora, Terra, Romulus, Libitina, Epona, Sol Invictus, Lares, Vulcan, Vesta, Laetitia, Bacchus, and all other Roman gods; terrors of the colosseum, gladiators, circus maximus, pantheon, sexual perversion, massacre of Jews and Christians, anger, hot tempers, vanity, matriarch worship, and impatience.

Native American (Indigenous people) ancestry- demon gods and idols of all the indigenous peoples including: Aleut, Algonquin, Apache, Arapaho, Biloxi, Blackfoot, Beaver, Catawba, Cherokee, Cheyenne, Chickamauga, Chickasaw, Chippewa, Choctaw, Comanche, Conestoga, Cree, Creek, Crow, Dakota, Delaware, Erie, Fox, Hopi, Illinois, Inuit, Iowa, Iroquois, Kiowa, Maya, Miami, Miwok, Mohawk, Mohican, Multnomah, Natchez, Navajo, Nez Perce, Nottaway, Oconee, Omaha, Ottawa, Pawnee, Pensacola, Powhatan, Rappahannock, Santee, Seminole, Seneca, Shasta, Shawnee, Shoshone, Sioux, Tillamook, Wampanoag, Washoe, Walla Walla, Wichita, Yuma, Zuni, and other indigenous peoples; I also renounce worship of nature, animal spirits, celestial spirits, and ancestors; spirit guides, smoking incense, murder, human and animal blood sacrifice, superstitious rituals, ritual dance, dream catchers, ritual beads, war paint, totem poles, scalping victims, kidnapping wives and children, conjuring demons, witchcraft practices, divination practices, sorcery, charms, gambling, alcoholism, and addiction.

After renouncing the specific demon gods, pray the following prayer:

In Jesus' name I renounce all forms of idolatry including all dark covenants, trades, dedications, sacrifices, and worship made with and to demon gods and supernatural beings of darkness by my paternal and maternal ancestors {as well as, any ancestry from adoptive parents and ancestry of my husband's bloodlines (if applicable)}. I repent for and renounce all blood sacrifice of humans, animals, and bloodletting.

I repent for these sins and renounce and cancel all oaths, vows, pledges, curses, blood covenants, agreements, acts of violence, sexual perversion, and violence associated with these demon gods.

I repent for and renounce all associated witchcraft, sorcery, incantations, formulas, spells, incense, candle lighting, immersions, sprinklings, burials, prayers, ceremonies, superstitions, and rituals. I renounce all occult supernatural powers gained by my ancestors through the worship of false gods.

I renounce the worship of idols, false gods, demons, entities, people, images, sacred pillars, standing stones, obelisks, poles, trees, totems, etc.

I renounce worship of the earth, sun, moon, stars, constellations, planets, and all gods associated with them.

I renounce animal worship, sexual and soul-ties with animals, and invoking animal spirits.

I renounce worship of the five elements of earth, wind, fire, water, and space/void, and all the spirits associated with them.

I renounce the worship of plants and any witchcraft using plants as medicine, charms, and alternative healing.

I renounce ancestor worship including all monuments, ceremonies, rituals, and sacrifices made to them at altars, tombs, and graveyards.

I reject worship and pride taken in my nationality, ethnicity, race, religion, and sex related to sin, human accomplishment, superiority, exclusivity, and degradation of others. I renounce the rebellion of God-given authority by my ancestors.

I renounce all secret and occult organizations entered into by my ancestors. I renounce all ideologies, holy days, festivals, customs, and superstitions that exalt themselves against the knowledge of God.

I renounce all evil altars and the priests/priestesses accompanying them. I renounce ties to temples, occult sacred grounds, and places of worship where false gods or idols are served. I renounce their festivals, paying homage to the gods through removing shoes, bowing, prostrating, gestures, handshakes, blood-letting, making sacrifices, lighting candles or incense, making oaths, eating food sacrificed to them, and sexual perversion.

I petition You, Yahweh God, to cut loose myself and my bloodline from all ties to idolatry and occult religions, groups, or organization. Sever us from any magic, psychic powers, or witchcraft that continues in the bloodline from these evil acts. Cleanse our spiritual gifts and talents that You have given our bloodline for Your kingdom.

I ask You to sever all soul-ties to any entities, humans, groups, or places involved in any of these dark covenants. I ask You to cancel all their claims on me and my bloodline. I petition to remove our names, images, DNA and representations from any evil altars and for all of our DNA, destinies, and parts to be released from any holding areas in any realm to be returned to me and all my living relatives, children, and future generations. I detach myself and my bloodline from any and all demonic forces that have had access to us from this idolatry. I command them to leave this bloodline now in the name of Jesus the Messiah.

I ask You Yahweh God to cleanse my bloodlines from all of this sin and iniquity and remove all legal rights of darkness to claim any place in myself or my generations. Remember the blood of Jesus that speaks on my behalf and the covenant I have with You. Remember Your plans for me and my bloodline. I petition that You revoke every curse that has been following us and restore the blessings You have planned for us. Restore all of us to a righteous relationship with You. Restore our shattered souls and free us from any bondage we have been in because of this sin. In Jesus' name, I take back any spiritual territory my ancestors have given to the kingdom of darkness and I now give it to Yahweh God. Please guard us with Your heavenly host and restore this bloodline to Your kingdom purpose.

Yahweh's calendar and appointed times

Now that you have renounced the occult worship and celebration of false gods, did you know the God of Israel has special times of celebration on His calendar? These set-times or appointed times are special seasons that He has set aside to be with His people which include those of us who are grafted into Israel. Most are tied to special celebrations or "feasts" that are to be repeated or rehearsed year after year. They were set up to help the Israelites remember who Yahweh was and what He had done for them. These times usually line up with events in the heavens, such as blood moons, which were created for signs and seasons.

> Then God said, "Let there be lights in the firmament of the heavens to divide the day from the night; and let them be for signs and seasons, and for days and years; and let them be for lights in the firmament of the heavens to give light on the earth"; and it was so. Genesis 1:14-15

> These are the feasts of the Lord, holy convocations which you shall proclaim at their appointed times. Leviticus 23:4

These feasts are called "Feasts of the Lord" and they are not only for the children of Israel, but for all who have been grafted in to the Tree of Israel through Messiah Jesus. Each feast reminds us of a Biblical event from the past, as well as, a prophetic event that is to come. They are celebrations of covenant. The weekly feast of "Shabbat' or Sabbath is held on the seventh day of the week when Yahweh God rested from His work of creation. Because Yahweh's calendar days are "evening and morning", the weekly Shabbat celebration begins at sundown on Friday night and goes until sundown on Saturday night. This day is an appointed time for rest and meeting with Yahweh God. He has special blessings for us when we choose to forego our own plans and meet with Him on this day.

> "If you turn away your foot from the Sabbath, from doing your pleasure on My holy day, and call the Sabbath a delight, the holy day of the Lord honorable, and shall honor Him, not doing your own ways, nor finding your own pleasure, nor speaking your own words, then you shall delight yourself in the Lord; and I will cause you to ride on the high hills of the earth, and feed you with the heritage of Jacob your father. The mouth of the Lord has spoken." Isaiah 58:13-14

The seasonal feasts, or seven feasts of the Lord, that were given to the Israelites in the wilderness all point prophetically to Jesus the Messiah. Each time the Israelites would celebrate the feasts, they would be rehearsing for the coming of Messiah. The spring feasts of Passover, Unleavened Bread, and First Fruits were fulfilled in the first coming of Jesus. The middle feast of Pentecost was fulfilled when the Holy Spirit was sent to the disciples. The fall feasts of Trumpets, Day of Atonement, and Tabernacles will be fulfilled when Jesus returns again. If the

Israelites had perpetually kept these appointed times, they would have recognized their Messiah when he came. You can read about the feasts in Leviticus 23.

Today, most of us no longer follow Yahweh's lunar calendar and His appointed times. We use the Gregorian solar calendar with months and days named after Roman and Greek gods and celebrate pagan holidays that have come through the Catholic church and the great melting pot of our country. The faith of the body of Messiah has been syncretized with many false religions and their celebrations.

Celebrations in Bible times were usually tied to worship, whether they were dedicated to Yahweh God or the gods of the pagan nations. The celebrations were a part of covenant fellowship. Great feasts were prepared as the covenant meal and activities were focused on worship. In Numbers 25, the Israelite men began to intermarry with the Moabite women and go to their feasts. The scriptures say that it caused Israel to be "joined to Baal of Peor", a demon god.

> Now Israel remained in Acacia Grove, and the people began to commit harlotry with the women of Moab. They invited the people to the sacrifices of their gods, and the people ate and bowed down to their gods. So Israel was joined to Baal of Peor, and the anger of the Lord was aroused against Israel. Numbers 25:1-3

As we join in with worldly festivals and feasts, we are taking part in covenant practices. Some of these holidays (taken from the words "holy days") are appointed times on the calendar of darkness and celebrations to dark gods. They are "holy days" on satan's calendar.

Some of this may be new information to you, but I hope the Holy Spirit will give you a witness of truth where these appointed times are concerned. If you would like to renounce the pagan holiday practices you or your ancestors have taken part in and refocus your covenant celebrations on Yahweh God's appointed times, pray the following prayer:

Father in heaven, I repent for the sins of my ancestors and myself for neglecting your appointed times that You have set as a perpetual statute in Your word. I also repent for choosing to celebrate the pagan festivals that the enemy has brought into my culture, knowingly and unknowingly, including Halloween, Pagan Easter and Christmas rituals, Mardi Gras, Mayday, Pagan Valentine's Day rituals, Day of the Dead celebrations, Epiphany, Pagan birthday rituals; and any festivals which involve drunkenness, licentiousness, superstitions, and occult activities. I repent for giving the enemy access to my identity by dressing in costumes of evil entities, animals, or in honor of false gods on these holidays. I repent for encouraging my family members, friends, and others to participate in these holidays and festivals.

I repent for any covenants that were made with darkness by participating in these events, even in ignorance. I ask You to forgive these sins and cleanse me and my bloodline. I choose to renounce and detach myself from the demon gods associated with these festivals and the Gregorian calendar that we use for our schedules. I command them to release me and my bloodline now in Jesus' name. I choose to forgive my ancestors and church leaders for leading me into worship of false gods whether knowingly or unknowingly. I choose to serve and worship You, Yahweh God, and You alone. I petition that You sever me and my bloodline completely from the darkness that had legal rights to us through this idolatry.

In Jesus' name, I petition that You free us from any future set-times or appointed times on the enemy's calendar. I ask that you would cancel them and erase those appointments. I dedicate all of our lives and life-cycle events to You.

Please Yahweh, give me a hunger and thirst for righteousness. Give me a desire for the things of Your kingdom. I choose to follow You and obey Your word and ask You to teach me how to worship You and meet with You on Your appointed times. I recognize that all the feasts on Your holy calendar have not been fulfilled, so we still need to rehearse and prepare for the second coming of Jesus the Messiah, King of Kings and Lord of Lords. Please show me how I can honor Your Shabbat (Sabbath) and put away my normal activities to meet with You. Let me find joy in Your feasts and appointed times.

Chapter 5:
Renouncing Dark Covenants and Occult Activities

We have already pointed out that our God requires us to worship Him only. Idolatry, or the worship of idols, is considered spiritual adultery in His eyes. Those who dwelled in the land of promise were idol worshipers. Yahweh God did not want His people to learn their practices. The following verses will give insight into occult activities involved in the worship of idols or false gods that were being practiced by the inhabitants of the promised land. Yahweh God refers to them as abominations.

> "When you come into the land which the Lord your God is giving you, you shall not learn to follow the abominations of those nations. There shall not be found among you anyone who makes his son or his daughter pass through the fire, or one who practices witchcraft, or a soothsayer, or one who interprets omens, or a sorcerer, or one who conjures spells, or a medium, or a spiritist, or one who calls up the dead. For all who do these things are an abomination to the Lord, and because of these abominations the Lord your God drives them out from before you. You shall be blameless before the Lord your God. For these nations which you will dispossess listened to soothsayers and diviners; but as for you, the Lord your God has not appointed such for you." Deuteronomy 18:9-14

> And take heed, lest you lift your eyes to heaven, and when you see the sun, the moon, and the stars, all the host of heaven, you feel driven to worship them and serve them, which the Lord your God has given to all the peoples under the whole heaven as a heritage. Deuteronomy 4:19

The term 'occult' means secret or hidden and usually refers to something supernatural or mystical. Most occult practices seek wisdom or power from a source other than Yahweh God. Our God wants us to seek Him for all our needs.

> And when they say to you, "Seek those who are mediums and wizards, who whisper and mutter," should not a people seek their God? Should they seek the dead on behalf of the living? Isaiah 8:19

Use the checklist at the end of this chapter to identify any occult involvement for yourself and your generational line. Some people choose to renounce all of it not knowing what all their ancestors have done. If you choose to do a general renunciation, go back and be specific about your known sins. Add anything to your personal checklist that the Holy Spirit brings to your mind. If you have questions about practices that are not in the Bible and are not listed below, there is an easy way to test them by looking at the roots and fruits of the practice. You also have the witness of the Holy Spirit. For example, here is a roots and fruits test for chiropractic which can be found in a quick internet search. The practice of chiropractic was started by a magnetic healer and occultist by the name of D.D. Palmer. Palmer claimed to get some of his principles from a séance. His work was rooted in vitalism, naturalism, magnetism, and spiritism. It is based on subluxations or "energies" flowing through the spine that can block and interfere with the bodies systems (occultic roots). People who see chiropractors for adjustments feel better temporarily, but rarely get healed. They must continue to go back for treatments for many years in a seemingly addictive pattern (bad fruits).

If you or your ancestors have been involved in any false religion or secret societies like the Shriners or Freemasons, it would be beneficial for you to pray through some deeper renunciation prayers. Also, if you have been greatly involved in Satanism or New Age practices, or have been an instructor in any of those practices, deeper renunciation prayers for those activities would be recommended. There are a few in the following chapter. You can find many deeper renunciation prayers through Kanaan Ministries and Jubilee resources.

After marking the checklist, pray the following prayer aloud, renouncing each separate type of occult activity:

"Father in heaven, I repent for the sins of idolatry for myself and my bloodline. Forgive me for breaking covenant with You. I recognize and confess _____ as a sin against you. I am deeply sorry for this sin and I repent of it. Please forgive me and my ancestors for seeking wisdom or power apart from You. Please wash and cleanse me with your blood.

I renounce satan in this area in all his ways; I reject and detach myself from any covenant, power, knowledge, wealth, spiritual guides, gifts, or abilities that I have received from him and my involvement with the occult."

After confessing and repenting of these sins, pray the following prayer aloud:

"In the name of Jesus the Messiah, I also repent for any idolatry and occult sins my ancestors have committed, known and unknown to me, especially _____. I renounce any dark covenants, trades, dedications, and sacrifices made by them on my behalf and on behalf of my generations. Yahweh God, you gave us power over the adversary. I therefore release and detach myself and my family from any hold which any of these occult activities have, or have had, on our lives. I sever myself and my bloodline from all evil spirits which entered through these sins and command them to release us now. I petition that You cancel any curse against me or against any member of my family brought about by this occult

activity. I ask that you serve eviction notice to any spirits that came into my life or my bloodline through any of this occult activity. I ask You to close these doors and seal them with the blood of Jesus, never to be opened again. In Jesus' name, I take back any spiritual territory I have given to the enemy, and I now give it to Yahweh God. I commit my life to Jesus, my covenant partner, and dedicate all areas of my life to Him. I claim the protection of the blood of Jesus over my mind, body, and spirit. Messiah Jesus, I claim and thank you for all of the blessings made available to me because of your death on the cross. Thank you for paying the price for my freedom. "

Occult activity checklist:

- Abstract art (under hallucinogenic stimulus)
- Acupuncture
- Alchemy (as a branch of occult philosophy and experimentation)
- Aliens, UFO's, extraterrestrials, Nordics, Grays, abductions
- Amulets (tiger's claw, shark's tooth, horseshoe over door, mascots, talisman, magic picture)
- Ancestor worship/ food and drink offerings to ancestors or their spirits
- Ankh (a cross with a ring top from Egypt used in satanic and fertility rites)
- Apparitions
- Astral travel
- Astrology
- Augury (interpreting omens)
- Automatic writing/ scratching out names
- Biofeedback
- Birth signs/ birthstones/ birth flowers, colors, etc.
- Boy Scouts order of the arrow and Native American lore/ceremonies
- Black arts/ Black magic
- Black mass
- Blood sacrifices (animal, human, self)
- Blood pacts
- Burning incense (sage and others)
- Burying objects for spells, magic, or witchcraft
- Cartomancy (using playing cards for divination)
- Chain letters (curses involved)
- Charms, Charming or enchanting (attempts to use spiritual power)
- Chinese astrology and zodiac
- Chiropractic (manipulating energy flow, DD Palmer)
- Clairaudience (ability to hear voices and sounds super-normally – spirit voices alleging to be those of dead people giving advice or warnings)

- Clairsentience (supernormal sense perception)
- Clairvoyance (ability to see objects or events spontaneously or supernaturally above their normal range of vision – second sight)
- Colour/color therapy
- Concept therapy philosophy
- Conjuration (summoning up a spirit by incantation)
- Costumes of an occult nature (wizards, witches, ghouls, devils, ghosts, etc.)
- Coven (a community of witches)
- Crystal ball gazing
- Crystals used for spiritual reasons
- Death magic (where the name of the sickness plus a written spell is cast into coffin or grave)
- Demon worship
- Disembodied spirits
- Divination
- Divining rod or twig or pendulum (Hosea 4:12)
- Dowsing or witching for water, minerals, under-ground cables, finding out the sex of unborn child using divining rod, pendulum, twig or planchette
- Dreamcatchers / talismans to ward off evil spirits
- Dream interpretation of an occult nature, as with Edgar Cayce books
- Dungeons and dragons (role-playing games)
- Eastern meditation (Gurus, Mantras, Yoga, Temples etc; also called contemplative prayer, clearing the mind)
- Ectoplasm (unknown substance from body of a medium)
- Enchanting
- E.S.P. (extra sensory perception)
- Evil eye
- False Religion (Hinduism, Buddhism, Islam, Rosicrucianism. New Age, Native American religion, Paganism, Bahai, Mormonism, Jehovah's Witness, Scientology, Hare Krishna, Moonies, Shamanism, etc.)
- Findhorn Community (spiritual utopian community in Britain)
- Floating trumpets (séance trick by mediums or spiritists)
- Folklore (fairies, spirits, gnomes, dragons, trolls, golems, mermaids)
- Fortune cookies
- Fortune telling (including carnivals and fortune telling games played by children)
- Freemasonry, Eastern Star, Shriners, secret societies, fraternity, sorority
- Gothic rock music
- Gurus (Yogis)
- Grave soaking, graveyard rituals, death rituals

- Gypsy curses
- Hallucinogenic drugs (cocaine, heroin, marijuana, sniffing glue, etc.)
- Handwriting analysis (for fortune telling)
- Hard rock music (Kiss, Led Zeppelin, Rolling Stones, Ozzy Osborne)
- Harry Potter
- Heavy metal music (AC/DC, Guns and Roses (all heavy rock)
- Hepatoscopy (examination of liver for interpretation)
- Hex signs (hexagrams)
- Horoscopes
- Hydromancy (divination by viewing images in water)
- Hypnosis
- Idols/ idolatry/ idol worship
- Incantations
- Invisible friends/ spirit guides
- Iridology (eye diagnosis)
- Japanese flower arranging (sun worship)
- Jonathan Livingston Seagull (Reincarnation, Hinduism, New Age, Self-actualization)
- Kabbalah (Jewish Occult Lore)
- Karma
- Levitation
- Love potions, spells, or curses
- Lucky charms, lucky numbers
- Magic (not sleight of hand but use of supernatural power)
- Magic potions, herbs, and powders
- Mantras
- Marine spirits and mermaids
- Martial arts (Aikido, Isshinryu, Judo, Karate, Kung fu, Tae Kwon Do, etc.)
- Matthew Manning (popular British psychic and healer)
- Mediums
- Mental suggestion, telepathy, or therapy
- Mesmerism
- Metaphysics (study of spirit world)
- Mind control, dynamics, or mediumship
- Mind reading
- Moonmancy
- Motorskopua (mechanical pendulum for diagnosing illness)
- Mysticism
- Mythological gods and creatures including chimeras or half-breeds

- Native American religious ceremonies, activities or objects (dreamcatchers, pow-wows, sweat lodge, peace pipe, boy scout order of the arrow)
- Necromancy (communicating with or conjuring up spirits of the dead)
- New Age
- Nightmares/ night terrors
- Numerology/ numerical symbolism
- Oaths made to occult groups/ demons/ Satan/ gangs/ darkness/ secret societies
- Occultic games/ video games (Ouija board, Pokemon, Yugioh, sorcery, curses, evil creatures, violence)
- Occult letters of protection
- Occult literature, ex: The Greater World, the 6th & 7th Book of Moses, The Other Side, The Book of Venus, Pseudo-Christian works of Jacob Lorber, works by Edgar Cayce, Alistair Crowley, Jeane Dixon, Levi Dowling, Arthur Ford (The Overt Worship of Spirit Beings), Johann Greber, Andrew Jackson Davis, Anton LeVay, Ruth Montgomery, John Newborough, Eric Von Daniken, Dennis Wheatley.
- Occult movies (renounce them by name)
- Omens
- Ouija boards
- Pagan fetishes, religious objects, artifacts and relics
- Pagan holy days (holidays)
- Pagan rites (Voodoo, Sing sings, Corroborees, Fire walking, Umbanda, Macumba)
- Palmistry (divination by the palm)
- PK or parakinesis (control of objects by the power of the mind and will)
- PS or parapsychology (especially study of demonic activity)
- Past life readings
- Pendulum diagnosis (divination)
- Pentagrams
- Phrenology (divining/analysis from the skull)
- Piercings (blood sacrifice)
- Planchette (divining)
- Precognition (foreknowledge of the occurrence of events)
- Psychic healing
- Psychics/ psychic sight
- Psychography (use of heart shaped board for automatic writing)
- Psychometry (telling fortunes by lifting or holding object belonging to the enquirer)
- Punk rock music
- Pyramidology (mystic powers associated with models of pyramids)
- Rebirthing
- Reflexology (healing by pressure points)

- Reiki (Japanese energy healing)
- Reincarnation
- Rhabdomancy (casting sticks into the air for interpreting omens)
- Rituals of all kinds
- Role-playing games/ avatars/ alternate personalities/ alias)
- Santeria (occult syncretism of African, Catholic, and spiritist religion)
- Satanism/ satanic Bible
- Scrying, peeping, looking into different mediums for divination
- Séances
- Self-hypnosis
- Self-mutilation
- Sexual dreams/ spirit husband or wife/incubus and succubus spirits
- Shamanism
- Shapeshifting/ morphing
- Shrines/ temples of any false religion
- Significant pagan days (Mardi Gras, Halloween, Santa, Easter Bunny/Easter)
- Silva Mind Control or SMC (psychorientology)
- Sleepover games of occult nature (Ouija board, bloody Mary, light as a feather, séance, fortune teller games, magic 8 ball)
- Sorcery
- Spells
- Spirit knockings or rappings
- Spirit guides
- Star signs
- Stichomancy (fortune telling from random reference to books)
- Stigmata (appearance of bodily wounds, scars, or pain in the area corresponding to the crucifixion wounds of Jesus)
- Superstitions (self or parents or grandparents)
- Table tipping
- Talismans
- Tarot cards (22 picture cards for fortune telling)
- Tattoos (blood sacrifice)
- Tea-leaf reading
- Temples of demon gods, removing my shoes to walk on unholy ground, bowing to demon gods
- Thought transference
- Throwing bones, runes, dice, etc. for divination
- TK or telekinesis (objects move around the room, instruments play, engines start...)
- TM (Transcendental Meditation)

- Trances, altered state of consciousness, passive mind, lucid dreaming, direct visualization, mantras
- Transmigration
- Travel of the soul
- Tribal dedications, names, medicines, idols, ingestions, tattoos, cuttings in the flesh
- UFO fixation
- Uri Geller (Israeli-British illusionist, magician, and psychic)
- Vampires, werewolves, ogres, gremlins, goblins, wraiths, ghosts, zombies, and other evil entities
- Vision quest
- Water witching
- White magic (invoking hidden powers for 'good ends')
- Wishing on a star, an eyelash, a daisy, candle blowing, etc.
- Witchcraft
- Witch doctor, sangoma, tribal doctor, naturalist, herbalist, traditional medicine (Africa)
- Yoga (involves Eastern demon worship), kundalini, third eye, chakras
- Zodiac charms, signs, and birthdates

Pray aloud:

"Father in heaven, I repent for using my body as an instrument of unrighteousness. I repent for spilling my blood in self-sacrifice and mutilating my body which was made in Your image. I repent for agreeing with death and demon gods and placing their marks upon my body, Your temple. Please forgive me. I cancel and renounce all blood covenants I have made with satan and darkness through my own living blood sacrifice. I declare that the blood of the Lamb, Jesus, was sacrificed on my behalf. That blood sacrifice is sufficient to set me free from all dark covenants. His blood speaks a stronger word than my own. I apply the blood of Jesus to these marks and declare that I am cleansed by Jesus' blood and made whole and forgiven for my sin. I declare now my covenant with Jesus. My body is a temple of His Holy Spirit. In Jesus' name, I detach and sever myself and my bloodline from all spirits associated with these acts, whether done by me or to me, to be cast out of my being; body, soul, and spirit never to return. I also sever any soul-ties to dark practitioners that put marks on me. I petition that You, Yahweh God, cleanse my body and destroy any and all touchpoints, connections, or portals provided by any of these marks. I ask You to close those portals and seal them with the Blood of Jesus. I ask You to destroy all tracking devices that were used against me through these marks and remove any branding from my body. I present my body to You to as a living sacrifice and an instrument of righteousness; holy, and set apart for Your kingdom in Jesus' name."

Cursed items-Open Doors for Demons

The Israelites were told not to bring accursed items into their homes as they possessed the land. These items would become a snare to them and allow the enemies to take ground in their lives and inheritance. These items that are used in idolatrous practices or the occult can also bring a snare to our lives. They are forbidden to us as believers.

> Nor shall you bring an abomination into your house, lest you be doomed to destruction like it. You shall utterly detest it and utterly abhor it, for it is an accursed thing. Deuteronomy 7:26

> And you, by all means abstain from the accursed things, lest you become accursed when you take of the accursed things, and make the camp of Israel a curse, and trouble it. Joshua 6:18

> Get up, sanctify the people, and say, 'Sanctify yourselves for tomorrow, because thus says the Lord God of Israel: "There is an accursed thing in your midst, O Israel; you cannot stand before your enemies until you take away the accursed thing from among you." Joshua 7:13

> So none of the accursed things shall remain in your hand, that the Lord may turn from the fierceness of His anger and show you mercy, have compassion on you and multiply you, just as He swore to your fathers. Deuteronomy 13:17

Any involvement with idolatry is spiritual adultery to our God, Yahweh. We must repent of our involvement and renounce these sins. We must remove any contact with them from our homes and consecrate our homes to Yahweh God, the God of Abraham, Isaac, and Jacob.

> For you were once darkness, but now you are light in the Lord. Walk as children of light (for the fruit of the Spirit is in all goodness, righteousness, and truth), finding out what is acceptable to the Lord. And have no fellowship with the unfruitful works of darkness, but rather expose them. For it is shameful even to speak of those things which are done by them in secret. But all things that are exposed are made manifest by the light, for whatever makes manifest is light. Ephesians 5:8-13

> Test all things; hold fast what is good. Abstain from every form of evil. 1 Thessalonians 5:21-22

Cursed items are demon magnets or demon doorways, sometimes referred to as a point-of-contact. They can allow demons to have legal rights to enter your home and cause chaos in your life. They can cause manifestations such as nightmares, night terrors, sleep paralysis, poltergeists, ghosts, physical ailments, emotional distress, or financial setbacks.

> Like a flitting sparrow, like a flying swallow, so a curse without cause shall not alight. Proverbs 26:2

If you have items or literature associated with any of the following, they should be removed from your home and burned/ passed through the fire just like we read about in the book of Acts. Please do this in a safe way according to your city laws.

And many who had believed came confessing and telling their deeds. Also, many of those who had practiced magic brought their books together and burned them in the sight of all. And they counted up the value of them, and it totaled fifty thousand pieces of silver. So the word of the Lord grew mightily and prevailed. Acts 19:18-20

Do not sell occult items or give them away as others can be affected or demonized by them. This is true for any related entertainment, as well…movies, music, video games. The word ENTER-tainment reminds us that it is a way for spirits to enter us. Also, remove anything from your home with occult symbols on it (shirts, notebooks, jewelry, art, photographs, etc.) Listen to the Holy Spirit as you go through this list. Pray through your house (or room) and He may lead you to something not listed. Obey Him and you will be blessed. If there are cursed items in your home that do not belong to you, you can ask Yahweh to bind the spirits attached to them and to forbid them from bringing you harm. If possible, move them to an area where they are apart from your daily life. Pray that the owner will choose to remove those items from your home.

False religion

- Artifacts/literature from false religions (Mormonism, Jehovah's Witness, Islam, Hare Krishna, Bahai, Hinduism, Buddhism, Christian science, Wicca, New Age, satanism, etc.)
- Native American (indigenous peoples) religious items (dream catchers, beaded items, war items, totems, etc.)
- Celtic items (Celtic cross, superstitious tokens, 4-leaf clover, Celtic knots, Celtic tree of life, Celtic triangle)
- Hindu and Buddhist items (prayer cloths, statues, paintings, jewelry, lucky charms, beads, tilaka)
- Egyptian items (ankh, jewelry, book of the dead, statues, eye of horus, isis, mummies, obelisk, pyramid, hieroglyphic art, sphinx, scarab, sun/solar crest or halo)
- Jewish Kabbalah (evil eye jewelry/ hamsa hand)
- Catholic items (rosary beads, saint statues, crucifix, Mary statues, candles burned to saints, paintings with solar crests or halos, mother and child paintings (Tammuz and Semiramis), etc.)
- Crosses or angels can be used as a superstitious protection
- Ancestral worship/ shrines/ altars
- Feng shui alignment in the home
- Martial Arts paraphernalia/ yin-yang
- African masks, carvings, and statues

New Age

- Yoga paraphernalia (from Hinduism) and lotus flowers
- Reiki, alternative healing items and literature

- Magnetic healing, aromatherapy healing, tai-chi healing
- Crystals for healing, protection, strength, etc.
- New age candles/ atmospheric incense
- Astrology books, images, pictures, clothing, zodiac signs
- Psychic readings/recordings
- Divination rods/ amulets/ runes/ talismans/ angel cards
- Essential oils used for superstitious protection (check the producer for occult ties)
- Angel worship
- Birthstones, flowers, numbers, etc. used as a form of protection or power

Occult/satanism/witchcraft

- Occult literature
- Demonic/horror movies and books
- Demonic video games
- Dungeons and dragons/role-playing games
- Pokemon/ Yugioh/ games that battle with demons (entry-level sorcery)
- Movies filled with witchcraft, sorcery, extreme violence
- Music that glorifies satan, man, drugs, sexual perversity, drinking, depression, etc.
- Harry potter books, movies, games, wands, etc.
- Tarot and/or angel cards
- Ouija boards
- Santeria beads, books, statues, ritual items
- Witchcraft items
- Pendulums and other divination items, runes, bones, dice
- Sage for burning/ atmospheric incense/ incense to false or demon gods
- Gargoyles/dragon statues
- Voodoo dolls
- Halloween décor and costumes
- Death images/ skulls/ tombstones/ graveyard dirt
- Any items with santanic or death symbols
- Sand, candles, graveyard dirt, etc. used for rituals
- Weapons used in rituals

Secret societies

- Masonic/ Shriners/ other lodges emblems and paraphernalia (even Bibles)
- Fraternity/sorority items
- Other items from initiations or ungodly brotherhood oaths
- Navy equatorial crossing/ baptism of Neptune
- Gang items

Other

- Superstitious items (rabbit's foot, horseshoe, 4-leaf clover, saint medal/pendant, lucky socks, etc.)
- Aliens
- Mermaids/water spirits/marine spirits/ sirens
- Mythological gods and creatures, especially half animal/half men hybrids
- Fairies, gnomes, goblins, trolls, etc.
- Superhero/supervillains with names of false gods (Thor, Loki, Hercules, etc.)
- Kachina dolls/ other dolls possibly
- Clowns
- Items with human blood on them—bloody shirts, etc. from accidents
- Hair/fingernails/ fingerprints of animals or people
- Swords, daggers, arrows, bullets, throwing stars, etc. used to murder or kill
- Drug paraphernalia/drugs, alcohol, cigarettes, pipes, incense burners
- Pornography
- Romance books
- Items affiliated with sexual perversion/ pornography/ toys
- Soul-tie items from old relationships
- Obsessive-compulsive items or collections
- Gifts that are cursed as a point-of-contact (from witches or bitter people)

Items that may be cleansed through prayer

- Some antiques/heirlooms can house demons but can be cleansed.
- Used clothing/items should be cleansed.
- Some items brought back from other countries that are not associated with false religions or intrinsically evil (such as dishes, household items, clothing, blankets, etc.) can be cleansed.

Cleansing Prayer

Some items that are not intrinsically evil or associated with false religion can be cleansed through prayer and anointed with oil to set them apart for the kingdom of God. Used clothing or items can be cleansed. Items brought back from other countries that are not religious can be cleansed. Many antiques and heirlooms can house demons and should be cleansed. Check them for hidden doors, drawers, and compartments that could hold cursed items. You can also pray cleansing prayers over used automobiles.

For these items pray the following:

Father in heaven, I repent for any sins that have been committed using this item while it was in the possession of another person. In Jesus' name, I detach and release it from any iniquity that would allow familiar spirits to be drawn to it or allow it to be a touch-point to continue a generational curse. I also release it from any prayers spoken over it to demon gods and any demons that have attached to it. I cancel any curses, spells, enchantments, hexes, vexes, and assignments over this item. In Jesus' name, I command any demonic forces that have taken a place in this item to leave it and this bloodline. I claim this item today for the kingdom of God as I have either purchased it or been given it as a gift. I set it apart for your kingdom and ask that You, Yahweh God, cleanse it with the blood of Jesus and make it fit for your kingdom. If the item is not able to be cleansed, please give me a witness in my spirit. I choose to serve You with my whole life including my earthly possessions. My possessions are Yours; we are one.

Chapter 6: Renouncing Common Eastern Occult Practices

This chapter had been added separately because so many believers are caught up in Eastern occult practices. They have infiltrated our Western culture in America where many don't understand their spiritual significance. These practices advertise good health and a balanced life, but there is a trade involved. Because they are rooted in the occult and false religion, they are open doors to evil spirits. You may be free from pain for a while, but you get a demon or two in return. It is very easy to look up the occultic roots of these practices, but many seem to be blinded to them. This makes it very simple for the enemy to get an open door to fill the lives of believers with demons and strongholds.

In the Psalms, we read that those who worship or trust in idols can become blind, deaf, and mute just like the idols themselves. Idolatry desensitizes us to our own God and brings us into delusion.

> Their idols are silver and gold, the work of men's hands. They have mouths, but they do not speak; eyes they have, but they do not see; they have ears, but they do not hear; noses they have, but they do not smell; they have hands, but they do not handle; feet they have, but they do not walk; nor do they mutter through their throat. Those who make them are like them; so is everyone who trusts in them. Psalm 115:4-8

Many who seek healing and peace through Eastern medicine and doctrines are desperate and haven't found the answers they need elsewhere. There is so much fear circulating of pharmaceuticals and the chemicals that they use. Medical establishments are known for their expensive bills, unfriendly manners, and unnecessary prescriptions. Many are looking for alternative treatments that are not invasive and more "natural." What they do not recognize, is that most of these "natural" treatments have a "supernatural" spiritual component because they are based in a false religion and occult rituals.

> Now the Spirit expressly says that in latter times some will depart from the faith, giving heed to deceiving spirits and doctrines of demons. 1 Timothy 4:1

63

Many practitioners use "energies" in their treatments. These have multiple names like chi, qi, prana, pneuma, innate intelligence, vital fluid, vital force, orgone, life fields, subluxations, etc. The treatments are used to restore the "balance and flow" of these energies and to remove blockages. These energies are demons.

Many of the practitioners are involved in Eastern religions and know they are inviting spirits into your body. It is part of their faith. Some practitioners may be Christians who don't recognize the spiritual significance of these "treatments" is in conflict with their own faith. They may be deceived into thinking they can practice this apart from the occult origin or take out the occult. Unfortunately, that is rarely possible.

Overall, the treatment is only a temporary fix like taking pain medication which only lasts a few hours until the pain returns. Most patients must come back at regular intervals to treat the symptoms, but true healing never comes. Many patients actually get worse over time or end up with new physical, spiritual, mental, or emotional problems.

It is hard to come up with a complete list of these practices. Some are seen as alternatives to medicine and some are seen as fitness practices. They include yoga, martial arts, tai-chi, traditional Asian medicine of any nationality, acupuncture, acupressure and other pressure techniques, reiki, chiropractic, applied kinesiology, reflexology, herbology that involves spiritual practice, crystal healing, magnetic healing, qigong, shiatsu, homeopathy, hypnosis, alchemy, iridology and other methods that read body parts like tea leaves (divination), macrobiotic diet, and visualization. There are many new alternative medicine practices that come out on a regular basis. Most are based in the spiritual with no scientific basis or studies. It is time to expose these works of darkness taking believers captive.

> For you were once darkness, but now you are light in the Lord. Walk as children of light (for the fruit of the Spirit is in all goodness, righteousness, and truth), finding out what is acceptable to the Lord. And have no fellowship with the unfruitful works of darkness, but rather expose them. Ephesians 5:8-11

Mind control

You may feel resistance and an urge to justify your choices when confronted with the following information. Please allow the Holy spirit to testify to the truth that follows. It is highly possible that there is a spirit that has blinded you to truth to keep you in bondage, as well as, in physical pain and illness. It is hard for you to live in victory and walk in your kingdom purpose if you are unhealthy or weak. The blinding spirit may have brought with it false wisdom. All "wisdom" does not come from Yahweh God. There is "wisdom" that is soulish and demonic.

> Who is wise and understanding among you? Let him show by good conduct that his works are done in the meekness of wisdom. But if you have bitter envy and self-seeking in your hearts, do not boast and lie against the truth. This wisdom does not descend from above, but is earthly, sensual, demonic. For where envy and self-seeking exist,

confusion and every evil thing are there. But the wisdom that is from above is first pure, then peaceable, gentle, willing to yield, full of mercy and good fruits, without partiality and without hypocrisy. Now the fruit of righteousness is sown in peace by those who make peace. James 3:13-18

The Israelites felt desperation in the wilderness. Moses had gone up on the mountain to receive instructions from Yahweh God. He was gone for 40 days. The people didn't know what had happened to him.

> Now when the people saw that Moses delayed coming down from the mountain, the people gathered together to Aaron, and said to him, "Come, make us gods that shall go before us; for as for this Moses, the man who brought us up out of the land of Egypt, we do not know what has become of him." And Aaron said to them, "Break off the golden earrings which are in the ears of your wives, your sons, and your daughters, and bring them to me." So all the people broke off the golden earrings which were in their ears, and brought them to Aaron. And he received the gold from their hand, and he fashioned it with an engraving tool, and made a molded calf. Then they said, "This is your god, O Israel, that brought you out of the land of Egypt!" So when Aaron saw it, he built an altar before it. And Aaron made a proclamation and said, "Tomorrow is a feast to the Lord." Then they rose early on the next day, offered burnt offerings, and brought peace offerings; and the people sat down to eat and drink, and rose up to play. Exodus 32:1-6

Even though they had just made covenant with Yahweh and agreed to obey His command to have no other gods before Him or make any idols, the Israelites made some very bad choices out of desperation. Aaron made a calf out of the gold from their jewelry and put an altar before it. They made offerings before the idol and had a celebration. Two of Aaron's statements seem to conflict with one another. He said, "This is your god, O Israel, that brought you out of the land of Egypt!" Then he said, "Tomorrow is a feast to the Lord." It appeared that they believed they could worship the calf and Yahweh at the same feast. Some Jewish teaching says that the calf was created to be a "mount' of Yahweh the invisible God. The Israelites had seen this in Egypt where some of the gods were depicted riding or standing on the backs of animals. Whether or not this was the case, Yahweh was not pleased by their going back so quickly to their old way of life. He sent Moses down the mountain to deal with the corruption.

> And the Lord said to Moses, "Go, get down! For your people whom you brought out of the land of Egypt have corrupted themselves. They have turned aside quickly out of the way which I commanded them. They have made themselves a molded calf, and worshiped it and sacrificed to it, and said, 'This is your god, O Israel, that brought you out of the land of Egypt!'" Exodus 32:7-8

Yahweh has declared that we should have no other gods before Him. We saw in Exodus 20 that a curse follows idolatry. Even today, Yahweh is the same. He will not be worshiped along with other gods. This spiritual adultery still brings a curse. We cannot worship Him and other gods. In 1 Corinthians chapter 10, Paul talks about how the idolatry of the Israelites is an example to us.

> Now these things became our examples, to the intent that we should not lust after evil things as they also lusted. And do not become idolaters as were some of them. As it is written, "The people sat down to eat and drink, and rose up to play." Nor let us commit sexual immorality, as some of them did, and in one day twenty-three thousand fell; nor let us tempt Christ, as some of them also tempted, and were destroyed by serpents; nor complain, as some of them also complained, and were destroyed by the destroyer. Now all these things happened to them as examples, and they were written for our admonition, upon whom the ends of the ages have come. 1 Corinthians 10:6-11

Back in chapter 8 of 1 Corinthians, Paul was addressing a question about eating meat sacrificed to idols. It appears that there was some disunity going on about eating meat from the marketplace. Many times, it was unknown as to whether this food had been sacrificed to idols. Some believers there were arguing that the idols were not real gods, and some had a conscience that was convicting them of eating that meat. Some may have even been going boldly into the temples of idols to eat. Paul encouraged those who had a stronger conscience to abstain from the practice so as not to be a stumbling block for their weaker brothers.

> However, there is not in everyone that knowledge; for some, with consciousness of the idol, until now eat it as a thing offered to an idol; and their conscience, being weak, is defiled. But food does not commend us to God; for neither if we eat are we the better, nor if we do not eat are we the worse. But beware lest somehow this liberty of yours become a stumbling block to those who are weak. For if anyone sees you who have knowledge eating in an idol's temple, will not the conscience of him who is weak be emboldened to eat those things offered to idols? And because of your knowledge shall the weak brother perish, for whom Christ died? But when you thus sin against the brethren, and wound their weak conscience, you sin against Christ. Therefore, if food makes my brother stumble, I will never again eat meat, lest I make my brother stumble. 1 Corinthians 8:7-13

In chapter 10, Paul revisits this theme and tells us in verse 14, "Therefore, my beloved, flee from idolatry." He follows that by saying:

> What am I saying then? That an idol is anything, or what is offered to idols is anything? Rather, that the things which the Gentiles sacrifice they sacrifice to demons and not to God, and I do not want you to have fellowship with demons. You cannot drink the cup of the Lord and the cup of demons; you cannot partake of the Lord's table and of the table of demons. Or do we provoke the Lord to jealousy? Are we stronger than He? 1 Corinthians 10:19-22

There may be times when some strong believers have participated in these occult practices and were not demonized. That is truly grace and mercy. The truth is, we as believers should not be tempting God. We need to test all these things and abstain from every form of evil. We are being held as role models by younger believers who may follow our lead. We do not want to cause them to stumble.

> Test all things; hold fast what is good. Abstain from every form of evil.
> 1 Thessalonians 5:21-22

We do not want to compromise our faith. Several churches addressed in the book of Revelation are told to repent from compromise. The church of Thyatira had become corrupt by sexual sin and idolatry. A woman, jezebel, had been teaching and seducing the believers there into these sins and would not repent. The One who is speaking to John of judgment to these churches is the glorified Messiah Jesus.

> "And to the angel of the church in Thyatira write, 'These things says the Son of God, who has eyes like a flame of fire, and His feet like fine brass: "I know your works, love, service, faith, and your patience; and as for your works, the last are more than the first. Nevertheless I have a few things against you, because you allow that woman Jezebel, who calls herself a prophetess, to teach and seduce My servants to commit sexual immorality and eat things sacrificed to idols. And I gave her time to repent of her sexual immorality, and she did not repent. Indeed I will cast her into a sickbed, and those who commit adultery with her into great tribulation, unless they repent of their deeds. I will kill her children with death, and all the churches shall know that I am He who searches the minds and hearts. And I will give to each one of you according to your works. Revelation 2:18-23

The church of Laodicea was also rebuked for being lukewarm, neither cold nor hot. If they didn't repent, they were to be vomited out of the mouth of God.

> "And to the angel of the church of the Laodiceans write, 'These things says the Amen, the Faithful and True Witness, the Beginning of the creation of God: "I know your works, that you are neither cold nor hot. I could wish you were cold or hot. So then, because you are lukewarm, and neither cold nor hot, I will vomit you out of My mouth. Because you say, 'I am rich, have become wealthy, and have need of nothing'—and do not know that you are wretched, miserable, poor, blind, and naked— I counsel you to buy from Me gold refined in the fire, that you may be rich; and white garments, that you may be clothed, that the shame of your nakedness may not be revealed; and anoint your eyes with eye salve, that you may see. As many as I love, I rebuke and chasten. Therefore be zealous and repent. Revelation 3:14-19

There was compromise in most of the churches addressed in the book of Revelation. They were all given the same charge…"Repent!" Let us not compromise our faith and drink the cup of demons along with the cup of the Lord.

Because you may have been blinded to the following occult practices and other activities that can open demonic doors, pray the following prayer to renounce any blinders, demonic wisdom, seducing spirits, or false beliefs that may be keeping you in captivity.

Father in heaven, I repent for seeking life, health, and peace from alternative spiritual sources instead of You. I admit my desperation drove me to occult practices and idolatry where I have opened doors to darkness in my life and my bloodline. Please forgive me. I also repent for the sins of my ancestors who looked to idols and false gods for help in these areas.

I repent for following trends and fads to keep up with my neighbors. I repent for any envy, jealousy, or self-seeking that may have led me to soulish wisdom. You tell us not to covet anything our neighbor has, but to be content with our own portion and with Your plan for us. I repent for seeking the acceptance of man and for leading my children in that way, especially when the activities are based in idolatry. I repent for ignoring Your still small voice that may have alerted me to danger or given me "red flags". Please forgive me and cleanse both me and my children. Give me the strength to cut these activities out of our lives no matter the financial loss or the loss of community. Please show us Your way for us. Please draw us to Your kingdom.

I renounce any wisdom that is earthly, soulish, or demonic. I petition that my mind be filled with wisdom from above. I ask You to open my eyes to see all the ways I have participated in these practices. I ask You to expose any areas where I have been walking in darkness. I ask you to remove the blinders that have been over my eyes and my mind. I renounce the spirit of mind control that has kept me in darkness. I ask you Father, to sever its ties to me. I petition that you cut off every tentacle reaching into every area of my body and soul and cut me free from the dark veil over my head and eyes and reaching into my brain and mind. I renounce any mind-binding spirits and the scrambler that keeps me confused and believing lies. I repent for having itching ears that looked for someone that would agree with me. I repent for agreement with the spirit of error, doctrines of demons, and any deceiving and seducing sprits that first opened my mind to deception. I renounce these spirits and detach myself from these spirits now in Jesus' name. I command them to release me and my bloodline now. I declare I have a sound mind, the mind of Messiah.

Please Yahweh fill me with Your discernment from this point on to have my spiritual eyes opened in Your kingdom. Please release all of my senses that have been dulled or desensitized to truth. Please fill me with boldness to make the right choice, even if I choose it alone.

Renunciation prayer for yoga

Many believers have chosen yoga as a low-impact exercise without knowing the spiritual side of it. Yoga means "yoked" and is a part of Hinduism. All the different parts of yoga including the breathing, positions, and meditation exercises are created to yoke you with the Hindu gods (of which there are 330,000,000) and bring you into god-consciousness, the realization that you are a god.

Some people have tried to separate the physical part of yoga from the spiritual, thinking they would do the breathing and stretching exercises and meditate on other things, even scripture. Unfortunately, every part of yoga is intended to yoke you with the Hindu gods. Yoga is inseparable from Hinduism.

In 1 Corinthians 10, Paul talks about eating meat sacrificed to idols in reference to the covenant meal of communion. He makes the parallel about pagan feasts being covenant meals with demons. We cannot partake of both covenants. The elements of yoga can be considered sacrifices or offerings to false gods.

> Therefore, my beloved, flee from idolatry. I speak as to wise men; judge for yourselves what I say. The cup of blessing which we bless, is it not the communion of the blood of Christ? The bread which we break, is it not the communion of the body of Christ? For we, though many, are one bread and one body; for we all partake of that one bread. Observe Israel after the flesh: Are not those who eat of the sacrifices partakers of the altar? What am I saying then? That an idol is anything, or what is offered to idols is anything? Rather, that the things which the Gentiles sacrifice they sacrifice to demons and not to God, and I do not want you to have fellowship with demons. You cannot drink the cup of the Lord and the cup of demons; you cannot partake of the Lord's table and of the table of demons. Or do we provoke the Lord to jealousy? Are we stronger than He? 1 Corinthians 10:14-22

The physical exercise and breathing in yoga are called asanas and pranayama. Each separate yoga position of the body is designed to be an invocation to different deities. They are very specific and you wouldn't "accidentally" do these stretches. Even the hands are in specific positions called mudras to invite certain gods. AUM chanting is an invocation to the three main deities of Hinduism (brahman, vishnu, shiva) to inhabit your body. The mantras given to focus you and clear your mind are repetitively spoken. A passive mind is an open door to demons.

> And when you pray, do not use vain repetitions as the heathen do. For they think that they will be heard for their many words. Matthew 6:7

Doing the yoga poses awakens the dormant occult power, or kundalini, at the base of the spine. This allows the spirit to rise through all the seven chakras, or energy centers formed by doing yoga, like a serpent until it reaches the crown chakra at the top of the head. This kundalini power is associated with the goddess shakti who is the female counterpart for the god shiva, god of destruction. When the power reaches the top, the highest level of consciousness or cosmic energy, the person will become yoked with shiva. This is the same idea as covenant oneness. The demon god shiva, also known as the lord of yoga, will enter you along with many other gods that will live in the open chakras.

> Do not be unequally yoked together with unbelievers. For what fellowship has righteousness with lawlessness? And what communion has light with darkness? And what accord has Christ with Belial? Or what part has a believer with an unbeliever? And

what agreement has the temple of God with idols? For you are the temple of the living God. As God has said:

"I will dwell in them and walk among them. I will be their God, and they shall be My people."

Therefore, "Come out from among them and be separate, says the Lord. Do not touch what is unclean, and I will receive you." "I will be a Father to you, and you shall be My sons and daughters, says the Lord Almighty." 2 Corinthians 6:14-18

Many people say they feel peaceful when they first start doing yoga, but eventually long-term yoga students complain of persistent headaches and chronic back and neck pain. Can you imagine why?

Even if you have only participated in yoga once or have only done the stretching poses and the breathing exercises, it is good to renounce these gods and close any doors that have been opened. The enemy of our soul does not care if you meant to worship or invoke these gods. He is a legalist and an opportunist. He doesn't play fair.

When you think about a physical yoke, it is a large crossbeam that is placed on the neck of two load-bearing animals that connects them to each other. It causes them to go in the same direction, one usually leading the other. When you are yoked to evil, it will lead you away from God's purpose and become a heavy burden on your shoulders. Jesus invited us to take up His yoke which is easy and light. He will bear the burden for us and guide us into truth.

"Come to Me, all you who labor and are heavy laden, and I will give you rest. Take My yoke upon you and learn from Me, for I am gentle and lowly in heart, and you will find rest for your souls. For My yoke is easy and My burden is light." Matthew 11:28-30

It is important to remove and burn all ties to yoga. To renounce yoga and all the Hindu gods, pray the following prayer aloud:

Father in heaven, I repent for participating in worship of and yoking with the Hindu gods through the practice of yoga. I renounce any dark covenants, dedications, trades, sacrifices, and worship of Hindu gods by me and my ancestors. I renounce yoga as a way to salvation, health, and perfect peace.

I renounce all the following forms of yoga: hatha yoga, hot yoga, laughing yoga, raj or raja yoga, tantra yoga, karma yoga, jnana yoga, integral yoga, patanjali yoga, bhakti yoga, shiva yoga, kundalini yoga, and any other form of yoga not mentioned.

I renounce all of the gods of Hinduism that I worshiped through the religious works, asceticism, mysticism, pranayama, asanas, mudras, mantras, and the meditation practices of yoga. I specifically renounce brahman, vishnu, shiva, kali, shakti, ganesh, surya, hanaman, khrishna, ramah, and saraswati. I also renounce all other Hindu gods that made a place in me through yoga. I detach myself from them now in Jesus' name.

I renounce the Hindu ideologies of reincarnation, becoming a god, and becoming one with the universe.

I renounce sun worship at sunrise, the moksa-karma wheel of reincarnation, and the belief that there is no heaven or hell.

I renounce the vital energy, kundalini force, which is the serpent that curls at the base of the spine and the seven chakras or strongholds of demons

I renounce the greeting namaste which means "the divine in me bows to the divine in you".

I renounce AUM and the invocation of the three deities, brahman, vishnu, and shiva.

I renounce the mantras that were repeated to bring me to union with brahman.

I renounce the secret mantra that was given to me _____.

I renounce astral projection, liberating the spirit body from the physical body.

I renounce being used to channel gods and goddesses, psychic visions, occult programming and mind-control, and the opening of the third eye with all its psychic power.

I renounce bending down to worship Hindu gods by bending my body in worship positions.

I renounce the gyan mudra- (first finger and thumb touching with other three fingers out) which represents the human soul coming into communion with brahman, an invocation to brahman.

I renounce the lotus position (sitting on the ground with legs crossed and hands resting on knees in gyan mudra) asking brahman to lift you up from a lowly level to higher levels of consciousness.

I renounce the tree pose (standing on one foot with other foot on knee, hands in prayerful position)-dedicated to Vishnu the preserver god.

I renounce the cosmic dancer pose (leaning on left foot with right foot curled up behind to right hand behind the head and left hand stretching out)-dedicated to shiva the destroyer god.

I renounce the warrior pose (one arm is stretched forward and one arm stretched back with the legs in a lunge)-dedicated to ganesh the elephant and man.

I renounce the splits pose (legs in splits with arms stretched up in prayer position)- dedicated to hanaman the monkey and man.

I renounce the standing pose (crossing the feet while standing erect with hands appearing to play the flute with first finger and pinky up and second and third fingers touching the thumb)- dedicated to krishna the god who had 16,108 wives.

I renounce the goddess pose with gyan mudra (squatting down with legs spread out and gyan mudra hands on knees)- dedicated to kali goddess of war.

I renounce the crocodile pose (lying flat on your stomach with your arms folded underneath your head)- dedicated to ramah an avatar of vishnu.

I renounce the cat/cow pose (on hands and knees with arching the back)- dedicated to Saraswati the goddess of learning and education.

I renounce the warrior poses-dedicated to virabhadra who was born out of anger and revenge.

I renounce the sun salutation poses (12 poses)- dedicated to surya the sungod.

I renounce all other yoga poses that invoke or invite Hindu gods into my being or life.

I renounce the four Hindu ages: the krita-yuga, treta-yuga, dwapara-yuga, and the kali yuga

I renounce honoring deceased masters by leaving offerings for them of flowers, fruit, and a white handkerchief on an altar.

I renounce the occult Eastern arts of transcendental meditation, hypnosis, self-hypnosis, trance states, silva mind-control, ESP, mantras, breathing techniques, occult philosophy, fire worship, visualization, astral projection, alpha and beta brain waves, biorhythm, homeopathy, acupuncture, holism, reflexology and aromatherapy.

I renounce all sickness, disease, and disorder that has entered my body through yoga including psychosis, schizophrenia, psychiatric disorders, Alzheimer's disease, senility, fear, anxiety disorders, depression, paralysis, nerve disorders, MS, fibromyalgia, chronic fatigue, dormant diseases, brain disturbance, vision problems, abnormal weight gain or loss, food cravings, desperation, distortion of time and space, trances, chaos, anorexia, bulimia, occult visions, hallucinations, dissociation, shortness of breath, suicidal thoughts, self-mutilation, hyperactivity, strange sounds coming from inside my body, profound stillness, chronic fatigue, and obsessions.

I renounce worship of lucifer and his tree of knowledge, the golden triangle in the chakras and the seat of lucifer that brings paralysis to the brain, the fire serpent in the pituitary gland and its demonic fire moving throughout the body, the spirit of death in the nose and the brow chakra, the pshycic pain and vibration from the pyramid, and the serpent and his seat in the mind. I renounce the un-Goldy passions and energies of lucifer connected to the throne of satan and the excitement of kundalini fire, tantric yoga, sex magic, serpent intimacy, seduction, eroticism, and perversion.

I repent for and renounce all worship of kali, the goddess of darkness, destruction, and death. I renounce all her other titles including lilith, venus, isis, semiramis, black madonna, inanna, black venus, goddess of love, fire witch, great mother, mother of yoga, mother nature, the grandmother - baba yaga, queen of Heaven, false virgin Mary. I renounce any songs sung to her or images made of her.

I renounce kali as mother over the cycle of creation and the natural realm. I renounce her elokshi or hair curtains of death, veils of death, and black coverings. I renounce her nakedness, garland of human heads, cup of blood, deadly weapons, snake bands, and her digambari. I renounce kali's ritual cycles and black nirvana.

I renounce inviting her into my home and channeling her secret force and occult powers for sexual bewitchment, whoredoms, enchantment, control, and manipulation. I renounce the declaration that she holds the seat of absolute knowledge. I repent for allowing her to use my mental faculties through yoga and wear my head as a trophy through mind-control. I renounce kali's entrance into my mind, memories, behaviors, and thoughts.

I repent for allowing kali to use the work of my hands through yoga as a girdle around her waist.

Father, I ask that the blood of Jesus cleanse me and my bloodline of this sin of idolatry and spiritual adultery erasing all iniquity. I choose to forgive anyone who led me into these sins and any teachers or yogis that taught me to worship idols.

I ask you Father to sever all soul-ties that have formed between me and my past Hindu gurus and yogis _____. I forgive _____ for leading me astray through occult practices. I now renounce this unholy bond and ask you Yahweh to cleanse and forgive me. I ask you to free me from any mind-control and unholy attachment to _____ and loose the bonding of our souls. I return any parts of _____ that have been attached to me, back to him/her. I ask You, Father, to restore to me any parts of myself that were tied to _____ through this bond

Please sever all soul-ties and umbilical cords between me and cosmic powers, Hindu gods, evil entities, demons, the wheel of rebirth, dead ancestors, people, objects, India and other places connected to yoga. I release any parts of them from my body and soul now and command them to leave. Father, please restore my shattered parts back to me cleansed by the blood of Jesus. Please redeem any parts that I willingly gave to the Hindu gods. I choose to return any gifts, abilities, rankings, jewelry, and paraphernalia I have received from yoga and the Hindy gods.

In Jesus' name, I ask you to break open any chakras formed in my body and soul, destroy the demons that reside there, and remove all trace of them. I ask you Father to close the third eye or psychic portal and detach me from any spirits or spiritual gifts that came in through the third eye. I ask you to cut me free from the wheel of life and rebirth attached to my spine. Please cleanse me with the blood of Jesus.

I choose to detach myself and my bloodline from all 330,000,000 Hindu gods that could have accessed me through yoga. I specifically detach myself from brahman, vishnu, shiva, kali, shakti, ganesh, surya, hanaman, khrishna, ramah, saraswati, lilith, venus, kundalini, lucifer, and the mother of yoga with all her titles. I command them to release me and my bloodline now in Jesus' name and come out!!!

I petition that all occult programming and mind-control be deleted, all demonic seals removed, and all magical cords be cut and my silver cord be cleansed and detached from any other being who has attached to it. I ask you to free me from any spirit of distraction, restlessness, *wandering, or vagabond that has entered me through astral projection. I ask that any dormant powers or evil devices set to activate in me be deactivated, cut off, and destroyed in Jesus' name.*

I petition that every seal of yoga and kundalini be broken off every system of my body. Please sever all controlling triggers to sickness and premature death. I ask that the blood of Jesus cleanse me fully and close every portal opened through yoga. I ask You to heal and restructure my body and soul back to Your perfect order of health, life, and youth.

Please cleanse my mind, senses, tongue, receptors, olfactory organs, limbic system, brain system and its five lobes, nerve centers, sacral plexus, nervous systems, navel cord, short and long-term memory banks, organs, pineal gland, pituitary gland, thalamus, hippocampus, amygdala, bones, marrow, spinal cord, spinal discs, muscles, tendons, ligaments, nerves, vessels, and every other part of my physical body and their functions. I detach myself from any psychic powers in these areas.

I petition you would send Your Holy spirit fire through all channels and meridians opened to demon gods or entities that were channeled through yoga. I ask You to shut down all those portals and seal them shut with the blood of Jesus. I petition that the only channel open in the spirit realm from me would be the one to You, Yahweh God.

I present myself to You as an instrument of righteousness, including my mind which I choose to focus on You, Your kingdom, and Your word. Help me learn to meditate only on You. Please remove any touchpoints on my body or soul that were created during yoga. Please erase any cellular memory of my participation of yoga and any pathways created through it. Please restructure and realign my body, soul, and spirit with You, Yahweh God and Your kingdom order. I petition You to restore my soul.

<u>Renouncing Martial arts</u>

(Much of this information about martial arts was gleaned from Selwyn Stevens of Jubilee Resources)

Many believers put their children in martial arts to help them learn respect and self-discipline. Others want their kids to learn to protect themselves if bullied or attacked. Some just join classes because friends have invited them. Many children then find an identity in the martial arts and dedicate their lives to it.

Although martial arts originated as an Eastern occult practice, many clubs or "dojos" call themselves "Christian." Unfortunately, this is an area of deception just like yoga. Martial arts are part of an Eastern religious lifestyle balanced by philosophy and discipline. Those training in martial arts in Asian countries, would also be training in yoga and other Eastern religious practices. Like yoga, the martial arts are not purely a physical practice, all parts are linked together both physically and spiritually. Katas and kicks are focused on the body learning to flow using the inner ki or psychic energy. Hand and body movements and war cries (like "kiai" and high-pitched screams) are used to summon demons and their powers. Most all forms of martial arts are commonly used as a way of spiritual growth.

There are many stories about where martial arts originated. Most agree it started with Buddhist monks in India and then travelled to China and later to Japan and Korea. The most famous Buddhist teacher, Bodhidharma, was an instructor of the earliest forms of martial arts taught at the Shaolin monastery. It was originally called Shaolin Kung Fu with a philosophy that is rooted in the occult through Buddhism and Taoism. Taoists believe that an energy called "chi" flows along meridians in the universe. It is balanced by the two opposing forces yin and yang that came from the Tao. This energy is supernatural and does not come from Yahweh God. It is demonic. The martial artist desires to achieve a perfect balance of yin and yang to control the life force and overcome the opponent. Some forms of martial arts include a type of solitary fighting in which they actually work to overcome an opponent spiritually.

Martial arts involve mind-body training so that the mind and body can perform as one. The body is instinctively and impulsively trained to react with certain stimuli and fight. This suspends rationalization and calculation from the mind so that reactions are impulsive and not given thought. The martial arts practitioner depends on muscle memory and practiced reactions rather than making contemplative choices according to the word of God. This is in conflict with the scriptural commands to take our thoughts captive and to have the mind of Messiah. Our minds and bodies should be fully surrendered to Yahweh. We should take up the mighty weapons and gear of His army. Our enemy is not flesh and blood but the powers of darkness in the realm of the spirit.

> Finally, my brethren, be strong in the Lord and in the power of His might. Put on the whole armor of God, that you may be able to stand against the wiles of the devil. For we do not wrestle against flesh and blood, but against principalities, against powers, against the rulers of [c]the darkness of this age, against spiritual hosts of wickedness in the heavenly places. Therefore take up the whole armor of God, that you may be able to withstand in the evil day, and having done all, to stand. Ephesians 6:10-13

> For though we walk in the flesh, we do not war according to the flesh. For the weapons of our warfare are not carnal but mighty in God for pulling down strongholds, casting down arguments and every high thing that exalts itself against the knowledge of God, bringing every thought into captivity to the obedience of Christ, and being ready to punish all disobedience when your obedience is fulfilled. 2 Corinthians 10:3-6

Another area of concern is violence. The constant training in warfare and weapons, opens the mind to violent spirits. The spirit of violence that comes in by training in martial arts actually attracts other violent spirits to the practitioner. "Martial arts" are named for the Roman god mars, god of war, and actually can be translated "killing arts." Although the teachers may keep things structured in class, the actions taught are intended to harm, maim, or kill.

Weapons are used in many forms of martial arts, but the killing arts were originally created by monks who weren't allowed to carry weapons. Through karate, or 'empty hand', the monks learned to defend themselves with only their own hands. It is taught when your chi comes into balance, you can do superhuman feats. Some forms of martial arts use psychic powers to break objects that are humanly impossible to break without personal injury. This superhuman power comes from demons.

A third area of concern is the soul-tie bond with the sen-sei master which gives him some mind-control over the students through the authority given to him. Just as bowing to each other in yoga recognizes the god of yoga in each other, bowing before the sensei is bowing before the spirit of violence in that person. Students are also asked to bow to past masters and the spirit of the art called a shomen. We should call no one master but One, Yahweh God.

Pride and superiority can be even another problem developed through martial arts. Belts and trophies are given individually, and although they are earned, can still be a source of envy and jealousy causing division. There is also the basis of winning at any cost. These problems can be seen in any individual sport, but are worth mentioning.

If you have been involved in the martial arts, it is important to renounce it and cut yourself free from these spirits. Like you learned in the last chapter, it is also important to destroy all physical ties to the practice including the yin/yang symbol, clothing, weapons, awards, and titles. No man can serve two masters.

> "No one can serve two masters; for either he will hate the one and love the other, or else he will be loyal to the one and despise the other. You cannot serve God and mammon." Matthew 6:24

Pray the following prayer aloud:

Father in heaven, I repent for participating in any Eastern occult activity including martial arts whose roots are idolatry and not compatible with faith in You. Please forgive me for opening occult doors in my life or the lives of my children through the spiritual and philosophical side of martial arts, as well as, the violent and prideful spirit involved. I also repent of any involvement of my ancestors in any form of Eastern occult religion.

I renounce the occult roots and teachings of martial arts from Hinduism, Buddhism, Taoism, and other pagan religions. I renounce the teachings of Bodhidharma and any link with the monasteries and temples where martial arts originated.

I repent for and renounce honoring Buddha, past martial arts masters, and calling any man master. I renounce the soul-tie between me and _____, the one I referred to as master (sen-sei.) I ask you Father to break all soul-ties that have formed between me and _____. I forgive _____ for leading me astray through occult practices. I now renounce this unholy bond and ask you Father to cleanse and forgive me. I ask you to free me from any mind-control and unholy attachment to _____ and loose the bonding of our souls.

I return any parts of _____ that have been attached to me, back to him/her. I ask You, Father, to restore to me any parts of myself that were tied to _____ through this bond

I renounce any Eastern meditation connected to my study or practice of martial arts including zen Buddhism, yoga, transcendental meditation and certain katas used for the purpose of enlightenment. I renounce any disciplines of the mind that do not come in line with Your word. I renounce meditation through the practice of basic karate principles. I renounce any new levels of consciousness that I developed through the practice of martial arts and Eastern mysticism. I renounce the "way of the empty mind." I also renounce any pride in my achievements and any superiority to which it opened the door.

I renounce the different forms of martial arts including ninjutsu, taijutsu, jiujitsu, karate, aikido, iaido, hapkido, judo, sambo, taekwondo, kung fu, isshinryu, wendo, kempo, kendo, muay thai, tai chi, kick boxing, military martial arts, ninja, and all other styles of martial arts (include the one in which you participated).

I renounce trying to overcome myself and my ego through principles of karate rather than submitting myself to You Yahweh and Your principles. I renounce karate as a way of life. Jesus the Messiah is the only way.

I renounce every weapon I wielded against physical opponents made in your image. I repent for any harm that came to them physically, spiritually or mentally. I repent for marking them with weapons, including chaka-sticks. I petition that all marks be erased from me and my opponents with the blood of Jesus. I renounce the use of chaka-sticks, bokken, swords, sticks, staffs, shuriken stars, poison, spears, naginata, halberd, chain, sickle, fire, and explosives.

I renounce the mind-body tie that has been formed in me and ask You to cut it now in Jesus' name. I renounce mind-control, hypnosis, and self-hypnosis used by me and against me. I renounce psychic powers used to break "unbreakable" objects with my hands and feet.

I renounce every position, every kick, every war cry that was used knowingly or unknowingly to summon demons and/or send them against an opponent. I renounce channeling "chi' or "ki" energy and shouting "kiai" to activate this energy. I renounce mystical hand positions used to channel and call demons. I renounce any demonic skills and fighting techniques I have learned.

I renounce visualization in the martial arts. I renounce any connection to the elementals of earth, water, fire, wind, and the void. I renounce the breathing techniques for hypnotic trance and coming into union with nature. I renounce uniting with animal spirits to learn the techniques of fighting including the snake, crane, crocodile, fish, camel, cat, cobra, lion, tiger, and eagle. I renounce the strongmen and spirits of buddha, zhen wu, mars, skanda, ares, takemikazuchi-no-okami, hercules, shiva, kali, leviathan, python, death, and suicide and cancel and break all covenants with them. I detach myself and my bloodline from them and command them to release us now.

I renounce every oath I made in martial arts or its degrees. I renounce any titles and rankings I have received. I lay down all physical items associated with the martial arts including symbols, clothing, belts, weapons, and awards.

<u>Ninjas</u>: I renounce the ninja code of honor, and any oaths made as a ninja. I renounce any ranks of war that I have received in the army of satan all the way up to the rank of _____. I lay down and destroy all ninja uniforms, paraphernalia, and weapons including the fighting sword and ritual sword. I renounce the suicide oath of a ninja, and I repent for any participation in the following: disguise and impersonation, stealth, superiority, self-exaltation, invincibility, breaking and entering, entrapment techniques, water training, war strategies, weaponry, combat, poison, psychological warfare, destruction, death, killing, suicide, self-destruction, murder, deception, concealment, invisibility techniques, espionage, secrecy codes, and suicide codes. I renounce all ninja gods of war and the holy four. I renounce all of these spirits in Jesus' name and the occult wisdom I have gained from them. I detach myself and my bloodline from them and command them to release us now. I renounce being a killing machine, mercenary, assassin, or spy.

Renouncing Eastern Traditional Medicine and Occult Alternative Medicine

Holistic healthcare covers the realm of body, soul, and spirit. This appeals to those who have been treated like a number in a medical healthcare perspective. It is truly important that all areas of a person be healthy, unfortunately the spiritual side of most holistic healthcare is occult in nature. The occult or new age spirituality is usually derived from Eastern religion. Most of these practices involve the "energy" flow mentioned at the beginning of the chapter which was determined to be demon spirits. Others involve divination which is seeking knowledge, power, or even healing from supernatural means other than Yahweh God. As you undergo these occult-based treatments, demons are given access to you. Because of the seriousness of this topic, it is important to read this scripture again:

> "When you come into the land which the Lord your God is giving you, you shall not learn to follow the abominations of those nations. There shall not be found among you anyone who makes his son or his daughter pass through the fire, or one who practices witchcraft, or a soothsayer, or one who interprets omens, or a sorcerer, or one who conjures spells, or a medium, or a spiritist, or one who calls up the dead. For all who do these things are an abomination to the Lord, and because of these abominations the Lord your God drives them out from before you. You shall be blameless before the Lord your God. For these nations which you will dispossess listened to soothsayers and diviners; but as for you, the Lord your God has not appointed such for you." Deuteronomy 18:9-14

Many of these therapies sound harmless when reading a description online. They do not always disclose the spirituality of the therapy. Because they are non-invasive and usually involve manipulation of muscles or massage, they may even seem relaxing. The problem is that the practitioner is not only massaging your soft-tissue, but is releasing spirits into you through touch to bring your systems into "balance." This is the counterfeit of the "laying on of hands" for healing which we read about in the gospel of Mark when Jesus gives the great commission:

> And He said to them, "Go into all the world and preach the gospel to every creature. He who believes and is baptized will be saved; but he who does not believe will be condemned. And these signs will follow those who believe: In My name they will cast out demons; they will speak with new tongues; they will take up serpents; and if they drink anything deadly, it will by no means hurt them; they will lay hands on the sick, and they will recover." Mark 16:15-18

Some of these treatments involving energy flow imbalances are acupuncture, acupressure, reiki, ayurveda, chiropractic, massage therapy, and applied kinesiology.

Other treatments consist of giving practitioners access to your mind through hypnosis, relaxation techniques, qi gong, guided imagery, biofeedback, or TM. A passive mind state can allow an open door for mind-control and entrance of demons. It can also form soul-ties with anyone who has this access to you.

Some alternative treatments involve divination to determine areas of sickness, disease, and blocked energy flow. Just like a fortune teller reads tea leaves or your palm, these practitioners read other parts of your body. These treatments include iridology, phrenology, reflexology, applied kinesiology, NAET, and swinging a pendulum over your body. The practitioners may tell you that all parts of your body are connected and they are using an external part to read a hidden part, but these practices are actually using your body like a large Ouija board. They look at or touch a part of you and allow a familiar spirit to give them knowledge. There is no true scientific method to these practices. Many practitioners don't need to even interact with you to have this knowledge. It is like going to a fortune teller where familiar spirits give information. If we choose to get occult knowledge from a fortune teller, there is a dark future that can be given to us to accept. Their predictions can come to pass if we accept them. The results or "future" they provide you is the plan of darkness for your life. It is not God's plan. Yahweh God has already paid a high price for your freedom. He came in the flesh and paid the punishment for your sin and iniquity so that you could be forgiven, cleansed, healed, and made new. When we turn to occult practitioners acting as mediums, we are committing spiritual adultery:

> And the person who turns to mediums and familiar spirits, to prostitute himself with them, I will set My face against that person and cut him off from his people. Consecrate yourselves therefore, and be holy, for I am the Lord your God. Leviticus 20:6-7

Some people justify these alternative techniques because they "worked" or made them feel good in the beginning. (This is also true for many forms of drugs.) Some believe that all healing comes from God. The truth is that alternative medicine doesn't heal. It temporarily stops the pain and torment which are being placed on you by the spirits already. These spirits are happy to give you a bit of relief knowing you will return for more treatments. You are trading temporary relief for a spiritual problem...more demons. Over time, you must continue the treatments or look for other alternative treatments to continue to feel "good" or "peaceful". (This is also true of drugs.)

Some of you may say, "But I see a Christian practitioner." Even Christians can be deceived. There are very rare cases where a chiropractor may actually use only spinal manipulative therapy which treats musculoskeletal problems causing headaches, back pain, or pinched nerves. Unfortunately, the same practitioner may also include other alternative therapies in their practice that use energy manipulation, such as muscle testing, or applied kinesiology. This is very widespread. You can probably pull up the website to see what is offered. It is very important to lay all of these practices at the feet of Jesus and ask Him to reveal the truth to you.

It is also important to make sure your holistic health practitioner is not using spirits to aid in wisdom, knowledge, and divination. For instance, there are many wonderful herbs that can help our bodies receive much needed supplements to our sometimes-unhealthy diets. These herbs are provided by our creator, Yahweh God, and there are wonderful books and Godly people who can share their knowledge with us in this area. Unfortunately, many practitioners who prescribe herbs and supplements are trained in the arts of traditional medicine which usually involves familiar spirits and knowledge from demons. They can also make use of divination, incantations, and superstition in their treatments. Remember that traditional medicine comes from cultures where every area is part of religion.

It is even important to research the companies and stores where you buy supplements and essential oils. Some are owned by occultists who curse the items they sell. Pray over your supplements as well as your food. Bless Yahweh for the provision and ask Him to cleanse it with the blood of Jesus, cancelling any curse over it and cleansing it from poisons and anything harmful.

Pray the following prayer aloud:

Father in heaven, I repent for myself and my ancestors for seeking healing and health in supernatural ways apart from You. Forgive me for not listening to Your warnings to me and following desperation. I repent for turning to mediums, familiar spirits, and demon guides whether knowingly or unknowingly. I ask You to forgive these sins and cleanse me and my bloodline.

I repent for participating in all areas of alternative medicine which involved energy flow and channeling demons including acupuncture, acupressure, reiki, ayurveda, chiropractic, massage therapy, applied kinesiology, and _____. I repent for participating in all areas of alternative medicine which involved divination including iridology, phrenology, reflexology, applied kinesiology, NAET, swinging a pendulum over the body, and _____. I repent for participating in all areas of alternative medicine which involved giving access of my mind to the practitioner including hypnosis, relaxation techniques, qi gong, guided imagery, biofeedback, TM and _____. I choose now to detach myself from all evil spirits that have gained access to me and my bloodline through these practices. I command them to release us now in Jesus' name.

Pray the following to break soul-ties with each practitioner.

I ask you Father to break all soul-ties that have formed between me and _____. I forgive _____for leading me astray through occult practices. I now renounce this unholy bond and ask you Father to cleanse and forgive me. I ask you to free me from any unholy attachment to _____ and loose the bonding of our souls. I return any parts of _____ that have been attached to me, back to him/her. I ask You, Father, to restore to me any parts of myself that were tied to _____ through this bond

If you have been a practitioner of these alternative therapies whether licensed or from home, pray the following:

Father in heaven, please forgive me for participating in sorcery, witchcraft, and divination through the practice of _____. Forgive me for committing spiritual adultery against You and leading others astray from Your truth, Your word, and Your kingdom. Forgive me for profiting from the spiritual addiction these practices caused. I repent for and renounce all these practices and the spirits behind them. I detach myself and my bloodline from them and command them to release us in Jesus' name. I also repent for any of my ancestors who have taught these practices. I release all the people to whom I made soul-ties through these practices. (Pray through the above prayer to break soul-ties with them.) I renounce and detach myself from any supernatural, psychic giftings I have received from darkness. I take back that spiritual territory from the enemy and give it to You Yahweh. Please Father, show me how I can use my talents, abilities, and gifts for Your kingdom and how I can give testimony against these practices to protect Your people from going into bondage.

Yahweh God blesses us with health

Our Creator, Yahweh God has given us His own wonderful blessings to help us relax and have peace including reading and meditating on His word, observing His beautiful creation including the animals, singing and praising with beautiful music that glorifies Him, wonderful smells, good food, good touch, laughter and joy, comfort and encouragement from friends, family time, etc. Relaxation and meditation are good when we do them God's way. He has also given us good food, plants, and herbs that can bring health to our bodies when used His way without being corrupted by incantations or occult involvement. Yahweh is the Healer of body, soul, and spirit.

> Now may the God of peace Himself sanctify you completely; and may your whole spirit, soul, and body be preserved blameless at the coming of our Lord Jesus Christ.
> 1 Thessalonians 5:23

> Beloved, I pray that you may prosper in all things and be in health, just as your soul prospers. 3 John 1:2

One of the benefits of the atonement sacrifice is that we are healed. It is Yahweh's will to heal you. He has paid a high price to destroy sickness, disease, and death. This healing is for all parts of us; body, soul, and spirit. Sometimes there is a curse working to keep this healing from manifesting. Sometimes healing can be blocked by seeking healing from other supernatural sources. When the legal rights are removed and the demons cast out, the healing can come. May your full healing manifest as you become free indeed!

Here are some verses about healing to meditate on and pray over yourself. Ask the Holy Spirit to fill you with His truth and health.

> Surely He has borne our griefs and carried our sorrows; yet we esteemed Him stricken, smitten by God, and afflicted. But He was wounded for our transgressions, He was bruised for our iniquities; the chastisement for our peace was upon Him, and by His stripes we are healed. All we like sheep have gone astray; we have turned, every one, to his own way; and the Lord has laid on Him the iniquity of us all. Isaiah 53:4-6

> Bless the Lord, O my soul; and all that is within me, bless His holy name! Bless the Lord, O my soul, and forget not all His benefits: Who forgives all your iniquities, Who heals all your diseases, Who redeems your life from destruction, Who crowns you with lovingkindness and tender mercies, Who satisfies your mouth with good things, so that your youth is renewed like the eagle's. Psalm 103:1-5

> So you shall serve the Lord your God, and He will bless your bread and your water. And I will take sickness away from the midst of you. Exodus 23:25

> Do not be wise in your own eyes; fear the Lord and depart from evil. It will be health to your flesh, and strength to your bones. Proverbs 3:7-8

> I will extol You, O Lord, for You have lifted me up, and have not let my foes rejoice over me. O Lord my God, I cried out to You, and You healed me. O Lord, You brought my soul up from the grave; You have kept me alive, that I should not go down to the pit. Psalm 30:1-3

> I shall not die, but live, and declare the works of the Lord. Psalm 118:17

> Heal me, O Lord, and I shall be healed; save me, and I shall be saved, for You are my praise. Jeremiah 17:14

> He heals the brokenhearted and binds up their wounds. Psalm 147:3

> My son, give attention to my words; incline your ear to my sayings. Do not let them depart from your eyes; keep them in the midst of your heart; for they are life to those who find them, and health to all their flesh. Proverbs 4:20-22

> And Jesus went about all Galilee, teaching in their synagogues, preaching the gospel of the kingdom, and healing all kinds of sickness and all kinds of disease among the people.

Then His fame went throughout all Syria; and they brought to Him all sick people who were afflicted with various diseases and torments, and those who were demon-possessed, epileptics, and paralytics; and He healed them. Matthew 4:23-24

When evening had come, they brought to Him many who were demon-possessed. And He cast out the spirits with a word, and healed all who were sick, that it might be fulfilled which was spoken by Isaiah the prophet, saying: "He Himself took our infirmities and bore our sicknesses." Matthew 8:16-17

Then Jesus went about all the cities and villages, teaching in their synagogues, preaching the gospel of the kingdom, and healing every sickness and every disease among the people. Matthew 9:35

And when He had called His twelve disciples to Him, He gave them power over unclean spirits, to cast them out, and to heal all kinds of sickness and all kinds of disease. Matthew 10:1

Jesus Christ is the same yesterday, today, and forever. Hebrews 13:8

For with God nothing will be impossible." Luke 1:37

Now to Him who is able to do exceedingly abundantly above all that we ask or think, according to the power that works in us, to Him be glory in the church by Christ Jesus to all generations, forever and ever. Amen. Ephesians 3:20-21

Ah, Lord God! Behold, You have made the heavens and the earth by Your great power and outstretched arm. There is nothing too hard for You. Jeremiah 32:17

But He said, "The things which are impossible with men are possible with God." Luke 18:27

"God is not a man, that He should lie, nor a son of man, that He should repent. Has He said, and will He not do? Or has He spoken, and will He not make it good? Numbers 23:19

Diet and Exercise

One more area that is worth mentioning is diet. So many people turn to changing their dietary habits to become healthier. Some diets do have short-term benefits, but why not look in the Word of God to see what He tells us to eat. In Genesis, Yahweh God gave Adam and Eve seed-bearing herbs and fruit:

And God said, "See, I have given you every herb that yields seed which is on the face of all the earth, and every tree whose fruit yields seed; to you it shall be for food. Genesis 1:29

He also gave us meat, but was specific about what meat was considered food and what was not. We can see a list of those in Leviticus 11:1-23. For most people, this list only cuts pork and shellfish out of their normal diets. When eating meat, Yahweh told His people not to eat fat or blood. Many people have seen a change in their health by merely following Yahweh's commands in this way.

> 'This shall be a perpetual statute throughout your generations in all your dwellings: you shall eat neither fat nor blood.' Leviticus 3:17

There are also many warnings about becoming drunkards or gluttons. Alcohol and food can become idols in our lives.

> Do not mix with winebibbers, or with gluttonous eaters of meat; for the drunkard and the glutton will come to poverty, and drowsiness will clothe a man with rags. Proverbs 23:20-21

Many have become caught up in addiction to alcohol and food. Some have been caught up in addiction to exercise, too. The word says that exercise has some profit for us, but godliness is most profitable. Exercise can also become a god.

> For bodily exercise profits a little, but godliness is profitable for all things, having promise of the life that now is and of that which is to come. 1 Timothy 4:8

The word says our bodies are not ours once we covenant with Yahweh:

> Or do you not know that your body is the temple of the Holy Spirit who is in you, whom you have from God, and you are not your own? For you were bought at a price; therefore glorify God in your body and in your spirit, which are God's. 1 Corinthians 6:19-20

If You choose to dedicate your body to Yahweh and turn to Him for your health and begin to follow His commands, pray the following prayer of repentance:

Father in heaven, I repent for any way I have mistreated my body which is Your holy temple. You say that I am not my own. I have been bought with the price of Jesus' precious blood. I repent where I and my ancestors did not seek You concerning dietary habits. I repent for eating unclean meats, fat, and blood. I repent for eating and drinking to excess and for looking to alcohol, food, or exercise as an idol. I renounce these actions and ask You to free me and my bloodline from any addictions to these things.

I repent for any idolatry in myself or my ancestors involving eating or drinking in communion with idolatry or false gods. I understand that eating can be a part of covenant, and I repent for any ways I have taken that lightly. Please forgive all these sins and cleanse my bloodline.

I choose today to follow Your Biblical commands about what is food and what is not. I ask for a Godly desire for the foods You have created for me. Please continue to teach me about this in

Your word. I detach myself and my bloodline from all evil spirits that are associated with these sins including the spirit of error, addiction, hoarding, poverty, pride, selfishness, rebellion, rejection, self-pity, drunkenness, gluttony, fear of starvation, fear of rejection, unclean spirits, idolatry, and false communion. I renounce them all and command them to leave us now in Jesus' name. I also ask You Yahweh to destroy any poisons or deposits of darkness in my body from my old eating habits.

Here is a prayer of blessing you can pray over your own body through the authority you have in Messiah Jesus. Your words have power as you have been made in the image of Yahweh God. He spoke the universe into existence. His words are living and powerful. May your own words agree with His to speak life and blessing into your being. Pray this prayer daily or whenever you choose.

In the name of Jesus the Messiah, I cancel all words of death spoken over my body including bad diagnoses, bad health, early aging, early death, or curses. I break my agreement with these words. I bless my body in the name of Jesus. I speak life, health, healing, wholeness, youth, and shalom to every cell, every tissue, every organ, every part, every area, every system of my body. I speak the proper pH to every area. I speak the proper amount of hormones, chemicals, electrolytes, and proteins being produced and received throughout. I speak health to my circulation. I receive Holy Spirit breath in my lungs. I speak life and strength to my immune system. It will recognize invaders and fight them. It will recognize my own cells and nourish them. It will not be compromised or confused.

I declare that my body is a temple of the Holy Spirit. I will not share it with darkness or the works of darkness. In Jesus' name, I curse to death and destroy any invading virus, bacteria, parasite, fungus or poison. In Jesus' name, I curse to death and destroy any invading prions, cancerous or precancerous cells, growths, or tumors. I command all these invaders to be removed from my body.

I speak the proper body weight for my frame distributed properly and the proper metabolism. I speak a desire for healthy foods and I break any agreement with unhealthy cravings and addictions.

I speak double blessing and healing to (parts that you have especially hated or spoken curses over.) I speak resurrection life into any areas that have died prematurely.

I bless my mouth to speak words of life and blessing. I bless my hands to heal and my feet to bring good news.

I repent for using any part of my body as an instrument of unrighteousness. I present my members to God as instruments of righteousness. I declare that I am healed by the stripes of Jesus! (Isaiah 53:5) I declare that my God forgives all my iniquity and heals all my disease (Psalm 103:3) I choose to forgive anyone who has hurt me and bless them in Jesus' name.

I speak blessing and favor into my day. The joy of the Lord is my strength (Nehemiah 8:10). Today I will delight myself in the Lord, and He will give me the desires of my heart (Psalm 37:4). Today God will be with me. He will strengthen me and help me. He will uphold me with His righteous right hand (Isaiah 41:10). Today I give all my worries to Him, for He cares for me (1 Peter 5:7). I trust in Him with all my heart. He will guide my paths (Proverbs 3:5-6). This is the day the Lord has made; I will rejoice and be glad in it (Psalm 118:24).

Chapter 7:
Renouncing Personal and Ancestral Sins

You may use the following list provided to give you some examples of generational sins that can provide legal rights for the operation of curses. The best place to look for a complete list is Yahweh's Torah, or holy way of living, written down by Moses (Genesis-Deuteronomy). This is where our God gave us instructions about righteous living. It is His "instruction book" for us. It is actually part of the covenant we have made with Him through the blood of His Son, Messiah Jesus. Throughout the Bible, Yahweh tells us to obey His commands. Messiah Jesus also said:

> "If you love Me, keep My commandments. And I will pray the Father, and He will give you another Helper, that He may abide with you forever. John 14:15-16

Yahweh God knew that we would need help obeying, so He prophesied how He would cleanse His people and give them a new spirit and heart of flesh, and He would put His Spirit in them:

> For I will take you from among the nations, gather you out of all countries, and bring you into your own land. Then I will sprinkle clean water on you, and you shall be clean; I will cleanse you from all your filthiness and from all your idols. I will give you a new heart and put a new spirit within you; I will take the heart of stone out of your flesh and give you a heart of flesh. I will put My Spirit within you and cause you to walk in My statutes, and you will keep My judgments and do them. Ezekiel 36:24-27

Jesus provided the way to God through His sacrificial death which allowed us to be born again and made new. He became a curse for us when He died so that we would be released from the curse.

> Christ has redeemed us from the curse of the law, having become a curse for us (for it is written, "Cursed is everyone who hangs on a tree"). Galatians 3:13

After He ascended, he sent the Holy Spirit to us to make us walk in His ways. If you have never been baptized in the Holy Spirit, please seek that baptism to be able to walk in God's ways. Also, if you have never been baptized in water in your own faith, you will need to obey in that way, too. You need both of these baptisms to walk in victory as a child of God.

Look through the list below for sin doors in your life or the lives of your ancestors that could allow a curse to operate. After you complete your list, pray the following prayer of repentance and renunciation for each personal or generational sin.

Father in heaven, I repent for myself and my ancestors where we have transgressed your holy way of living and sinned against you, whether knowingly or in ignorance. I repent especially for breaking covenant with you and committing spiritual adultery or idolatry.

I specifically repent for the sins of_____ in my life or my bloodline. I come into agreement with you that they are wrong according to your Word. I renounce these sins and actions and break any agreement I have had with them. I renounce agreement with the following spirits: the spirit of divination, familiar spirits, the spirit of jealousy, lying spirits, perverse spirits, the spirit of haughtiness, the spirit of heaviness, the spirit of whoredoms, the spirit of infirmity, deaf and dumb spirit, the spirit of bondage, the spirit of fear, seducing spirits, the spirit of anti-Christ, the spirit of error, and the spirit of death. I detach myself from all these spirits and their kingdoms in the mighty name of Jesus' the Messiah and command them to release me and my bloodline.

I choose to forgive my ancestors for their sins that brought the iniquities on our family bloodlines. I release any lingering traces of those ancestors, or familiar spirits, that came into the bloodline through these sins, and I commit them to you. I especially ask you to release me from any namesake attachments, witchcraft attachments, or evil assignments coming through the bloodline. I relinquish any supernatural abilities or giftings that have come into my family line through the kingdom of darkness. I break agreement with any destiny assigned to me by the kingdom of darkness and choose to walk only in the purpose You, Yahweh God, have assigned to me.

I choose to commit myself and my bloodline to you Yahweh God, creator of the universe, and your kingdom. I choose to covenant with you and keep your commands. Please forgive these sins I have confessed today. I ask you to cleanse my body, soul, spirit, and bloodline and remove these sins from me as far as the east is from the west. I ask that you remember them no more and no longer hold the judgment for these sins against me and my bloodline. I ask that you would remember the blood and sacrifice of your Son that paid the penalty for these sins and how that blood speaks for me through covenant in your heavenly courts. Please rule on my behalf and remove the legal rights the enemy has against me and free us from the curse of these sins. I sever and detach myself and my bloodline from any demons, familiar spirits, human spirits, entities, forces, energies, frequencies, or anything else that has gained access to us and our lives through these sins and curses. I cast them out in Jesus' name. Please Yahweh God would you close and seal with the blood of Jesus any doors, portals, or openings that have allowed these curses to operate in me and my bloodline.

I give every area of my life to you Yahweh God. I ask that the blessings of Your kingdom be restored to me and my bloodline along with all the talents, abilities, and spiritual gifts that you have for us. Please use me for your kingdom plan and purpose. Please clear my path of any roadblocks that the enemy has placed before me and lead me in the way everlasting.

These categories are listed under the spirit strongmen found in scripture. Feel free to add anything the Holy Spirit brings to your mind.

Familiar spirit (Leviticus 19:31)

Necromancy

Mediums/psychics

Yoga/Transcendental meditation

Spiritism

Seeking knowledge from other supernatural sources

False prophets/ peeping and muttering

Voodoo/ santeria/ conjuring spirits

Double-mindedness

Mind-control

Role-playing games

Spirit guides

New Age

Clairvoyants

Passive mind-states

Spirit of jealousy (Numbers 5:14)

Revenge/retaliation

Feuding

Anger/rage

Strife/contention

Envy

Competition

Jealousy

Murder

Hatred

Division

Cruelty

Violence/gangs

Lying spirit (2 Chronicles 18:22)

Deception

Superstitions

Accusations

Slander

False teachers

Flattery

Religious bondage

Gossip

Lies

Spirit of haughtiness (Proverbs 16:18)

Pride/arrogance	Obstinate attitude
Self-righteousness	Scornful
Idleness	Disobedience

Perverse spirit (Isaiah 19:14)

Sexual perversion (homosexuality, bestiality, adultery, fornication)

Filthy mind/ profanity

Pornography	Child abuse
Incest/ molestation/ rape	Evil actions
Atheism	Abortion
Twisting the Word	Foolishness
Contention	Reprobate mind
Contention/strife	Vanity
Rebellion/defiance	Rejection of God
Racism/prejudice	Grudge-holding/ bitterness
bitterness/ unforgiveness	Judging unrighteously/ criticism

Spirit of heaviness (Isaiah 61:3)

Sorrow/ grief /excessive mourning	Insomnia
Self-pity	Broken heart
Despair/ hopelessness	Rejection
Depression	Suicide
Inner wounds	Heaviness
Broken relationships	

Spirit of whoredoms (Hosea 5:4)

Idolatry

Lust

Adultery/ unfaithfulness

Worldliness

Prostitution of the body, soul, or spirit

Reprobate mind

Love of money

Greed/materialism

Gluttony/ Excessive appetite

Fornication/ promiscuity

Chronic dissatisfaction

False religion/ cults/ false doctrines

Deaf and dumb spirit (Mark 9:17-29)

Mental illness

Deafness/ ear problems

Muteness

Drowning

Blindness/ eye problems

Crying

Tearing

Seizures/epilepsy

Foaming at the mouth/ Gnashing teeth

Burns

Suicidal

Pining away/ grief

Prostration

Infirmity

Spiritual blindness and deafness

Dementia

Spirit of infirmity (Luke 13:11-13)

Weakness

Oppression

Lame/frailness/impotence/bent body

Pain/torment

Asthma/allergies

Arthritis

Chronic or lingering disorders or disease

Cancer

Spirit of divination (Acts 16:16-18)

Fortune-telling

Sorcery

Astrology

Magic

Drugs

Rebellion

Occult games

Martial arts

Occult activities and groups

Witchcraft

Movies and media associated with the occult

Spirit of bondage (Romans 8:15)

Addiction/ alcoholism/ drugs

Fear

Captivity

Compulsions

Perfectionism

Domination/ control

Bondage to sin

Corruption

Eating disorders

Poverty/financial lack

Spirit of death (1 Corinthians 15:26)

Death/ early death

Bodily death

Body parts that have stopped functioning

Destruction

Death to relationships or other parts of life

Seducing spirits (1 Timothy 4:1)

Deception

Seared conscience

Hypocrisy

Fascination with evil

Seducers/ enticers

Wandering from truth

False religion

Music and frequencies of evil nature

Hypnotism

Mind control

Spirit of fear (2 Timothy 1:7)

Fears/phobias

Torment/horror

Terror/nightmares

Anxiety/ worry

Secret societies

Mind-control organizations

Fear of death

Fear of man

Stress

Doubt

Heart failure

Spirit of anti-Christ (1 John 4:3)

Lawlessness

Witchcraft

satanism

Humanism

Denying Jesus/ coming against Jesus

Deception

Atheism

Legalism

Worldly speech and actions

Heresies

False doctrine

Treason/rebellion/defiance

Spirit of error (1 John 4:6)

Errors

False doctrines

Unteachable spirit

Unsubmissiveness

Corruption

Contention

Defensive/argumentative

New age movement

Lying

Cults/ False religion

Chapter 8:
Breaking Unholy Unions of the Soul (Soul Ties)

In Genesis 2, we find that a suitable helper was not found for Adam among all the animals Yahweh God had created.

> And the Lord God caused a deep sleep to fall on Adam, and he slept; and He took one of his ribs, and closed up the flesh in its place. Then the rib which the Lord God had taken from man He made into a woman, and He brought her to the man. And Adam said: "This is now bone of my bones and flesh of my flesh; She shall be called Woman, because she was taken out of Man." Therefore, a man shall leave his father and mother and be joined to his wife, and they shall become one flesh. Genesis 2:1-24

Yahweh created woman as a suitable helper for man from one of his own ribs and declared that the two would become one flesh. The soul union of marriage of a man and wife is blessed by God to join the two people together. This union is a Godly covenant.

We can see covenant practices in the traditional American wedding ceremony. The wedding witnesses, the family and friends of the bride and groom, are seated on two sides of the aisle. A white runner usually runs down the aisle to form a sacred path. This is similar to the door made in the ancient covenant. The bride is walked down the aisle by her father to be given to the groom. The bride and the groom join right hands to say their vows, committing themselves and all their possessions to one another, "until death do we part." The bride and groom exchange rings and names and are pronounced man and wife. At the wedding reception, the bride and groom and the wedding witnesses share a meal together and watch the bride and groom share a cup of wine and feed each other cake, a covenant meal. The blood of the covenant happens as the two consummate the marriage on the wedding night to show the two have become one flesh. Sometimes the couple will plant a tree to remember their wedding day.

We also find an example of a holy union or covenant of friendship between David and Jonathan in 1 Samuel 18:1-4:

> Now when he had finished speaking to Saul, the soul of Jonathan was knit to the soul of David, and Jonathan loved him as his own soul. Saul took him that day, and would not let him go home to his father's house anymore. Then Jonathan and David made a covenant, because he loved him as his own soul. And Jonathan took off the robe that was on him and gave it to David, with his armor, even to his sword and his bow and his belt.

Paul teaches us in 1 Corinthians 6:13-20 that sexual immorality can join two people together in an unholy union. It is a sin against your own body which is the temple of Yahweh's Holy Spirit.

> Now the body is not for sexual immorality but for the Lord, and the Lord for the body. And God both raised up the Lord and will also raise us up by His power. Do you not know that your bodies are members of Christ? Shall I then take the members of Christ and make them members of a harlot? Certainly not! Or do you not know that he who is joined to a harlot is one body with her? For "the two," He says, "shall become one flesh." But he who is joined to the Lord is one spirit with Him. Flee sexual immorality. Every sin that a man does is outside the body, but he who commits sexual immorality sins against his own body. Or do you not know that your body is the temple of the Holy Spirit who is in you, whom you have from God, and you are not your own? For you were bought at a price; therefore, glorify God in your body and in your spirit, which are God's.

We see the power of the unholy union in Genesis 34:1-4 where Dinah went out into the surrounding lands and was taken by the prince into sexual immorality and defilement.

> Now Dinah the daughter of Leah, whom she had borne to Jacob, went out to see the daughters of the land. And when Shechem the son of Hamor the Hivite, prince of the country, saw her, he took her and lay with her, and violated her. His soul was strongly attracted to Dinah the daughter of Jacob, and he loved the young woman and spoke kindly to the young woman. So Shechem spoke to his father Hamor, saying, "Get me this young woman as a wife."

The sexual union was formed through fornication and Shechem was 'strongly attached' to Dinah. He loved her and wanted to marry her but this is not always the case. We see another instance of rape in the story of Amnon and Tamar in 2 Samuel 13. Amnon was 'sick with love' for Tamar. He could have asked David to marry her, but instead, he deceived her to come into his house by pretending to be sick. Then he raped her, and the 'love' he had for her turned to 'hatred'. After the unholy sexual union, he put Tamar out of his house, shamed and defiled with no hope of having a husband.

In these two instances, we see how sexual immorality can bring unholy unions of the soul which can manifest differently. The second example might be considered what some would call a 'love-hate' relationship. This type of unholy union can bond women to abusive men. Though they desperately want to escape the abuse, they are continually drawn back to the abuser.

Proverbs 6:32 tells us adultery can destroy the soul.

> Whoever commits adultery with a woman lacks understanding; He who does so destroys his own soul.

Another problem of unholy sex, sex outside of marriage (husband and wife), is the transference of demons. Perverted sex opens doors to demonic forces as a sin door. It also opens a door to the demons already inside the sexual partner. This is how victims of rape and molestation can have demons enter them. The one flesh spiritual law is in effect.

In order to be free from unholy soul unions and the demons that entered through them, there must be repentance, renunciation, and forgiveness, before the breaking of the bonds. It is also important to pray for healing of the shattered soul. Read through the following prayers as they relate to you:

For each unholy soul union for which you willingly participated, pray the following:

Father, I repent for sinning against my body, your temple, and using it as an instrument of unrighteousness through fornication and sexual perversity with _____. I forgive _____ for any betrayal, hurts, and wounds that came through this unholy union. I forgive myself for failing to keep the purity You have given me for marriage. I now renounce this unholy bond and ask you Father to cleanse and forgive me. I ask you to free me from any unholy attachment to _____ and loose the bonding of our souls. I return any parts of _____ that have been attached to me, back to him/her. I ask You, Father, to restore to me any parts of myself that were tied to _____ through this bond.

For each unholy soul union that happened through trauma of molestation or rape, pray the following:

Father, I renounce the trauma and sexual perversion that came into my life through _____ with _____. In no way do I justify the treacherous act, but I choose as an act of my will to forgive _____ for sinning against me and defiling me and for any betrayal, hurts and wounds that came through this unholy union. I ask you to forgive me Father if I have held onto bitterness from this trauma. I now renounce this unholy bond and ask you Father to cleanse and forgive me. I ask you to free me from any attachment to _____ and loose the bonding of our souls. I return any parts of _____ that have been attached to me, back to him/her. I ask You, Father, to restore to me any parts of myself that were tied to _____ through this bond.

If you have been through a divorce, you need to repent for breaking the oath you made before God and forgive your spouse. This does not justify any wrong that your spouse committed against you. We will go deeper into forgiveness in the next chapter.

Father, I ask you to forgive me for failing to keep my covenant oaths, vows, or promises to _____. I ask you to forgive me for every offense on my part against _____ that played a part in our marriage vows being broken. I ask you to forgive me for any gossip, slander, anger, or hatred I have used against _____, as well as, any curse this may have brought upon his/her life. I cancel those words and bless _____ in Jesus' name. I ask you to free me from any attachment to _____ and loose the bonding of our souls. I return any parts of _____ that have been attached to me, back to him/her. I ask You, Father, to restore to me any parts of myself that were tied to _____ through this bond.

For each <u>unholy soul union that was not sexual</u>; ex. Yoga or martial arts instructor, bonds with club members or societies, or worldly friendships that formed an unholy bond, pray the following:

Father, I repent for (practicing yoga) and the unholy soul union that formed with (my yogi) _____. I forgive _____ for any betrayal, hurts, and wounds that came through this unholy union (and for leading me into worship of demon gods). I repent for any broken vows with _____. I now renounce this unholy bond and ask you Father to cleanse and forgive me. I ask you to free me from any attachment to _____ and loose the bonding of our souls. I return any parts of _____ that have been attached to me, back to him/her. I ask You, Father, to restore to me any parts of myself that were tied to _____ through this bond.

After praying to break all the unholy soul unions, pray the following:

Father, forgive me for holding any bitterness or unforgiveness against any one of these people who has hurt or defiled me. Today I choose to obey You and forgive them just as You have forgiven me. I ask that You would restore my fragmented soul to wholeness and bring Your healing power to my memories and emotions and body. I ask that every muscle memory of any traumatic event will be removed now. Whether good or bad, I release every relational or romantic memory formed through these unholy unions to You so that the enemy can no longer use them to torment me. I ask You to wipe them from my remembrance along with any pain from soul wounds. I choose to detach myself from all unclean and sexual spirits that have come into my life through the sin of fornication and sexual perversity, along with any other demons that have transferred to me through these unholy unions. I command them to release me now in Jesus' name! I ask You, Yahweh God, to serve them an eviction notice from me and my bloodline forever. I ask You to close the doors that were opened to darkness through these acts and seal them with the blood of Jesus.

I also renounce any unholy ties to any place or object including_____. I repent Father, for walking on any ground considered 'holy' by darkness. I repent for removing my shoes or other actions of respect on these unholy grounds. I repent for eating at unholy festivals or feasts, bowing down to false gods or false religions. I repent for wearing 'holy items' from false religion or lucky charms or talismans. I repent for oaths and vows that would attach me to places or items. I choose to detach myself from these places and items now in Jesus' name and command all demons associated with them to release me now.

If you are <u>single</u>, pray the following:

Father, I believe and agree with Your command to reserve sexual intimacy for marriage and commit myself to wait for marriage to the one You have chosen for me. I declare that my body is Your temple, and I am not my own. I present my body to You as a living sacrifice, holy and acceptable to You, and present my members as instruments of righteousness. I renounce the lie that my body is unclean or dirty and accept the cleansing of the blood of Jesus to make me clean and pure again. Please sing over me songs of deliverance and cause the awakened love and desire to fall back asleep until the time for my marriage that You have chosen.

If you are <u>married</u>, pray the following:

Father, I believe Your command to reserve sexual intimacy for marriage and commit myself to my husband and the holy union that You have given me. I declare that my body is Your temple, and I am not my own. I present my body to You as a living sacrifice, holy and acceptable to You, and present my members as instruments of righteousness. I renounce the lie that my body is unclean or dirty and accept the cleansing of the blood of Jesus to make me clean and pure again. Please sing over me songs of deliverance and create in my marriage a path to the beautiful gift that sex in marriage was always intended to be. Remove any hindrance to the soul bonding and oneness that You intend for my spouse and I to have together. Strengthen our covenant and restore what the enemy has stolen. Let the blood of Jesus consecrate this marriage as holy before You.

If married to an <u>unsaved spouse</u> also add:

Father, please place the blood of Jesus as a barrier between me and any demons that have had access to me through my one-flesh union with my husband. As we are one flesh, I repent on his behalf. I ask You to grant _____ repentance and remove the veil the enemy has placed over him/her so that he/she doesn't see the glory of Your gospel. Please draw _____ to You and bring him/her into Your kingdom that we might be equally-yoked in marriage and set-apart for You.

Chapter 9:
Freedom from Spiritual Spouses and Their Covenants

I included the spiritual spouse in this manual because it is one of the main spirits that works to prevent and destroy marriages because marriage is God-ordained and a picture of Messiah and His bride. The spiritual spouse is commonly known among people living in Africa, but many in the western world have never heard of it even though it affects many of them.

Because it so commonly comes at night, the spirit spouse may be referred to in Isaiah 34:14 as the night creature which is the word "Lilith" or "Lilit" in Hebrew.

> The wild beasts of the desert shall also meet with the jackals, and the wild goat shall bleat to its companion; also the night creature shall rest there, and find for herself a place of rest.

Like all darkness, these evil spirits come to steal, kill, and destroy. They can come in generationally through dedications of the bloodline or through sexual perversion. They usually manifest with some type of perverse or early sexual encounter, but some are present from the womb. These spirits can make themselves known in dreams and can manifest as invisible friends to children who can see into the spirit realm. They may appear as friends early on and even as children themselves.

If you are a dreamer, these spirits usually appear in dreams as a husband or wife would…getting married, having sex, living together, having children, eating together, making a home together. They may take on the appearance of someone you know or someone unknown. Look for covenant practices in your dreams.

Although marriage between humans and demons is illegal in God's kingdom, the spiritual husband claims to be a true husband and wants to keep the woman chained to him. He doesn't want her to marry in the physical world and will do everything possible to stop her. The spiritual husband scares away any prospects for marriage, but pushes the woman to commit masturbation, fornication and sexual immorality, opening the door to more demons as the spiritual husband is usually a strongman building his kingdom in the woman. The same spirit as a spiritual wife can cause a man to be addicted to pornography and masturbation which is actually sex with demons. It will try to block marriage for the man, as well. It can also cause him to be jealous and controlling and fill him with lust leading to all kinds of sexual sin.

The spiritual spouse can cause disease and problems with the reproductive tract including heavy periods, severe pain, abnormal cycles, foul-smelling discharge, fibroids, cancer, and signs of a false pregnancy with "spiritual babies" such as bloating or feeling movement in the abdomen like a baby kicking or moving. It can also cause low sperm count and impotence in men.

It can cause miscarriages, early and late. It is a major cause of infertility and barrenness. Though the women can get pregnant and have babies, even nursing them, in their dreams, they are barren in the physical.

This spirit strives to cause division between the physical wife and husband, a major cause of separation and divorce. It can steal affection and attraction and cause hatred between man and wife. It can cause women to become feminists taking the role of the man of the house and focusing on career, jobs, rising to the top, equality and power, and riches and wealth. It may cause the wife to feel prideful and superior to the true husband. The wife can become authoritative and controlling, seeing the husband as useless. She can be disrespectful and unsubmissive. Husbands are sometimes forced to take the wife's role in her absence. The role reversal can turn into homosexuality for either true spouse.

Spirit spouses hate Jesus and persecute His followers, the Bible, anything connected to Yahweh God. This can manifest with great persecution of the person affected or their actual physical spouse. It will try to block intimacy with Yahweh God and with fellowship among the members of the body of Messiah.

The spiritual spouse doesn't want the person to find pleasure in anything or anyone else, causing life to be filled with disappointment, delay, and despair. It brings sickness and accidents to eventually cause death which is the end goal. Because this spirit makes a claim on the person it has "married," it is best to declare a divorce from it in the courts.

Before reading the declaration below, make sure you have completed the previous steps of repenting for and renouncing all sexual sin in your life and your ancestral lines, and cancelling any agreements or covenants that your ancestors may have made with demons linking you to spiritual spouses. You also need to have already broken any demonic or unholy soul ties made through sexual sin.

You will also be declaring your betrothal to your physical husband or wife (if you are married) and your true spiritual husband as the bride of Messiah Jesus.

> Husbands, love your wives, just as Christ also loved the church and gave Himself for her, that He might sanctify and cleanse her with the washing of water by the word, that He might present her to Himself a glorious church, not having spot or wrinkle or any such thing, but that she should be holy and without blemish. Ephesians 5:25-27

Let us be glad and rejoice and give Him glory, for the marriage of the Lamb has come, and His wife has made herself ready." And to her it was granted to be arrayed in fine linen, clean and bright, for the fine linen is the righteous acts of the saints.
Revelation 19:7

If you need freedom from this spirit, pray the following petition and declaration aloud:

I hereby declare that _____ is my legal physical husband/wife under God. I am one with him/her. My covenant is with _____ and Yahweh God, the God of Abraham, Isaac, and Jacob.

I declare, before heaven and earth, that I am betrothed to Yeshua haMaschiach, Jesus the Messiah, as my spiritual husband. I have made covenant with Him through the shedding of His blood. I am His bride and He is my Bridegroom. He has paid the bride price for me. He has traded my life of sin and shame for His life without sin. He has cleansed me and given me a robe of righteousness. He has crowned me with mercy and lovingkindness. He has placed His seal upon my heart and life. He has given me His name which is above all names and the authority that comes with His name. He proclaims that He will never leave me. His covenant protects me and my family. His angels encamp around me. He has placed His powerful sword in my hand, the Word of God. It is living and powerful, it is fire, and a hammer that shatters rock.

Every spiritual marriage with darkness is illegal in the courts of heaven. I come before the throne of mercy and grace petitioning the God of Israel for a complete divorce and release from the unholy covenants with the spiritual spouse. I repent for participating in this marriage through deception, as well as, all my sins known and unknown and all the sins of my ancestors all the way back to Adam, especially known covenants that have allowed this bondage. I ask that the blood of Jesus cleanse my bloodline from iniquity and curses coming from these sins. I ask that the power of the Living Word of God divide me now from these dark covenants and the evil spirits operating through them. I ask that a verdict of divorce be given and enforced from the courts of heaven along with my complete freedom and release; body, soul, and spirit; from all dark covenants, trades, dedications, altars, curses, and soul ties, that have allowed the entrance and operation of the spiritual spouse in my life. I ask that the courts of heaven command every curse to cease operations against me and all plans, purposes, destinies, appointments, and assignments from darkness be cancelled against me, my life, my God-ordained marriage, and my family line.

Now read this declaration aloud with boldness:

Before the heavenly courts and as I am seated in the heavenly realms in Messiah, I renounce and break all covenants made by me or on my behalf with the spirit husband (or wife) in the spirit world or dream world, in the name of Jesus.

In Jesus' name, I divorce and renounce my marriage with the spirit husband (or wife), calling it null and void. I renounce and break every blood covenant offering and soul-tie covenants with the spirit husband (or wife). I renounce and reject the name given to me by the spirit husband (or wife).

I remove the following items from my spiritual and physical bodies and command them to burn to ashes by the fire of God (remove them prophetically as you say it): crown, wedding gown, veil, ring, chains, beads, belts, shackles, shoes, marriage certificate, photographs, bridal gifts, dowry, trademarks, engravements, tattoos, jewelry, adornments, false armor, and all other materials used for the marriage, in Jesus' name.

I command every deposit of the spirit husband (or wife) in my life, spirit, soul, or body, especially the reproductive and sexual organs, to burn to ashes by Holy Spirit fire and to be removed right now in Jesus' name. This includes any spiritual food ingested by me in dreams. I also command death out of my womb and reproductive tract.

I break any agreement I have made with disease or acceptance I have made with a diagnosis of disease. I command every disease or symptom of disease, including _____ (be specific to mention each type of affliction, especially of the reproductive and sexual organs...fibroids, endometriosis, fertility problems, heavy or painful periods, low sperm count, blockages, cancer, etc.) placed in my body or soul by the spirit husband (or wife) to be consumed by Holy Spirit fire and to be removed right now in Jesus' name.

I destroy by Holy Spirit fire any spiritual children, snakes, fish, eggs, or marine spirits resulting from this unholy marriage in Jesus' name.

In the name of Jesus, I withdraw any part of myself that has been given to or stolen by the spirit spouse or has been deposited on any evil altar on my behalf. I command those altars to be destroyed now.

I take back and possess all my earthly belongings and spiritual blessings that have been stolen and are in the custody of the spirit husband (or wife), in Jesus' name.

I reject and declare cancelled every curse, evil pronouncement, hex, vex, spell, jinx, enchantment, assignment, attachment, and incantation placed upon me or my God-ordained marriage by the spirit husband (or wife), in the name of Jesus.

I declare my freedom from the stronghold, domineering power, and bondage of the spirit husband (or wife), in the name of Jesus.

I serve the spirit husband (or wife) a notice of eviction and restraint against me, my body, my marriage, my life, and my family line from now until eternity. I bind you, spirit spouse, to all your kingdom, your deposits, and disease. I cast you out, in the mighty name of Jesus, and forbid you from ever entering my dreams, marriage, or my life again!

(At this point, you can agree with this deliverance by blowing out a hard breath or coughing purposefully to expel the spirit. Because "ruach", the word for spirit in the Bible, also means breath, the spirits usually leave on the breath. This is your way to force the spirit out.)

Holy Spirit, I ask You to send Your cleansing fire into all parts of my life, body, soul, and spirit, and into my God-ordained marriage to burn out all traces of the covenant with the spirit spouse. I ask You to send Your healing and consecrating waters to repair and restore every damage done by this evil in my life, body, soul, and spirit and to my God-ordained marriage. I ask You to release every blessing that You have destined for me that has been blocked by the spirit spouse. I ask You to close and seal any doors opened by the spirit spouse and open any heavenly doors that it has been blocking. I put on the full armor of God to protect me from the enemy. I receive all that You have planned for me, my life, my God-ordained marriage, my family, my ministry, and my destiny in Jesus' name. Let Your armies make a hedge around me and my family. Release me to and equip me for your purposes. Amen.

Be sober and alert that the spirit spouse does not try to re-covenant with you in your dreams. If you find yourself interacting with it in any way, cancel those plans on waking. Announce to him/her that you will never marry again, that you are already betrothed to Jesus. It is helpful to seek out a deliverance minister to agree with you to cast out this spirit. Be persistent! Fight the good fight as you wrestle for your freedom.

Chapter 10:
The Power of Forgiveness

We have discussed our need to confess our sins and the iniquities of our bloodlines, repent, and be forgiven by God. There are many scriptures that speak of God's great mercy to forgive, without which we would all be condemned to death. This forgiveness comes through the blood of Jesus.

> This is my blood of the covenant, which is poured out for many for the forgiveness of sins. Matthew 26:28

> In him we have redemption through his blood, the forgiveness of sins, in accordance with the riches of God's grace. Ephesians 1:7

Remember that He is the door. Without His sacrifice we could not be forgiven. He paid the price for our sins to be remitted, to cancel the debt that we owed. There are many scriptures that talk about the forgiveness and mercy of Yahweh God.

> The Lord our God is merciful and forgiving, even though we have rebelled against him; Daniel 9:9

> Whoever conceals their sins does not prosper, but the one who confesses and renounces them finds mercy. Proverbs 28:13

> Then I acknowledged my sin to you and did not cover up my iniquity. I said, "I will confess my transgressions to the LORD." And you forgave the guilt of my sin. Psalm 32:5

> Who is a God like you, who pardons sin and forgives the transgression of the remnant of his inheritance? You do not stay angry forever but delight to show mercy. You will again have compassion on us; you will tread our sins underfoot and hurl all our iniquities into the depths of the sea. Micah 7:18-19

> Repent, then, and turn to God, so that your sins may be wiped out, that times of refreshing may come from the Lord. Acts 3:19

Peter replied, "Repent and be baptized, every one of you, in the name of Jesus Christ for the forgiveness of your sins. And you will receive the gift of the Holy Spirit. Acts 2:38

If we confess our sins, he is faithful and just and will forgive us our sins and purify us from all unrighteousness. 1 John 1:9

Now that we have been forgiven, what does Yahweh God require of us? He requires us to forgive as we have been forgiven.

And when you stand praying, if you hold anything against anyone, forgive them, so that your Father in heaven may forgive you your sins." Mark 11:25

"Do not judge, and you will not be judged. Do not condemn, and you will not be condemned. Forgive, and you will be forgiven. Luke 6:37

For if you forgive other people when they sin against you, your heavenly Father will also forgive you. But if you do not forgive others their sins, your Father will not forgive your sins. Matthew 6:14-15

Wow! Those verses have a strong message! It appears that forgiveness is not an option for those of us in covenant with Yahweh God. It is a command! Choosing forgiveness is a serious matter! In chapter 2, we read the parable of the unforgiving servant in Matthew 18:21-35. We learned that holding unforgiveness against our brother can allow the tormentors to have legal rights to us. Those tormentors can torment our minds, bodies, and lives. To be free from the torment, we must choose forgiveness.

Believe it or not, Yahweh also commands us to love our enemies, do good to them, bless them, and pray for them. We are His children, His covenant partners, and we should be forgiving and merciful just like Him. As we become one with Yahweh, we should be taking on His characteristics.

But to you who are listening I say: Love your enemies, do good to those who hate you, bless those who curse you, pray for those who mistreat you. If someone slaps you on one cheek, turn to them the other also. If someone takes your coat, do not withhold your shirt from them. Luke 6:27-29

But love your enemies, do good to them, and lend to them without expecting to get anything back. Then your reward will be great, and you will be children of the Most High, because he is kind to the ungrateful and wicked. Be merciful, just as your Father is merciful. Luke 6:35-36

How many times should we forgive? Jesus essentially told Peter to forgive as many times as needed.

> Then Peter came to Jesus and asked, "Lord, how many times shall I forgive my brother or sister who sins against me? Up to seven times?" Jesus answered, "I tell you, not seven times, but seventy-seven times. Matthew 18:21-22

Now that you know that you are commanded to forgive as you have been forgiven as many times as needed, how do you do that? You have undoubtedly been hurt by many people and some of those wounds may still be festering and painful. Does forgiveness mean the offender gets off without punishment? That doesn't seem very fair.

Actually, God's mercy for us isn't fair, either. Our sins against Him deserved the death sentence. His mercy spared us. When you choose, as an act of your will, to forgive those who have hurt you, you choose to be obedient to God. Instead of taking your own vengeance, you turn the offender over to the Great Judge of All the Earth.

Remember that Yahweh is your covenant partner. In the Ancient covenant, when the two became one, they pledged to protect each other from their enemies. If one man was hurt or killed by an enemy, the covenant partner would become the Avenger of Blood. Yahweh God will take up your case when you turn the matter over to him.

> Repay no one evil for evil. Have regard for good things in the sight of all men. If it is possible, as much as depends on you, live peaceably with all men. Beloved, do not avenge yourselves, but rather give place to wrath; for it is written, "Vengeance is Mine, I will repay," says the Lord. Romans 12:17-19

Forgiveness does not justify any sin committed against you by the offender. It only turns that offender over to the righteous Judge who will deal with him righteously. The offender may never apologize to you and may never deserve forgiveness, but neither did you. Forgiveness is a choice, an act of obedience.

When Yahweh God forgives us, He chooses to "remember our sins no more."

> "This is the covenant that I will make with them after those days, says the Lord: I will put My laws into their hearts, and in their minds I will write them," then He adds, "Their sins and their lawless deeds I will remember no more." Hebrews 10:16-17

This means He will no longer hold us accountable for theses sins or use them against us ever again. He separates us from those sins as far as the east is from the west.

> For as the heavens are high above the earth, so great is His mercy toward those who fear Him; as far as the east is from the west, Psalm 103:11-12

You may think that you could never forget the sins committed against you, but you can choose not to hold those sins against the offender, just like Yahweh does for you. Once the painful soul wound is healed, the pain will leave your memories. Those memories will then serve as a reminder of your freedom. They will become a testimony of overcoming.

You may not feel like you want to forgive the offender, but you do not need to wait until you feel like forgiving. Your emotions are likely tied to the festering wound. Hebrews 12:15 talks about a root of bitterness that can grow when there is no repentance:

> Pursue peace with all people, and holiness, without which no one will see the Lord: looking carefully lest anyone fall short of the grace of God; lest any root of bitterness springing up cause trouble, and by this many become defiled;

This root can bring trouble and defilement to your soul. By choosing to forgive with your will instead of your feelings, your obedience will remove any barriers to allow Yahweh God to pull out that bitter root and release His healing power that can cleanse and restore all the pain and hurt from the offense.

So, now is the time for action. Ask the Holy spirit to reveal to you all those you need to forgive. The list may be quite long. Trust that He will bring to you the name of every person you need to forgive. Some names may be from childhood and some may seem insignificant, but be faithful to choose forgiveness for each one. Most everyone needs to forgive those who have been closest to you like your mother, father, siblings, grandparents, and spouse. Because you have been together so much, there is a greater chance that these people have hurt you at some point. You will also need to forgive yourself for the failures that have been bringing guilt and shame upon you. Take time to allow the Holy Spirit to bring back the hurt and pain of the offense as you pray through each one allowing Yahweh to deal with it all.

Pray the following for each offender:

In the name of Jesus, I choose as an act of my will to forgive _____ for _____even though it made me feel _____. I choose no longer to hold this sin against him/her. I cut the chain binding us together through unforgiveness and release him/her to the great Judge of all for just judgment. I release him/her from any debt to me. I will not take vengeance on _____. I choose to bless _____ in Jesus' name and cancel any curses I have spoken against him/her. I ask You Father to draw _____ to you.

After you have finished forgiving all persons on your list, pray:

Forgive me Father for holding unforgiveness or bitterness in my heart toward all these people. I repent of and renounce any hatred, resentment, offense, anger, and vengefulness of which I had come into agreement. I also ask You to pull up any root of bitterness that has been planted in me causing trouble and defilement (Hebrews 12:15). I ask You to cleanse me and heal me from the wounds and scars I have received and make me whole. I open the door of my heart and soul to You and invite You in. I renounce and cancel any unholy soul ties between me and all these people. I now detach myself from any pain, tormentors, and torturers that have had a legal right to my life through unforgiveness. I cast them out in Jesus' name! My debt has been paid by Jesus the Messiah. He has paid the price for my sin. He took my punishment upon Himself. I now receive the peace Jesus paid for on my behalf. Please fill me Father with your hope and joy through the Holy Spirt.

Yahweh God has given us a ministry of reconciliation.

> Now all things are of God, who has reconciled us to Himself through Jesus Christ, and has given us the ministry of reconciliation. 2 Corinthians 5:18

It is so important to Yahweh that we have unity and reconcile with our brother that He commands us to do it before we offer Him gifts.

> So, if you are offering your gift at the altar and there remember that your brother has something against you, leave your gift there before the altar and go. First be reconciled to your brother, and then come and offer your gift. Matthew 5: 23-24

If there is someone to whom you need to apologize and seek forgiveness, that is the next step. There are some people to whom we cannot be reconciled, because of death or danger. Trust the Holy Spirit's leading on that. Sometimes it may also be best to take a friend or mediator along with you.

> Be kind to one another, tenderhearted, forgiving one another, as God in Christ forgave you. Ephesians 4:32

> Above all, keep loving one another earnestly, since love covers a multitude of sins."
> 1 Peter 4:8

> Get rid of all bitterness, rage and anger, brawling and slander, along with every form of malice. Be kind and compassionate to one another, forgiving each other, just as in Christ God forgave you. Ephesians 4:31-32

Chapter 11:
Freedom from Trauma

Trauma can be an open door to demonic control in our lives. It can be a symptom of a generational curse, personal sin, the sin of another, or an evil attack. Although traumatic events happen to you and are out of your control, they can open the door to agreement with bitterness, unrighteous anger, fear, despair, depression, and even revenge. Some people even blame God for these events or become angry at Him for allowing them to happen. The truth is that most of these events happen because of legal rights through sin or iniquity in the family line, or through human freewill decisions.

Trauma can cause much brokenness in our lives. It can trouble our hearts and shatter our souls. It can cause us to withdraw and build up walls to others and to Yahweh God. It can bring pain and torment to our bodies and souls and keep us bound in captivity. All of this can keep us from walking in the plans and purposes of God and from having a close, personal relationship with Him and with others.

Isaiah 61 tells us that Jesus the Messiah came to heal the broken-hearted and to set the captives free.

> "The Spirit of the Lord God is upon Me, because the Lord has anointed Me to preach good tidings to the poor; He has sent Me to heal the brokenhearted, to proclaim liberty to the captives, and the opening of the prison to those who are bound; to proclaim the acceptable year of the Lord, and the day of vengeance of our God; to comfort all who mourn," Isaiah 61:1-2

Jesus has power to free you and heal you from the trauma in your life. If you will choose to trust Him, He can begin that work today. Ask the Holy Spirit to help you make a list of traumatic events that have happened in your life from childhood into adulthood; physical, emotional, spiritual, and sexual. Include any major event that had an extreme, negative or traumatic impact on you, such as: near death experiences, death of a loved one, accidents, a significant move from your home to another community, divorce, assault, sexual assault, surgeries, major illness, abuse, major rejections or abandonment, traumatic events you have witnessed, broken relationships, problems or traumas in the womb, attempted suicide, etc.

Before you pray through the prayers to be free from trauma; make sure you have worked through the steps for forgiveness, breaking soul unions, and renouncing sin and occult involvement to make sure all legal rights of darkness have been broken. You are expected to have some overlapping events here. If there is a new event that you haven't dealt with yet, you may need to take that event back through the previous steps.

Pray the following prayer out loud:

Father in heaven, I choose to release the following times of my life to you in their fullness:

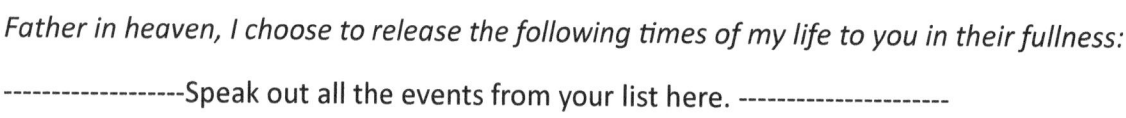

-------------------Speak out all the events from your list here. ---------------------

I ask that You would free me from any trauma or demonic forces that have collected in my body, soul, or spirit from these events. I choose to forgive my ancestors for any sin or iniquity that has allowed these events to happen through a generational curse. I also choose to forgive any other person whom I have blamed for these events, including myself. I repent for any ways I have agreed with the enemy where these events are concerned. I repent for and break agreement with any trauma, unforgiveness, bitterness; unrighteous anger toward you, other men, or myself; despair, depression, suicidal thoughts, thoughts or actions of revenge, fear, jealousy, or other negative emotions or actions. I also repent for the times I blamed You for these traumatic events or the times I was angry at You for allowing them to happen. Please forgive me and cleanse me with the blood of Jesus.

I ask You to rule on my behalf to abolish all legal rights the adversary has held against me through these traumatic events. I petition that all assignments and curses of darkness associated with these traumatic events be severed from me and my bloodline. I ask You to disconnect me from all earthly darkness and powers from the second heavens that have gained access to me through these traumatic events. I command all demonic forces related to these events to release me now in Jesus' name. I ask You to close and erase any portals, targets, touchpoints, pathways, marks, or any means of access to evil men, familiar spirits, demonic forces, principalities, powers, thrones, or rulers of darkness that were used for communication, spying or torment in my being: body, soul, or spirit. May they forever be closed in Jesus' name.

I request a permanent restraining order from heaven against any tormenting spirits or dreams. I request that You send Your heavenly host to collect and remove all pain, torment, torture, terror, fright, fear, anxiety, panic, worry, stress, tension, shame, guilt, and fear from every area of body and soul where they have held residence down to the atomic/cellular level. I ask You to disconnect and release any parts of my body and soul from any place, space, time, or dimension they have been held in captivity, a snare, prison, or trap. I ask You Father to cleanse and reunify my shattered soul to perfect restoration from the time of conception to the present and to break down any self-preservation or protective barriers against You that I have erected in response to trauma. You are my Covenant Partner. I choose to welcome You into all these areas and turn over all this territory to You. I surrender all parts of myself to You.

I ask You to remove from my body, soul, and spirit all dark deposits and all weapons of darkness that have been operating against me. I also ask that all soul and cellular memories and triggers from these traumatic events be completely erased from all parts of me including my senses. I ask that you destroy and remove any chemicals, drugs, poisons or toxins my body has either produced naturally and retained as a result of trauma, or that were ingested, injected, or placed in my body.

I petition that You would bring all of my body systems and their components into Your perfect order for life, health, and youth. Please send the fire of Your Holy Spirit to cleanse, heal, and restore in all parts and areas of my life that were once affected by darkness. Please fill me with Your Holy Spirit and Your shalom.

Please heal my brain and restore its hemispherical connections, as well as, it's connections to all systems and components of my body. Please establish perfect sleep patterns and Godly dreams. Please restore all my bodily systems to Your perfect order of life, health, youth, and peace.

Chapter 12:
Renouncing Rejection Through
Anti-Semitism and Illegitimacy

There are two curses we find in the scriptures that seem to play a great part in allowing the spirit of rejection to operate in a bloodline. The first curse is found in Genesis 12:

> Now the Lord had said to Abram: "Get out of your country, from your family and from your father's house, to a land that I will show you. I will make you a great nation; I will bless you and make your name great; and you shall be a blessing. I will bless those who bless you, and I will curse him who curses you; and in you all the families of the earth shall be blessed." Genesis 12:1-3

A curse comes on those who curse Israel. We call this hatred "anti-Semitism". Many of us have ancestors who were prejudiced or racist. You may have been taught this hatred yourself. Hatred of Israel, God's chosen people, can also bring a curse of disease:

> And the Lord will take away from you all sickness, and will afflict you with none of the terrible diseases of Egypt which you have known, but will lay them on all those who hate you. Deuteronomy 7:15

The second curse that opens the door to rejection is the curse of illegitimacy found in Deuteronomy 23:

> One of illegitimate birth shall not enter the assembly of the Lord; even to the tenth generation none of his descendants shall enter the assembly of the Lord. Deuteronomy 23:2

These curses often continue for hundreds of generations. In the family line; you may see hatred, anger, and prejudice projected on others. There can be much unfaithfulness and divorce in the family. Most feel isolated and rejected by everyone. No one seems to find true love and keep it. No one seems to feel loved by God. Love is always out of reach.

These curses can also manifest in our lives today by intense rejection or perceived rejection by the church, or its leaders or members. It can manifest in feelings of rejection by God and lack of intimacy with Him. Many under these curses struggle with praying, reading the Bible, listening to teachers and preachers of the Word, receiving the baptism of the Holy Spirit, and making friendships within the congregation. It seems like there is a barrier between them and blessing. They feel unloved, unwanted, and abandoned.

Praise God, we can be free from these curses and accepted back into the assembly because Jesus traded His blessing for our curse when He took our place! Not only did He free us from the curse, but He redeemed us to the blessing of Abraham and the promise of the Spirit.

> Christ has redeemed us from the curse of the law, having become a curse for us (for it is written, "Cursed is everyone who hangs on a tree"), that the blessing of Abraham might come upon the Gentiles in Christ Jesus, that we might receive the promise of the Spirit through faith. Galatians 3:13-14

Through the sacrifice of Jesus, we have been adopted into the family of God as sons. We can cry out, "Abba, Father." We can be led by His Spirit and be a joint-heir with Messiah Jesus.

> For as many as are led by the Spirit of God, these are sons of God. For you did not receive the spirit of bondage again to fear, but you received the Spirit of adoption by whom we cry out, "Abba, Father." The Spirit Himself bears witness with our spirit that we are children of God, and if children, then heirs—heirs of God and joint heirs with Christ, if indeed we suffer with Him, that we may also be glorified together. Romans 8:14-17

Pray the following prayers to repent for these sins:

Renunciation for Anti-Semitism

Father in heaven, I repent for the sins of myself and my ancestors which involve anti-Semitism. Your Word tells us in Genesis 12:3 that those who bless Israel will be blessed and those who curse Israel will be cursed. I repent for and renounce any time I or my ancestors have shown contempt toward Israel, cursed them, persecuted them, hated them, treated them unfairly, have been jealous of them, or did not stand with them or bless them. I repent for the sins of the church where it has tried to replace Israel instead of accepted being grafted into Israel through Messiah Jesus. I also repent for the rejection of Your Torah or Your teachings from the Old Testament, and the error that Your holy way of living found in the Old Testament is not for today. Please forgive these sins and cleanse our bloodline.

Today I choose to support and bless Israel. I pray for their peace, protection, and abundance in Your holy land. I pray that Your chosen people will find their Messiah. I petition that You would lift the curse that has been over me and my bloodline because of these sins. Please restore us to a right relationship with You and Your congregation. Please restore the blessing of Abraham to me and my future generations. Please restore our health and free us from the diseases of the curse and any evil spirits that have taken a place in my bloodline through anti-Semitism. I detach myself and my bloodline from any evil spirits associated with anti-Semitism in Jesus' name. I command them to release us now.

Renunciation for Illegitimacy

Father in heaven I repent for all sexual sin and perversion in my life and my bloodline; especially adultery, fornication, rape, incest, sexual abuse, and _____. I repent for the sexual lust that has caused my forefathers (and myself) to conceive illegitimate children outside of marriage. I repent for any abortions that were a result of this sexual sin which were actually sacrifices to Molech. I repent for any rape of slaves, mentally handicapped people, or the poor. I also repent where believers have chosen to be unequally yoked to unbelievers bringing up their children apart from You. I renounce all these sins and iniquities in Jesus' name. I ask You to forgive these sins and cleanse me and my bloodline.

I petition to remove the curse over our bloodline that says one of illegitimate birth or descendants of an illegitimate child cannot enter the assembly of the Lord. I bring the evidence that Jesus became a curse for us when He hung upon a tree and redeemed us from this curse into the blessing of Abraham and into a spirit of adoption into Your family. I receive the trade He made on my behalf and ask You to restore intimacy with You and the assembly to me and my bloodline.

Father God, I ask You to revoke the curse that brings rejection, self-rejection, perceived rejection, and rejection from the church and not being accepted by the congregation. Please break the curse that will make the heavens like iron and the earth like bronze.

Please restore the spirit of adoption and sonship including sweet fellowship with You, Abba. Please restore fellowship between us and our brothers in Messiah. I petition You to remove all hindrances to worship, prayer, singing, reading Your word, hearing Your voice, using our gifts and talents for Your kingdom, giving, acts of charity, fellowship in the congregation, corporate meetings, and intimacy with You and Your body. I petition that my bloodline be restored to the congregation of the Lord as a member of the family of God with all rights that implies.

I detach myself and my bloodline from this curse and any demons working through it including illegitimacy, bastard, fatherless, worthless, dog, abandonment, outcast, exile, shunned, sexual perversion, rape, incest, sexual abuse, molestation, shame, guilt, ba'al, molech, jezebel, and all forms of rejection. I command them to release us now in Jesus' name. I petition that the curse would be lifted along with all habits and mindsets that have formed in us from being hurt by the rejection and shunning of the assembly brought about by the curse. I ask You to erase all spiritual targets on our backs that draw rejection to us. I also ask that You remove any polarity over our lives that repels people from us and give us favor with God and man.

I choose to forgive all those who have hurt me or rejected me; especially all people, leaders, and groups from the church. I will not hold these sins against them, and I bless them in Jesus' name.

I choose to enter Your courts with praise and a grateful heart. Receive the praises we lift up to You and let them be a sweet-smelling fragrance before You. I petition that You would restore to me and my bloodline all the years of favor the enemy has stolen from us in all areas of our lives.

Chapter 13:
Renouncing Rebellion and Pride

(Important note: This chapter deals with the pride and rebellion in our hearts against authority figures which we all need to confront. There are some instances, though, where abuse comes from these figures. If this is the case with you, abuse is not condoned by Yahweh God. Please seek help and a safe place to heal and find freedom. If you are free from your abusers, it is still important to allow the Holy Spirit to show you the times in your life when you have given place to rebellion and pride, as all of us were born with a sin nature which gives rise to these sins. They are common to all men.)

Back in chapter one, we learned that each one of the ten commandments shared a part of Yahweh God's heart and character. We see in the fifth commandment that God has put us all under authority and we are expected to honor and obey them.

> Honor your father and mother, so that you may live long in the land which Adonai your God is giving you. Exodus 20:12

As we discussed before, Yahweh's commands were not a few simple rules to follow, but a new way of life, a way to become One with Him and take on His characteristics. God is the One who sets authority in place over us, whether it be parents, husbands, church leaders, work or government leaders. To honor the authority is to honor God Himself. When we resist them or rebel against them, we are resisting God.

> Let every soul be subject to the governing authorities. For there is no authority except from God, and the authorities that exist are appointed by God. Therefore whoever resists the authority resists the ordinance of God, and those who resist will bring judgment on themselves. For rulers are not a terror to good works, but to evil. Do you want to be unafraid of the authority? Do what is good, and you will have praise from the same. For he is God's minister to you for good. But if you do evil, be afraid; for he does not bear the sword in vain; for he is God's minister, an avenger to execute wrath on him who practices evil. Therefore you must be subject, not only because of wrath but also for conscience' sake. For because of this you also pay taxes, for they are God's ministers

attending continually to this very thing. Render therefore to all their due: taxes to whom taxes are due, customs to whom customs, fear to whom fear, honor to whom honor. Romans 13:1-7

Resistance to God-given authority causes judgment to fall on us. Yahweh calls us to submit to and honor authority in joy as that authority is placed over us for our protection.

> Obey those who rule over you, and be submissive, for they watch out for your souls, as those who must give account. Let them do so with joy and not with grief, for that would be unprofitable for you. Hebrews 13:17

> Therefore submit yourselves to every ordinance of man for the Lord's sake, whether to the king as supreme, or to governors, as to those who are sent by him for the punishment of evildoers and for the praise of those who do good. For this is the will of God, that by doing good you may put to silence the ignorance of foolish men— as free, yet not using liberty as a cloak for vice, but as bondservants of God. Honor all people. Love the brotherhood. Fear God. Honor the king. 1 Peter 2 :13-17

We are also commanded to pray and give thanks for the authorities over us and not to speak slander against them. This can lead to a quiet and peaceable life.

> Remind them to be subject to rulers and authorities, to obey, to be ready for every good work, to speak evil of no one, to be peaceable, gentle, showing all humility to all men. Titus 3:1

> Therefore I exhort first of all that supplications, prayers, intercessions, and giving of thanks be made for all men, for kings and all who are in authority, that we may lead a quiet and peaceable life in all godliness and reverence. For this is good and acceptable in the sight of God our Savior, who desires all men to be saved and to come to the knowledge of the truth. 1 Timothy 2:1-4

The only time we are instructed to disobey leaders is if their instructions are in conflict with obedience to Yahweh God. In the book of Acts, the religious authorities had put the apostles in prison for teaching in the name of Jesus. They forbade them to speak again in His name which went against the command of Yahweh. When brought before the council, the apostles said they must obey God rather than men.

> But Peter and the other apostles answered and said: "We ought to obey God rather than men. Acts 5:29

In 1 Samuel 15, Yahweh compares rebellion to witchcraft:

> So Samuel said: "Has the Lord as great delight in burnt offerings and sacrifices, as in obeying the voice of the Lord? Behold, to obey is better than sacrifice, and to heed than the fat of rams. For rebellion is as the sin of witchcraft, and stubbornness is as iniquity

and idolatry. Because you have rejected the word of the Lord, He also has rejected you from being king." 1 Samuel 15:22-23

There is a warning for rebellion in Proverbs 17:

> An evil man seeks only rebellion; therefore a cruel messenger will be sent against him. Proverbs 17:11

Whether this cruel messenger is physical or spiritual remains to be seen. Either way, it is not something to be desired. We have already seen how obedience to Yahweh God brings blessings and disobedience brings curses. Therefore, we should not harden our hearts in rebellion.

> If you will fear the Lord and serve him and obey his voice and not rebel against the commandment of the Lord, and if both you and the king who reigns over you will follow the Lord your God, it will be well. But if you will not obey the voice of the Lord, but rebel against the commandment of the Lord, then the hand of the Lord will be against you and your king. 1 Samuel 12:14-15

> If you are willing and obedient, you shall eat the good of the land; but if you refuse and rebel, you shall be devoured by the sword; for the mouth of the Lord has spoken." Isaiah 1:19-20

> While it is said, "Today, if you will hear his voice, do not harden your hearts as in the rebellion." Hebrews 3:15

Pride is one of the main sources of rebellion. It is sometimes called original sin because it was pride that caused the fall of lucifer, then he led Adam and Eve to rebel.

> "You were the anointed cherub who covers; I established you; you were on the holy mountain of God; you walked back and forth in the midst of fiery stones. You were perfect in your ways from the day you were created, till iniquity was found in you. "By the abundance of your trading you became filled with violence within, and you sinned; therefore I cast you as a profane thing out of the mountain of God; and I destroyed you, O covering cherub, from the midst of the fiery stones. "Your heart was lifted up because of your beauty; you corrupted your wisdom for the sake of your splendor; I cast you to the ground, I laid you before kings, that they might gaze at you. Ezekiel 28:17

There are many proverbs about pride.

> Pride goes before destruction, and a haughty spirit before a fall. Proverbs 16:18

> Everyone proud in heart is an abomination to the Lord; Though they join forces, none will go unpunished. Proverbs 16:5

> The fear of the Lord is to hate evil; pride and arrogance and the evil way and the perverse mouth I hate. Proverbs 8:13

The Lord will destroy the house of the proud, but He will establish the boundary of the widow. Proverbs 15:25

Yahweh God will exalt those who humble themselves before Him, but He will oppose and humble the prideful. In essence, we can make God our enemy.

For whoever exalts himself will be humbled, and he who humbles himself will be exalted." Luke 14:11

Likewise you younger people, submit yourselves to your elders. Yes, all of you be submissive to one another, and be clothed with humility, for "God resists the proud, but gives grace to the humble." Therefore humble yourselves under the mighty hand of God, that He may exalt you in due time, casting all your care upon Him, for He cares for you. 1 Peter 5:5-7

But He gives more grace. Therefore He says: "God resists the proud, but gives grace to the humble." Therefore submit to God. Resist the devil and he will flee from you. Draw near to God and He will draw near to you. Cleanse your hands, you sinners; and purify your hearts, you double-minded. Lament and mourn and weep! Let your laughter be turned to mourning and your joy to gloom. Humble yourselves in the sight of the Lord, and He will lift you up.   James 4:6-10

I will break the pride of your power; I will make your heavens like iron and your earth like bronze. Leviticus 26:19

But they rebelled and grieved his Holy Spirit; therefore he turned to be their enemy, and himself fought against them. Isaiah 63:10

Sometimes pride may cause us to forget God when things are going well for us. We can begin to think that our own abilities are the source of our strength and blessing.

"Beware that you do not forget the Lord your God by not keeping His commandments, His judgments, and His statutes which I command you today, lest—when you have eaten and are full, and have built beautiful houses and dwell in them; and when your herds and your flocks multiply, and your silver and your gold are multiplied, and all that you have is multiplied; when your heart is lifted up, and you forget the Lord your God who brought you out of the land of Egypt, from the house of bondage; who led you through that great and terrible wilderness, in which were fiery serpents and scorpions and thirsty land where there was no water; who brought water for you out of the flinty rock; who fed you in the wilderness with manna, which your fathers did not know, that He might humble you and that He might test you, to do you good in the end— then you say in your heart, 'My power and the might of my hand have gained me this wealth.' Deuteronomy 8:11-17

All of us have had pride and rebellion in our lives at some time. The enemy wants us to forget those times in the past where we rebelled against God or some authority He has placed in our lives. That way He can keep us in bondage. Ask the Holy Spirit to reveal to you all the times in your life where pride and rebellion led you to sin. Pray the prayer of repentance and include each event you remember:

Father in heaven, I and my ancestors have sinned before you in pride and rebellion. You tell us rebellion is as the sin of witchcraft. I repent for dishonoring and disobeying You and all those You have put in authority over me throughout my life. Forgive me for disobeying and dishonoring my parents, (husband), teachers, pastors, employers, and government leaders. Forgive me for times I have spoken against them in slander and lies. Forgive me for times that I have led others to do the same. Forgive me for the times I didn't pray for them or show gratitude for them. I especially repent for _____.

I also repent for thinking that I could run my life without You or save myself. I repent for and renounce all rebellion, pride, selfishness, self-centeredness, self-pity, arrogance, flattery, self-gratification, stinginess, hoarding, bragging, and exalting myself. I break agreement with all these actions and choose to humble myself before You. I need You in all areas of my life and I choose to surrender them to You. Please come into every room of "my house" which is Your Holy temple. Please remove all the filth from each room and fill them with Your love, light, and peace. I want my life to be a reflection of You.

I choose to cancel every negative word I have spoken over my parents and grandparents, (my husband), my teachers, employers, pastors, church leaders, and government officials and choose to bless each one of them now in Jesus' name. I cancel and break every demonic assignment related to those negative words and command those demons to cease and desist tormenting them.

I renounce every spirit associated with pride and rebellion including lucifer, leviathan, satan, python, anti-Christ, mind-control, prejudice, superiority, mutiny, uprising, insurrection, defiance, anarchy, riot, apostasy, insurgency, disobedience, insubordination, heresy, resistance, dissension, and schism. I detach myself from them and command them all to leave me and my bloodline in Jesus' name.

I petition for freedom from all curses and demonic assignments associated with pride and rebellion in my life and my bloodline, especially that of the cruel messenger. I petition that you, Yahweh God, would no longer oppose me, but would give me grace and take Your proper place as King of my life. Please restore a humble and contrite spirit to me and allow me to have beautiful communion with You in the secret place. Please cleanse all areas of my body, soul, spirit, mind, will and emotions from any pride or rebellion and make them fit for Your kingdom.

The Holy Spirit may lead you to ask for forgiveness from your parents or another authority figure. This can bring much healing to a God-given relationship. He may ask you to go in person or write a letter, just be willing to obey His leading.

Chapter 14:
Freedom from Anger, Hatred, and Bloodshed

The first time we hear of anger in the Bible is Genesis 4. Cain and Abel both brought offerings to the Lord. When Cain's offering wasn't accepted, he grew angry. Yahweh God spoke to Cain about how he would be accepted if he did well. He warned Cain that sin was crouching at his door if he chose not to do well. Sin desired to rule over Cain, but God told Cain that he should rule over sin instead.

> Now Adam knew Eve his wife, and she conceived and bore Cain, and said, "I have acquired a man from the Lord." Then she bore again, this time his brother Abel. Now Abel was a keeper of sheep, but Cain was a tiller of the ground. And in the process of time, it came to pass that Cain brought an offering of the fruit of the ground to the Lord. Abel also brought of the firstborn of his flock and of their fat. And the Lord respected Abel and his offering, but He did not respect Cain and his offering. And Cain was very angry, and his countenance fell. So the Lord said to Cain, "Why are you angry? And why has your countenance fallen? If you do well, will you not be accepted? And if you do not do well, sin lies at the door. And its desire is for you, but you should rule over it." Now Cain talked with Abel his brother; and it came to pass, when they were in the field, that Cain rose up against Abel his brother and killed him. Then the Lord said to Cain, "Where is Abel your brother?" He said, "I do not know. Am I my brother's keeper?" And He said, "What have you done? The voice of your brother's blood cries out to Me from the ground. So now you are cursed from the earth, which has opened its mouth to receive your brother's blood from your hand. When you till the ground, it shall no longer yield its strength to you. A fugitive and a vagabond you shall be on the earth." Genesis 4:1-12

Cain allowed his anger to rise up and kill his brother. He not only took his brother's life, but also the lives of all his future children. The word translated "blood" is actually "bloods'" representing Abel's offspring. This blood cried out to God from the ground. Cain was cursed to be exiled as a vagabond and a fugitive and the ground would not yield to him. This was on top of the original curse on Adam in which the ground would produce thistles and thorns, and he would work hard to eat bread from it. Cain would work hard amongst the thistles and thorns and the ground would still not yield its strength.

The kingdom of Judah was also sent into exile for the innocent blood shed by Manasseh that went unpardoned.

> Surely at the commandment of the Lord this came upon Judah, to remove them from His sight because of the sins of Manasseh, according to all that he had done, and also because of the innocent blood that he had shed; for he had filled Jerusalem with innocent blood, which the Lord would not pardon. 2 Kings 24:3-4

A curse came over Simeon and Levi, two of Jacob's sons, because of their anger and murderous rage. At a time they should have received a father's blessing, they received a prophecy of division and scattering.

> Simeon and Levi are brothers; instruments of cruelty are in their dwelling place. Let not my soul enter their council; let not my honor be united to their assembly; for in their anger they slew a man, and in their self-will they hamstrung an ox. Cursed be their anger, for it is fierce; and their wrath, for it is cruel! I will divide them in Jacob and scatter them in Israel. Genesis 49:5-7

It is clear that when anger is allowed to fester in the heart, it grows and turns to hatred and murder. Jesus spoke about this sin in Matthew 5:

> You have heard that it was said to those of old, 'You shall not murder, and whoever murders will be in danger of the judgment.' But I say to you that whoever is angry with his brother without a cause shall be in danger of the judgment. And whoever says to his brother, 'Raca!' shall be in danger of the council. But whoever says, 'You fool!' shall be in danger of hell fire. Therefore if you bring your gift to the altar, and there remember that your brother has something against you, leave your gift there before the altar, and go your way. First be reconciled to your brother, and then come and offer your gift. Matthew 5:21-24

The one who hates his brother is called a murderer.

> Whoever hates his brother is a murderer, and you know that no murderer has eternal life abiding in him. 1 John 3:15

> If someone says, "I love God," and hates his brother, he is a liar; for he who does not love his brother whom he has seen, how can he love God whom he has not seen? And this commandment we have from Him: that he who loves God must love his brother also. 1 John 4:20-21

The anger or wrath of man does not produce righteousness. We are told to cease from anger and forsake wrath because it causes harm. We are not to take our own vengeance. That is set aside for Yahweh God.

So then, my beloved brethren, let every man be swift to hear, slow to speak, slow to wrath; for the wrath of man does not produce the righteousness of God.   James 1:19-20

Cease from anger, and forsake wrath; do not fret—it only causes harm.   Psalm 34:8

"Beloved, do not avenge yourselves, but rather give place to wrath; for it is written, "Vengeance is Mine, I will repay," says the Lord.   Romans 12:19

'You shall not hate your brother in your heart. You shall surely rebuke your neighbor, and not bear sin because of him. You shall not take vengeance, nor bear any grudge against the children of your people, but you shall love your neighbor as yourself: I am the Lord. Leviticus 19:17-18

"You have heard that it was said, 'You shall love your neighbor and hate your enemy.' But I say to you, love your enemies, bless those who curse you, do good to those who hate you, and pray for those who spitefully use you and persecute you, that you may be sons of your Father in heaven; for He makes His sun rise on the evil and on the good, and sends rain on the just and on the unjust.   Matthew 5:43-45

Do not say, "I will recompense evil"; wait for the Lord, and He will save you. Proverbs 20:22

There are several proverbs that give us instruction on anger:

Do not hasten in your spirit to be angry, for anger rests in the bosom of fools. Proverbs 19:11

Make no friendship with an angry man, and with a furious man do not go. Proverbs 22:24

Whoever has no rule over his own spirit is like a city broken down, without walls. Proverbs 25:28

He who is slow to anger is better than the mighty, and he who rules his spirit than he who takes a city. Proverbs 16:42

A wrathful man stirs up strife, but he who is slow to anger allays contention. Proverbs 15:18

We are commanded to be angry and do not sin. How do we do this? We must take righteous anger to Yahweh. He is our covenant partner. He will deal with it righteously. He may tell us to forgive the offender, or He may give us instruction for the situation. We need to bring it to Him before the day is over or the sun goes down. We cannot let it fester in our hearts. It gives the adversary a place in us. It can allow a bitter root to begin to grow. It can allow hatred and murder to be birthed.

"Be angry, and do not sin": do not let the sun go down on your wrath, nor give place to the devil. Ephesians 4:26-27

Blood, bloodshed, and bloodguilt

Blood is sacred to Yahweh God. The blood is the life. The Israelites were told not to eat blood. If they did not eat blood, it would go well with them. If they did eat blood, they would be cut off from the people.

> Only be sure that you do not eat the blood, for the blood is the life; you may not eat the life with the meat. You shall not eat it; you shall pour it on the earth like water. You shall not eat it, that it may go well with you and your children after you, when you do what is right in the sight of the Lord. Deuteronomy 12:23-25

> This shall be a perpetual statute throughout your generations in all your dwellings: you shall eat neither fat nor blood. Leviticus 3:17

> Moreover you shall not eat any blood in any of your dwellings, whether of bird or beast. Whoever eats any blood, that person shall be cut off from his people. Leviticus 7:26-27

> 'And whatever man of the house of Israel, or of the strangers who dwell among you, who eats any blood, I will set My face against that person who eats blood, and will cut him off from among his people. For the life of the flesh is in the blood, and I have given it to you upon the altar to make atonement for your souls; for it is the blood that makes atonement for the soul.' Therefore I said to the children of Israel, 'No one among you shall eat blood, nor shall any stranger who dwells among you eat blood.' Leviticus 17:10-12

Because the life was in the blood, any man or beast who took the life of another man would in turn be killed. The people were commanded not to overlook the sin of murder.

> But you shall not eat flesh with its life, that is, its blood. Surely for your lifeblood I will demand a reckoning; from the hand of every beast I will require it, and from the hand of man. From the hand of every man's brother I will require the life of man. Whoever sheds man's blood, by man his blood shall be shed; for in the image of God He made man. Genesis 9:4-6

> "But if anyone hates his neighbor, lies in wait for him, rises against him and strikes him mortally, so that he dies, and he flees to one of these cities, then the elders of his city shall send and bring him from there, and deliver him over to the hand of the avenger of blood, that he may die. Your eye shall not pity him, but you shall put away the guilt of innocent blood from Israel, that it may go well with you." Deuteronomy 19:11-13

Innocent blood cries out to God from the ground. It defiles the land.

Moreover you shall take no ransom for the life of a murderer who is guilty of death, but he shall surely be put to death. And you shall take no ransom for him who has fled to his city of refuge, that he may return to dwell in the land before the death of the priest. So you shall not pollute the land where you are; for blood defiles the land, and no atonement can be made for the land, for the blood that is shed on it, except by the blood of him who shed it. Numbers 35:31-33

They did not destroy the peoples, concerning whom the Lord had commanded them, but they mingled with the Gentiles and learned their works; they served their idols, which became a snare to them. They even sacrificed their sons and their daughters to demons, and shed innocent blood, the blood of their sons and daughters, whom they sacrificed to the idols of Canaan; and the land was polluted with blood. Thus they were defiled by their own works, and played the harlot by their own deeds. Therefore the wrath of the Lord was kindled against His people. Psalm 106:31-40

Bloodguilt can keep God from hearing prayers.

When you spread out your hands, I will hide My eyes from you; even though you make many prayers, I will not hear. Your hands are full of blood. Isaiah 1:15

But your iniquities have separated you from your God; and your sins have hidden His face from you, so that He will not hear. For your hands are defiled with blood, and your fingers with iniquity; your lips have spoken lies, your tongue has muttered perversity. Isaiah 59:2-3

Yahweh God hates feet that run to evil and hands that shed innocent blood.

Their feet run to evil, and they make haste to shed innocent blood; their thoughts are thoughts of iniquity; wasting and destruction are in their paths. Isaiah 59:7

These six things the Lord hates, yes, seven are an abomination to Him: a proud look, a lying tongue, hands that shed innocent blood, a heart that devises wicked plans, feet that are swift in running to evil, a false witness who speaks lies, and one who sows discord among brethren. Proverbs 6:16-19

"Yet your eyes and your heart are for nothing but your covetousness, for shedding innocent blood, and practicing oppression and violence." Jeremiah 22:17

Yahweh God made the land desolate before the Israelites because of idolatry, bloodshed, and eating the blood.

Then the word of the Lord came to me, saying: "Son of man, they who inhabit those ruins in the land of Israel are saying, 'Abraham was only one, and he inherited the land. But we are many; the land has been given to us as a possession.' "Therefore say to them, 'Thus says the Lord God: "You eat meat with blood, you lift up your eyes toward your idols, and shed blood. Should you then possess the land? You rely on your sword, you commit abominations, and you defile one another's wives. Should you then possess the land?"' For I will make the land most desolate, her arrogant strength shall cease, and the mountains of Israel shall be so desolate that no one will pass through. Then they shall know that I am the Lord, when I have made the land most desolate because of all their abominations which they have committed."' Ezekiel 33:23-26, 28-29

"Woe to him who builds a town with bloodshed, who establishes a city by iniquity! Habakkuk 2:12

Bloodlust and violence

Bloodlust can be passed down through the bloodline or entered into through the sin of rage that leads to slaughter and killing. History reveals many wars and genocides resulting from bloodlust. Many people groups like the Norwegian Vikings were known for it. The Roman Coliseum was also known for its many displays of bloodlust and acts of violence.

In this generation, you may find agreement with bloodlust through watching violent movies, videos games, music, or even violent sports. How many times have you seen football fans speaking hate toward the other team, coaches, or referees. Many have become desensitized to violence, death, and destruction. Psalms 11 says Yahweh hates the wicked and the one who loves violence:

> The Lord tests the righteous, but the wicked and the one who loves violence His soul hates. Upon the wicked He will rain coals; fire and brimstone and a burning wind shall be the portion of their cup. Psalms 11:5-6

> A violent man entices his neighbor, and leads him in a way that is not good. Proverbs 16:29

> Do not enter the path of the wicked, and do not walk in the way of evil. Avoid it, do not travel on it; turn away from it and pass on. For they do not sleep unless they have done evil; and their sleep is taken away unless they make someone fall. For they eat the bread of wickedness, and drink the wine of violence. Proverbs 4:14-17

> My son, if sinners entice you, do not consent. If they say, "Come with us, let us lie in wait to shed blood; let us lurk secretly for the innocent without cause; let us swallow them alive like Sheol, and whole, like those who go down to the Pit; we shall find all kinds of precious possessions, we shall fill our houses with spoil; cast in your lot among us, let us all have one purse"—My son, do not walk in the way with them, keep your foot from their path; for their feet run to evil, and they make haste to shed blood. Surely, in vain the net is spread in the sight of any bird; but they lie in wait for their own blood, they lurk secretly for their own lives. So are the ways of everyone who is greedy for gain; it takes away the life of its owners. Proverbs 1:10-19

It is so important to renounce these sins. When we humble ourselves and turn away from them and seek God's forgiveness, He will forgive our sins and heal our land. He will again be attentive to our prayers. The blood of Jesus can speak on our behalf.

> If My people who are called by My name will humble themselves, and pray and seek My face, and turn from their wicked ways, then I will hear from heaven, and will forgive their sin and heal their land. Now My eyes will be open and My ears attentive to prayer made in this place. 2 Chronicles 7:14-15

> But you have come to Mount Zion and to the city of the living God, the heavenly Jerusalem, to an innumerable company of angels, to the general assembly and church of the firstborn who are registered in heaven, to God the Judge of all, to the spirits of just men made perfect, to Jesus the Mediator of the new covenant, and to the blood of sprinkling that speaks better things than that of Abel. Hebrews 12:22-24

> But now you yourselves are to put off all these: anger, wrath, malice, blasphemy, filthy language out of your mouth. Colossians 3:8

> Finally, all of you be of one mind, having compassion for one another; love as brothers, be tenderhearted, be courteous; not returning evil for evil or reviling for reviling, but on the contrary blessing, knowing that you were called to this, that you may inherit a blessing. 1 Peter 3:8-10

As you prepare to repent for these sins, ask the Holy Spirit to reveal the generational iniquity in these areas. You may see anger and rage following your bloodline. Maybe it has been called an 'Irish temper' or 'seeing red.' You may see hatred, prejudice, or racial superiority there, too. Some of you may have an ancestor that committed murder or sacrificed children to false gods. Abortion as a form of birth control may run in your family line. Maybe your great-grandfather owned slaves or was a member of the KKK. These sins can bring curses over us that remain generation after generation. The blood from these sins, cries to Yahweh God for justice.

Pray the following prayer aloud:

Father in heaven, I repent for myself and my ancestors for any ways we have agreed with anger, rage, abuse, cruelty, violence, vengeance, hatred, murder, abortion, unholy blood sacrifice, bloodshed, and bloodlust. I renounce all of these sins and the spirits behind them in Jesus' name.

I repent for violent sins of anger, rage, destruction, and abuse. I repent for emotional, verbal, sexual, physical, and ritual abuse. I repent for and renounce any slavery and trafficking in my family line. I specifically repent for _____.

I repent for and renounce the shedding of innocent blood. Life is sacred to You Yahweh. You have breathed life into Your creation. You are the One Who decides when it begins and ends. Forgive me and my ancestors for disregarding the sanctity of life. I repent for the mistreatment of animals. I repent for any murder of a person made in Your image whether it be intentional, accidental, or forced. I specifically repent for _____. I repent for wartime killing of soldiers or civilians. I repent for any murder of babies and children including child sacrifice and abortion. I renounce these sins and any demons with those functions including Molech, Ares, Kali, Ba'al, Tlaloc, Chernabog, satan, the grim reaper; all demons of murder, war, and death; murder, homicide, suicide, abortion, frenzy, and death. I detach myself and my bloodline from all these demons and command them to leave us now in Jesus' name.

Yahweh God, please silence the cries of the blood of the innocents that cry out for justice against me and my bloodline. Please allow the blood of Jesus the Messiah to speak for us.

I repent for and renounce any familial involvement with secret societies that have taken innocent lives including freemasonry, KKK, nazis, luciferians, satanism, illuminati, and the new world order. I repent for any programming and mind-control experiments performed on people. I repent for any heinous crimes and torture against people or people groups. I repent for any time me or my ancestors looked away from any type of violence or abuse and didn't take a stand for the innocent.

I repent for myself and my ancestors for any sins of bloodlust. I repent for watching acts of violence in person or on a movie/video game and consenting to those acts. I repent of bloodlust at sporting events, for choosing a side and sending actions of violence in the spirit realm through words and curses toward the other side. I repent for allowing violence in through my eye and ear gates. Please forgive me and help me to be sensitive again to your thoughts, Yahweh.

I repent for all the times I and my ancestors took vengeance into our own hands. Forgive us for the times that we have allowed bloodlust to overwhelm us. I specifically repent for _____.

I repent for the bloodshed of our nation through land clearances, wartimes, crimes, and legalized abortion. Please break this cycle of bloodshed in our land, Yahweh. Please forgive these sins and heal the land.

I repent and renounce any eating or drinking of blood that defiles the body. I repent for vampirism. I repent for any unholy blood rituals or covenants. I repent for any times me and my ancestors shed our own blood through pagan practices of bloodletting which is a sacrifice to demon gods.

I repent for hatred of my brother. I choose to forgive anyone that has hurt me or betrayed me. I bless each of them in Jesus' name. I choose to forgive all those who committed violence against my family line and took the lives of my family members and friends or who committed crimes against us. I choose not to take vengeance on them, Yahweh, and turn them over to You.

Yahweh God, please forgive all these sins and cleanse my bloodline with the blood of Jesus. Please turn away Your wrath and hear our prayers and cries again. I petition You would free me and my bloodline from the curse that would cause us to wander and be fugitives. Please restore to my bloodline an ability to settle, be content, and for our souls to be restored. Where we have been divided and scattered, please restore us to each other and to You, Yahweh. Please guide us as the Good Shepherd guides and cares for His sheep. I petition You would restore to us a good yield from the land, that it would yield its strength to us.

I ask You to remove the curse of bloodguilt on the land and my bloodline. I repent for any bloodshed that happened on my land whether it be from wartime, fighting, accidental or premeditated murder, or the sacrifice of humans or animals. Please take away the desolation and cleanse my land with the blood of Jesus. Please close any portals that were opened there through bloodshed or sacrifice and set Your host around my land to protect it from the enemy. Please bring Your blessing on me and my bloodline, my life, my finances, the work of my hands, my relationships, and my communion with You. May the following blessings of Deuteronomy 28 be true of me and my bloodline:

"Now it shall come to pass, if you diligently obey the voice of the Lord your God, to observe carefully all His commandments which I command you today, that the Lord your God will set you high above all nations of the earth. And all these blessings shall come upon you and overtake you, because you obey the voice of the Lord your God:

"Blessed shall you be in the city, and blessed shall you be in the country.

"Blessed shall be the fruit of your body, the produce of your ground and the increase of your herds, the increase of your cattle and the offspring of your flocks.

"Blessed shall be your basket and your kneading bowl.

"Blessed shall you be when you come in, and blessed shall you be when you go out.

"The Lord will cause your enemies who rise against you to be defeated before your face; they shall come out against you one way and flee before you seven ways.

"The Lord will command the blessing on you in your storehouses and in all to which you set your hand, and He will bless you in the land which the Lord your God is giving you.

"The Lord will establish you as a holy people to Himself, just as He has sworn to you, if you keep the commandments of the Lord your God and walk in His ways. Then all peoples of the earth shall see that you are called by the name of the Lord, and they shall be afraid of you. And the Lord will grant you plenty of goods, in the fruit of your body, in the increase of your livestock, and in the produce of your ground, in the land of which the Lord swore to your fathers to give you. The Lord will open to you His good treasure, the heavens, to give the rain to your land in its season, and to bless all the work of your hand. You shall lend to many nations, but you shall not borrow. And the Lord will make you the head and not the tail; you shall be above only, and not be beneath, if you heed the commandments of the Lord your God, which I command you today, and are careful to observe them. So you shall not turn aside from any of the words which I command

you this day, to the right or the left, to go after other gods to serve them."
Deuteronomy 28:1-14

Personal renunciation prayer for abortion

Many women have been deceived by the enemy to abort their child(ren). Some have been forced into an abortion. Whatever the reason, the aftermath of abortion is guilt, shame, pain, and regret. This heaviness hangs over women for most of their lives as they hide this tormenting sin from even their closest friends and loved ones. The sin seems unforgivable, but thankfully we have a loving compassionate Father who is full of mercy and grace. He has paid the price for our sin with His own blood so that we can be forgiven and cleansed. If you have committed the sin of abortion, you can be forgiven and healed. Bring it to the cross where it has been marked "paid in full."

Father in heaven, I come to You in the name of Jesus the Messiah. I repent for the sin of abortion and/or using abortive birth control methods. I confess this as murder and shedding innocent blood. Your word says the baby's blood cries out to You for justice against me. I am guilty of this sin, Father, and I have justified it by _____. I ask for Your forgiveness and cleansing of myself, my womb, and my bloodline.

I ask You to break all curses over my womb from the abortions I have committed, as well as, any other abortions or sacrifice of children to false gods in my family line. I renounce abortion, murder, child sacrifice, death, Ba'al, Molech, Jezebel, and any other gods of death that were served by my ancestors or by this abortion. I detach myself and my bloodline from these spirits and command them to release us in Jesus' name!

I ask forgiveness from my aborted child(ren). I release my aborted child(ren) to You Father. I know that You love each one of them and are caring for them in heaven. I give my mother's blessing to my child(ren). (You may also choose to name them.) I choose now to forgive myself and anyone who I blamed for this act (God, the baby's father, doctors, parents, anyone who pressured you to get the abortion, anyone who rejected you for becoming pregnant).

I dedicate all the babies I aborted to You, Father. I also dedicate to You all my children that were miscarried or died prematurely, and all of my living children. (Name each of Your children here, even the aborted or miscarried babies.) I ask that You cleanse each child from any defilement from my sins or the sins of my ancestors that brought death into our bloodline. I ask that You cancel any legal rights the enemy has over my life and all my children from these curses. Please send Your host to collect every part of our souls that has been held in captivity of the enemy through these sins.

Because You have forgiven me, Father, I detach myself from guilt and shame and command them to loose me now in Jesus' name. Please heal my heart of all the pain, grief, sorrow, loss, and mourning.

I rebuke death off my womb in Jesus' name. I dedicate my womb to You, Yahweh God, Creator of life. I ask that You cleanse my womb and reproductive tract from all this defilement and restore it to a healthy, safe place for children to be conceived and nurtured before birth. Fill it with love, compassion, purpose, justice, and fruitfulness. Fill it with Your life for any future children You have planned for me.

Personal renunciation prayer for wartime killing

Father in heaven, I come to You in the name of Jesus the Messiah. I repent for any way I was involved with the bloodshed of killing enemy soldiers or innocent civilians during wartime. I chose to serve my country with honor during the war. Your word says there is a time for war, and I know that war is full of death. I also know that many times even soldiers are pawns and victims of a war that is fought between two greater parties that may not be concerned about individual lives.

Life is sacred to you, so I repent of taking the lives of those I killed during wartime. Although I completed my commission, I have endured great guilt for taking their lives. I also saw many soldiers and civilians die which has brought trauma into my life. I repent for any part I played in training or combat that did not bring you glory. I repent for times that I did not represent You or reflect Your light. I repent for times that I did not share the good news of the gospel with those around me. I especially repent of the following sins that have been heavy on my heart_____.

Please forgive me Yahweh God for all of these sins. I know Your word says that You are faithful to forgive and cleanse me when I confess my sins. I ask You to heal my wounded heart. I choose to forgive every offense that I acquired during war times. Please set me free of tormenting thoughts, anxiety, physical pain, nightmares, and flashbacks. I know You are the One who can heal me and make me whole again.

I release to You all trauma, fear, anxiety, panic attacks, nightmares, night terrors, flashbacks, tormenting memories, torture, guilt, shame, regret, loss, mental pain, emotional pain, and physical pain. I release to You any anger, rage, hatred, murder, violence, revenge, retaliation, rejection, betrayal, abandonment, and walls of self-preservation. I renounce all these and the spirits behind them. I detach myself from these spirits and command them to leave me now in Jesus' name.

I choose to forgive myself as You have forgiven me. I release to You Yahweh any souls of those people that I fear I have failed. I especially release _____. I do not want to carry them around with me anymore through pain, guilt, shame, and regret. You, Yahweh God, are the One Who can help each one of them. I ask You to cleanse and restore all my Godly relationships.

I also release those whom I have killed or watched being killed. I ask You to cut me free from all unholy soul-ties and chains that I have acquired through holding these people in my mind through trauma. Please restore my soul back to wholeness. I know that Jesus paid the price for all my sin. He has taken the punishment upon Himself so I can be free. I choose to break agreement with the tormenting spirit that has been keeping me in a prison.

I petition that You remove all pain and torment from my memories of these terrors. I also ask that You remove all the muscle memory from my body and any trauma that has made its home in me. (Please pray the trauma prayer over yourself in chapter 10). Yahweh, you spared my life for a reason. You bought me with a price. I am not my own, I am Yours. I want to be free to walk in the plan and purpose to which You have called me while on this earth.

I choose to submit myself to You Yahweh God.... every area of myself. Create in me a clean heart and restore a right spirit in me. Let Your Holy Spirit cleanse me with fire and wash me with water. Anoint me with healing oil and fill me again with peace and joy. Set my feet again on the solid rock of Your foundation. Give me strength and ability to rise up as a soldier in Your army, Yahweh. Our battle is not against flesh and blood, but against the kingdom of darkness.

Chapter 15:
Lashon Hara or Evil Speech

"Lashon hara" is a Hebrew term translated "evil speech" or "evil tongue". It refers to spreading negative speech or slander about someone that is harmful to the person's reputation. We think of gossip and slander as spreading lies, but lashon hara is negative speech that is true. Both parties, the teller and the listener, are considered guilty of this sin. In Bible times, the sin of lashon hara was also linked to the skin disease leprosy. We can see this in numbers 12 when Miriam and Aaron spoke against their brother Moses.

Then Miriam and Aaron spoke against Moses because of the Ethiopian woman whom he had married; for he had married an Ethiopian woman. So they said, "Has the Lord indeed spoken only through Moses? Has He not spoken through us also?" And the Lord heard it. (Now the man Moses was very humble, more than all men who were on the face of the earth.) Suddenly the Lord said to Moses, Aaron, and Miriam, "Come out, you three, to the tabernacle of meeting!" So the three came out. Then the Lord came down in the pillar of cloud and stood in the door of the tabernacle, and called Aaron and Miriam. And they both went forward. Then He said,

"Hear now My words: If there is a prophet among you, I, the Lord, make Myself known to him in a vision; I speak to him in a dream. Not so with My servant Moses; he is faithful in all My house. I speak with him face to face, even plainly, and not in dark sayings; and he sees the form of the Lord. Why then were you not afraid to speak against My servant Moses?"

So the anger of the Lord was aroused against them, and He departed. And when the cloud departed from above the tabernacle, suddenly Miriam became leprous, as white as snow. Then Aaron turned toward Miriam, and there she was, a leper. So Aaron said to Moses, "Oh, my lord! Please do not lay [e]this sin on us, in which we have done foolishly and in which we have sinned. Please do not let her be as one dead, whose flesh is half consumed when he comes out of his mother's womb!" So Moses cried out to the Lord, saying, "Please heal her, O God, I pray!" Then the Lord said to Moses, "If her father had but spit in her face, would she not be shamed seven days? Let her be shut out of the camp seven days, and afterward she may be received again." So Miriam was shut out of the camp seven days, and the people did not journey till Miriam was brought in again. Numbers 12:1-15

Miriam and Aaron spoke against Moses in two matters; they criticized him about his wife and about his position in leadership. Yahweh God heard them and called them out. He stood in defense of Moses and rebuked his siblings. Miriam was struck with leprosy for her sin, but Moses cried out to God for mercy on her, and she was cleansed after a seven-day period of discipline. Thus, we see that critical, negative speech against God's covenant partners is a serious offense.

Remember back in chapter two, we studied the covenant in the Ten commandments? We learned that God's name and reputation were very important to Him. He also gave His name to those in covenant with Him, so their reputations were also important to Him. When we speak against another believer through criticism, gossip, or slanderous speech; we are coming against that person as an enemy. Yahweh God will come to the aid of His covenant partner just as He has promised. If you are the one who is fighting against that person with your negative words, you are fighting God! What a sobering thought!

Messiah Jesus shares in the gospels that a house divided cannot stand. He was being verbally attacked by some religious leaders who were accusing Him of casting out demons by the power of satan.

> But Jesus knew their thoughts, and said to them: "Every kingdom divided against itself is brought to desolation, and every city or house divided against itself will not stand. If Satan casts out Satan, he is divided against himself. How then will his kingdom stand? Matthew 12:25-26

The adversary will try to divide us as the body of Messiah. He will use pride, rebellion, jealousy, envy, and offense to provoke us to speak evil against each other, knowing our words can bring life or death, blessings or curses.

> Death and life are in the power of the tongue, and those who love it will eat its fruit. Proverbs 18:21

> But no man can tame the tongue. It is an unruly evil, full of deadly poison. With it we bless our God and Father, and with it we curse men, who have been made in the similitude of God. Out of the same mouth proceed blessing and cursing. My brethren, these things ought not to be so. Does a spring send forth fresh water and bitter from the same opening? James 3:8-11

The book of James is filled with encouragement and warning about our words. The tongue can be used as an instrument of evil. As a believer, we should not allow cursing and evil speech to come out of our mouths. This is a matter of self-control which is grown in us as a fruit of the Spirit, but it also involves the state of our hearts.

How can you, being evil, speak good things? For out of the abundance of the heart the mouth speaks. A good man out of the good treasure of his heart brings forth good things, and an evil man out of the evil treasure brings forth evil things. But I say to you that for every idle word men may speak, they will give account of it in the day of judgment. For by your words you will be justified, and by your words you will be condemned." Matthew 12:34-37

Therefore we make it our aim, whether present or absent, to be well pleasing to Him. For we must all appear before the judgment seat of Christ, that each one may receive the things done in the body, according to what he has done, whether good or bad. 2 Corinthians 5:9-10

The treasure of our hearts can be good or evil, and it is expressed in our speech. On the day of judgment, you will give account for your words. They will justify or condemn you. Idle words are words that are pointless or without purpose. When we speak idle words, we just let them flow out without thinking about the purpose or effect of what we say. When we do not take our thoughts captive before we speak, it can be very dangerous.

When we hold bitterness and offense in our hearts, our thoughts will not be filled with wisdom from above, but with earthly, sensual, and demonic thoughts. This wisdom is deceptive and does not accomplish the purposes of Yahweh God. When we speak out these thoughts, they will go forth with death to bring harm to their targets.

Who is wise and understanding among you? Let him show by good conduct that his works are done in the meekness of wisdom. But if you have bitter envy and self-seeking in your hearts, do not boast and lie against the truth. This wisdom does not descend from above, but is earthly, sensual, demonic. For where envy and self-seeking exist, confusion and every evil thing are there. But the wisdom that is from above is first pure, then peaceable, gentle, willing to yield, full of mercy and good fruits, without partiality and without hypocrisy. Now the fruit of righteousness is sown in peace by those who make peace. James 3:13-18

There is one who speaks like the piercings of a sword, but the tongue of the wise promotes health. Proverbs 12:18

A man who bears false witness against his neighbor is like a club, a sword, and a sharp arrow. Proverbs 25:18

Not only can our words do damage to others, but they can also bring defilement to the speaker and give the enemy a place in us.

But those things which proceed out of the mouth come from the heart, and they defile a man. For out of the heart proceed evil thoughts, murders, adulteries, fornications, thefts, false witness, blasphemies. These are the things which defile a man, but to eat with unwashed hands does not defile a man." Matthew 15:18-20

Therefore, putting away lying, "Let each one of you speak truth with his neighbor," for we are members of one another. "Be angry, and do not sin": do not let the sun go down on your wrath, nor give place to the devil. Ephesians 4:25-27

Jesus prayed that we, His body, would be one like he and the Father are One. We are to love each other, not devour each other. We should release any bitterness and anger toward other believers and seek the unity Jesus prayed for. It is powerful.

"I do not pray for these alone, but also for those who will believe in Me through their word; that they all may be one, as You, Father, are in Me, and I in You; that they also may be one in Us, that the world may believe that You sent Me. And the glory which You gave Me I have given them, that they may be one just as We are one: I in them, and You in Me; that they may be made perfect in one, and that the world may know that You have sent Me, and have loved them as You have loved Me. John 17:20-23

For you, brethren, have been called to liberty; only do not use liberty as an opportunity for the flesh, but through love serve one another. For all the law is fulfilled in one word, even in this: "You shall love your neighbor as yourself." But if you bite and devour one another, beware lest you be consumed by one another! Galatians 5:13-15

There are many scriptures that speak about our words.

Who is the man who desires life, and loves many days, that he may see good? Keep your tongue from evil, and your lips from speaking deceit. Depart from evil and do good; seek peace and pursue it. Psalm 34:12-14

Let the words of my mouth and the meditation of my heart be acceptable in Your sight, O Lord, my rock and my Redeemer. Psalm 19:14

Set a guard, Adonai, over my mouth; keep watch at the door of my lips. Psalms 141:3

Pleasant words are like a honeycomb, sweet to the taste and healing for the body. Proverbs 16:24

"Whoever guards his mouth and tongue keeps his soul from troubles." Psalm 21:23

You shall not go about as a talebearer among your people; nor shall you take a stand against the life of your neighbor: I am the Lord. Leviticus 19:16

Bless those who persecute you; bless and do not curse. Romans 12:14

Let no corrupt word proceed out of your mouth, but what is good for necessary edification, that it may impart grace to the hearers. And do not grieve the Holy Spirit of God, by whom you were sealed for the day of redemption. Let all bitterness, wrath, anger, clamor, and evil speaking be put away from you, with all malice. And be kind to one another, tenderhearted, forgiving one another, even as God in Christ forgave you. Ephesians 4:29-32

If anyone among you thinks he is religious, and does not bridle his tongue but deceives his own heart, this one's religion is useless. James 1:26

Keep your tongue from evil, and your lips from speaking deceit. Psalm 34:13

We can also speak evil against ourselves. Almost everyone has found fault with some past sin or action or even with their own bodies. We can speak blessing or curse against ourselves and our lives. These curses can manifest through troubles, sickness, disease, or pain. All these negative words need repentance and renunciation. Replace them with words that speak God's truth over your life and destiny.

Some believers who have had a roadblock from receiving the baptism of the Holy Spirit and the gift of tongues were able to receive it after repenting for these sins. Once the spring of bitter water was cut off, the river of Living Water could flow.

Will you choose today to repent for and renounce any evil speech that has come out of your mouth? It is your choice. Just like the Israelites were given a choice in the wilderness to follow and serve Yahweh or other gods, you are given the choice to choose life or death.

I call heaven and earth as witnesses today against you, that I have set before you life and death, blessing and cursing; therefore choose life, that both you and your descendants may live; that you may love the Lord your God, that you may obey His voice, and that you may cling to Him, for He is your life and the length of your days; and that you may dwell in the land which the Lord swore to your fathers, to Abraham, Isaac, and Jacob, to give them." Deuteronomy 30:19-20

If you choose life today, ask the Holy spirit to show you the times you have spoken death and cursing out of your mouth. Be faithful to repent for each one, and forgive each person that has hurt you. It's important to break any word curses you have spoken over yourself, as well. Also, choose to cancel those curses and replace them with blessings. You may be led by Yahweh to seek forgiveness from those whom you have slandered.

Pray the following aloud:

Father in heaven, in Jesus' name, I repent for all the sins of the mouth and heart for me and my bloodline, and I repent for the control or witchcraft which was involved. I believe my words can bring life and death according to Your Holy scriptures. I confess I have spoken evil words and curses against myself and others. I renounce and cancel the negative words and demonic assignments I have spoken over _____ and I choose today to bless _____ and his/her life with favor, peace, joy, love, and goodness. I forgive _____ for any hurt or offense and commit _____ to you.

I repent for and renounce for myself and my ancestors all the sins of the mouth including slander, gossip, criticism, judgment, negative words, curses, complaining, whining, murmuring, hatred, anger, rage, bitterness, corrupt words, malice, lying, deceit, sowing discord, murdering someone's reputation, profanity, filthy talk, blasphemy, and inner vows. I detach myself and my bloodline from all the spirits associated with these sins and command them to loose us in Jesus' name.

I am not my brother's judge. That is Your role, Yahweh. Forgive me for pointing out the sins of my brother instead of looking at my own heart. Forgive me for any agreement I made with demons when speaking these words. I cancel that agreement and detach myself from them in Jesus' name. I ask you to revoke any legal rights the adversary held against me and my bloodline through these sins. I choose from this day forth to use my mouth as an instrument of righteousness for Your kingdom. Please touch my heart, mouth, lips, tongue, vocal cords, and mind with Your hot coal of righteousness and sanctify them and make them holy before You. Let the blood of Jesus cleanse me from all unrighteousness. Set a guard over my mouth so that I will only speak Your words. Let my words be kind, tenderhearted, and edifying. Let my words and the meditations of my heart be acceptable to You.

Please free me and my bloodline from any physical or spiritual leprosy that has come over us because of these sins. Please restore our health and senses in both realms and make us whole.

Please release any spiritual gifts such as prophecy, words of wisdom, words of knowledge, and tongues that have been delayed because of these sins. Please baptize me in Your Holy Spirit with the evidence of tongues and give me a heavenly language with which to pray in the spirit and minister in the congregation.

Breaking word curses over yourself

The word of God tells us to bless those who curse us. This is a key to breaking free from any curses others send toward us.

> "But I say to you who hear: Love your enemies, do good to those who hate you, bless those who curse you, and pray for those who spitefully use you. Luke 6:27-28

Ask the Holy Spirit to remind you of all negative words that have been spoken over your life (even from your own mouth). Pray the following prayer for each remembrance to cancel those negative words, then speak truth over your life instead.

In Jesus' name I bless those who have persecuted me or spoken evil, negative words against me. I cancel all those evil words, curses, and assignments over my life in Jesus' name. I cancel the words of _____ spoken over my life by _____. I renounce any agreement with those words and choose to forgive the one who spoke them. I detach myself now from those words and curses along with any demonic assignments associated with them in Jesus' name. I command all demons associated with those curses to loose me now in Jesus' name. I petition that all those curses by revoked over me and my bloodline and all effects of them be cancelled in Jesus' name. I declare _____ as truth over myself.

Chapter 16:
Renouncing Fear and Superstition

Almost everyone deals with some level of controlling fear. According to the Bible, fear is a spirit.

> For God has not given us a spirit of fear, but of power and of love and of a sound mind. 2 Timothy 1:7

Fear manifests in worry, anxiety, panic attacks, superstitions, and many specific phobias. These feelings cause us to fall into other sins. The bottom line is that fear is not putting our trust in Yahweh God, our covenant partner, and can bring a curse.

> Thus says the Lord: "Cursed is the man who trusts in man and makes flesh his strength, whose heart departs from the Lord. For he shall be like a shrub in the desert, and shall not see when good comes, but shall inhabit the parched places in the wilderness, in a salt land which is not inhabited.

> "Blessed is the man who trusts in the Lord, and whose hope is the Lord. For he shall be like a tree planted by the waters, which spreads out its roots by the river, and will not fear when heat comes; but its leaf will be green, and will not be anxious in the year of drought, nor will cease from yielding fruit. Jeremiah 17:5-8

Just like the ten Israelite spies, we are not always convinced that Yahweh God will protect us and provide for us. We often put our trust in something or someone else; medical professionals, homeopathic medicine, diet, new age practices, false religion, mentors, counselors, TV personalities, self-help books, or even our own abilities. Although some of these options are not intrinsically evil, they should not be our first step in seeking help. Fear tries to drive us away from God as our source of help. When we put our trust in man or something else, our heart departs from Yahweh God who is our hope and strength.

Yahweh has spoken to us in His word about trusting in Him. It is clear that when we do, He will strengthen us, give us peace and light, direct us, supply our needs, be our helper, walk with us through troubles and trials, and be our salvation. He is trustworthy, and His love can set us free from slavery to fear.

Trust in the Lord with all your heart, and lean not on your own understanding; In all your ways acknowledge Him, and He shall direct your paths. Proverbs 3:5-6

You will keep him in perfect peace, whose mind is stayed on You, because he trusts in You. Isaiah 26:3

Be anxious for nothing, but in everything by prayer and supplication, with thanksgiving, let your requests be made known to God; and the peace of God, which surpasses all understanding, will guard your hearts and minds through Christ Jesus. Philippians 4:6-7

Fear not, for I am with you; Be not dismayed, for I am your God. I will strengthen you, yes, I will help you, I will uphold you with My righteous right hand.' Isaiah 41:10

And my God shall supply all your need according to His riches in glory by Christ Jesus. Philippians 4:19

Some trust in chariots, and some in horses; but we will remember the name of the Lord our God. Psalm 20:7

Behold, God is my salvation, I will trust and not be afraid; 'For Yah, the Lord, is my strength and song; He also has become my salvation.' Isaiah 12:2

When you pass through the waters, I will be with you; and through the rivers, they shall not overflow you. When you walk through the fire, you shall not be burned, nor shall the flame scorch you. Isaiah 43:2

Remember that Yahweh God is our covenant partner and will come to our rescue. Even His name is a strong tower of refuge and safety.

The name of the Lord is a strong tower; the righteous run to it and are safe. Proverbs 18:10

He is our protector and defender. He will deliver us, be a shield for us, and fight our battles. When we trust in Yahweh, we do not need to fear man or the powers of darkness.

So we may boldly say: "The Lord is my helper; I will not fear. What can man do to me?" Hebrews 13:6

The fear of man brings a snare, but whoever trusts in the Lord shall be safe. Proverbs 29:25

You must not fear them, for the Lord your God Himself fights for you.' Deuteronomy 3:22

No weapon formed against you shall prosper, and every tongue which rises against you in judgment You shall condemn. This is the heritage of the servants of the Lord, and their righteousness is from Me," says the Lord. Isaiah 54:17

The Lord is my light and my salvation; whom shall I fear? The Lord is the strength of my life; of whom shall I be afraid? Psalm 27:1

But let all those rejoice who put their trust in You; Let them ever shout for joy, because You defend them; Let those also who love Your name be joyful in You. Psalm 5:11

Every word of God is pure; He is a shield to those who put their trust in Him.
Proverbs 30:5

I sought the Lord, and He heard me, and delivered me from all my fears. Psalm 34:4

Many are the afflictions of the righteous, but the Lord delivers him out of them all.
Psalm 34:19

"If you lie down, you will not be afraid; when you lie down, your sleep will be sweet.
Proverbs 3:24

Whenever I am afraid, I will trust in You. Psalm 56:3

When we abide in Him, Yahweh's perfect love casts out fear.

And we have known and believed the love that God has for us. God is love, and he who abides in love abides in God, and God in him. Love has been perfected among us in this: that we may have boldness in the day of judgment; because as He is, so are we in this world. There is no fear in love; but perfect love casts out fear, because fear involves torment. But he who fears has not been made perfect in love. 1 John 4:16-18

If you are ready to be free from fear and put your trust fully in Yahweh God, pray the following:

Father in heaven, I come before Your courts in the name of Jesus the Messiah. I repent on behalf of myself and my bloodline for trusting in anyone or anything besides You. I specifically repent for trusting in _____. I renounce that false trust along with the following fears that have tormented me:

- *Fear of man*
- *Fear of death and hell*
- *Fear of sickness and disease*
- *Fear of losing a loved one*
- *Fear of suffering*
- *Fear of never finding a husband or wife*
- *Fear of not being accepted or loved by Yahweh God*
- *Fear of rejection*
- *Fear of failure*
- *Fear of financial problems*
- *Fear of insanity or being hopeless*
- *Fear of satan and demons*

- *Fear of the dark*
- *Fear of heights*
- *Fear of small spaces*
- *Fear of _____*

I cancel my agreement with fear and all its terror and horror. I renounce the spirit of fear and all the demons that have afflicted me with nightmares, sleep paralysis, insomnia, panic attacks, anxiety, agitation, nervousness, adrenaline attacks in my body, tormenting thoughts, evil images, shortness of breath, vertigo, compulsive behaviors, attention problems, double-mindedness, mental distress, mental disorders, and dreadful expectations. I detach myself from these afflictions, the spirit of fear, and all the separate phobias I just renounced. I command them to release me and my bloodline in Jesus' name! I declare that God has not given me a spirit of fear, but of power, love, and a sound mind. I ask You, Yahweh God, to revoke the rights of the adversary over my bloodline where fear is concerned and evict all evil spirits that gained a place through fear. I petition that You would rule on my behalf to free me and my bloodline from all forms of fear and its power over us.

I will no longer be afraid of the terror by night, the arrow that flies by day, the pestilence that walks in darkness, or the destruction that lays waste at noonday because Yahweh God is my refuge and my fortress; In Him I will trust. I declare that I will lie down and sleep in peace, for You alone, O God, make me dwell in safety. I will trust in Yahweh God for my protection and my provision. I will allow His perfect love to cast all fear out of me.

Renouncing Superstitions

Many of our ancestors turned to superstitious practices in their daily lives for good luck and to ward off evil spirits. This might have involved possessing good-luck charms or amulets, making wishes, doing prophetic acts, or avoiding bad luck. These superstitious acts have their roots in the worship and appeasement of false gods. It is actually a form of idolatry. Even though our culture doesn't put the same significance on superstition, many of the practices are still around today. You may have seen superstitious practices in your own life or in your family line.

When we do these acts for fun or out of fear, we are essentially choosing to trust in these acts rather than our Heavenly Father. Jeremiah called the people to repentance from idolatry and superstitious acts, but they refused to stop them. They felt like these acts were bringing them prosperity and protection. They rejected their God and His covenant.

> As for the word that you have spoken to us in the name of the Lord, we will not listen to you! But we will certainly do whatever has gone out of our own mouth, to burn incense to the queen of heaven and pour out drink offerings to her, as we have done, we and our fathers, our kings and our princes, in the cities of Judah and in the streets of Jerusalem. For then we had plenty of food, were well-off, and saw no trouble. But since we stopped burning incense to the queen of heaven and pouring out drink offerings to her, we have

lacked everything and have been consumed by the sword and by famine."
Jeremiah 44:16-18

Today, most people don't use superstitious acts for the purpose of worshipping false gods; in fact, many don't know why they do them at all. They are traditions passed down from generation to generation or learned in childhood. Some superstitions can become compulsive. There is an understood fear that something bad could happen if the behavior stops. It is essentially a fear of tempting fate. It can become a type of unseen slavery.

Compulsive behaviors can mimic superstitious acts. Some people don't know why they have compulsive behaviors. They are driven to do things without any understanding. This may come as a curse from years of idolatry and superstition in the family line. Some deal with double-mindedness when they profess faith in Messiah Jesus and are still driven to practice superstition or compulsive behaviors. Timothy may have seen this double-mindedness when he told his congregation to reject old wives' fables.

> But reject profane and old wives' fables, and exercise yourself toward godliness.
> 1 Timothy 4:7

To renounce superstition and compulsive behavior, read the following prayer out loud:

Father in heaven, I come before Your courts in the name of Jesus the Messiah. I repent for myself and my bloodline for practicing idolatry and for the belief that superstitious acts and words can save us from evil circumstances or bring us good luck. By doing this, we have put our trust in fate and other supernatural forces rather than You. In Jesus' name, I renounce trusting and acting according to superstition on behalf of me and my ancestors. I renounce the fear of tempting fate and the appeasement of idols or false gods through these practices. I ask You to forgive these sins and cleanse my bloodline. Please bring to my mind every superstitious act and belief that I have participated in so I can renounce them now.

I specifically renounce _____.

I renounce the belief that superstitious acts can protect me from bad luck, evil circumstances, demons or satan. In Jesus' name, I also renounce Lady Luck and all "good luck" charms and amulets including: rabbit's foot, shamrock, 4-leaf clover, lucky 7, lucky numbers, horseshoe, acorn, bamboo, evil eye charm, lucky socks, ladybug, dreamcatcher, white elephant, maneki-neko the luck cat, cornicello, Chinese luck dragon, and medals of patron saints or other religious charms worn for luck.

I renounce making wishes on stars, candles, dandelions, daisies, eyelashes, wishbones, pennies, white horses, rainbows, and wells.

I renounce the common superstitions of avoiding black cats, walking under ladders, throwing salt over the shoulder, knocking on wood, fingers crossed, jinx, avoiding cracks, avoiding 13, throwing coins in a fountain, using oils or objects to scare away demons, and compulsively using "bless you" when someone sneezes.

I also renounce any agreement with bad luck through superstition or events that I believed cause bad luck including, breaking mirrors, saying something positive that might tempt fate, hearing the call of a raven, magpie, or a crow, seeing the groom before the wedding, and not eating black-eyed peas on New Year's Day. I cancel any bad luck spoken over me by others or myself.

I repent for holding these actions and objects as a false comforter in the place of the Holy Spirit. I cut myself free from all these superstitions now with the sword of the Spirit. I petition for an eviction notice for all darkness related to superstition. I choose today to trust completely in You, Yahweh God, and in the sacrifice made by Your Son, Messiah Jesus. I trust that You have good plans for me, plans to give me a hope and a future. I choose Your purpose for my life. I will use Your Holy Scriptures as a template on how to live rather than superstition.

I detach myself and my bloodline from any compulsive behaviors, torment, and evil spirits that have had access to me from opening the door to superstition. I command those evil spirits to leave me and my bloodline now in Jesus' name! I ask You, Yahweh, to close those doors now and seal them with the blood of Jesus. I also choose to destroy all superstitious items in my possession.

Please cleanse me, renew my mind, and give me discernment in the future. Please come Holy Spirit and be my comforter. Please fill the places where the false comforters have been removed. Please send Your healing power into my mind, my brain and all its pathways, reconnecting them to each other and to Your truth. Please erase the old pathways that led to compulsive behaviors and wrong thinking and create new pathways of truth. Please erase all muscle memory of the compulsive behaviors and fill me and my bloodline with Your supernatural peace. Give me a sound mind, the mind of Messiah. Let my life be set-apart for Your kingdom and bring You glory.

Chapter 17:
Birth, Life-Cycle Events, and the Firstborn

Dedication of the firstborn

Yahweh God instructed in His Word that the first and best was to be given to Him. This included firstborn sons, firstborn animals, and the first fruits from each harvest. He even claimed the first city taken by the Israelites in the land of Canaan.

We see these instructions in Exodus, before the tenth plague in Egypt, the death of the firstborn. Yahweh God calls Israel His firstborn son when He is preparing their redemption from Egypt. He gave Pharoah a warning that if His own firstborn Israel was not released, God would kill the firstborn son of Egypt.

> "Then you shall say to Pharaoh, 'Thus says the Lord: "Israel is My son, My firstborn. So, I say to you, let My son go that he may serve Me. But if you refuse to let him go, indeed I will kill your son, your firstborn."'" Exodus 4:22-23

It is throughout this story that God shares how He has sanctified all the firstborn to Himself.

> Then the Lord spoke to Moses, saying, "Consecrate to Me all the firstborn, whatever opens the womb among the children of Israel, both of man and beast; it is Mine." Exodus 13:1-2

Yahweh God claimed all the firstborn of the Israelites, both men and beasts. He called them set apart.

> "And it shall be, when the Lord brings you into the land of the Canaanites, as He swore to you and your fathers, and gives it to you, that you shall set apart to the Lord all that open the womb, that is, every firstborn that comes from an animal which you have; the males shall be the Lord's. But every firstborn of a donkey you shall redeem with a lamb; and if you will not redeem it, then you shall break its neck. And all the firstborn of man among your sons you shall redeem. Exodus 13:11-13

Even though Yahweh declared that firstborn sons were to be consecrated to Him, He allowed the fathers to redeem them, or buy them back.

> So it shall be, when your son asks you in time to come, saying, 'What is this?' that you shall say to him, 'By strength of hand the Lord brought us out of Egypt, out of the house of bondage. And it came to pass, when Pharaoh was stubborn about letting us go, that the Lord killed all the firstborn in the land of Egypt, both the firstborn of man and the firstborn of beast. Therefore, I sacrifice to the Lord all males that open the womb, but all the firstborn of my sons I redeem.' It shall be as a sign on your hand and as frontlets between your eyes, for by strength of hand the Lord brought us out of Egypt."
> Exodus 11:14-16

Eventually the Levites were sanctified unto God to take the place of the firstborn when all the other tribes worshiped the golden calf in the wilderness. The people were still required to bring their firstborn sons and animals to God, but the clean sacrificial animals would be eaten by the Levites and the redemption money for the firstborn sons and unclean animals would be given to the Levites.

> Then the Lord spoke to Moses, saying: "Now behold, I Myself have taken the Levites from among the children of Israel instead of every firstborn who opens the womb among the children of Israel. Therefore, the Levites shall be Mine, because all the firstborn are Mine. On the day that I struck all the firstborn in the land of Egypt, I sanctified to Myself all the firstborn in Israel, both man and beast. They shall be Mine: I am the Lord." Numbers 3:11-13

> "Everything that first opens the womb of all flesh, which they bring to the Lord, whether man or beast, shall be yours; nevertheless, the firstborn of man you shall surely redeem, and the firstborn of unclean animals you shall redeem. Numbers 18:15

We see Joseph and Mary bringing Jesus to the temple for His "Pidyon Haben" or "redemption of the son" when He was 31 days old. Joseph would have paid five silver shekels to a cohen or priest to redeem Him.

> Now when the days of her purification according to the law of Moses were completed, they brought Him to Jerusalem to present Him to the Lord (as it is written in the law of the Lord, "Every male who opens the womb shall be called holy to the Lord"), and to offer a sacrifice according to what is said in the law of the Lord, "A pair of turtledoves or two young pigeons." Luke 2:22-24

> You shall take five shekels for each one individually; you shall take them in the currency of the shekel of the sanctuary, the shekel of twenty gerahs. Numbers 3:47

In Bible times, legitimate, firstborn males were given both a birthright (bechora) and a blessing (berachot). Both were usually reserved for the firstborn son who would be both spiritual leader and head of the family on the death of the father (birthright) and would inherit a double-portion of the land and property (blessing).

Much was expected of the firstborn son. He would take over the family business and would eventually be the patriarch of the family, the one to whom the rest of the family looked for wisdom and the final word. This was an honor and a responsibility.

This special purpose is still on the life of the firstborn today. Because the firstborn is special to God, the enemy wants to bring each of them to destruction. This is even more beneficial to the enemy because of the influence the firstborn child has on the younger siblings. It is a strategic way to destroy the entire family. Even during Bible times, we can read about several firstborn sons drawn away by the flesh and the enemy (Cain, Esau, Reuben).

Because there is a special blessing on the firstborn, it is easy for pride and arrogance to pull that child toward self-centeredness and the world. Another problem is that some of our ancestors may have dedicated all the firstborn children in their family line to false gods or idols in exchange for power, money, or fame. This gives the enemy legal rights or ties to these children.

How can we take this special blessing back out of the hands of darkness?

Just like the Israelites were spared the death of their firstborn by making a covenant with Yahweh using the blood of the lamb; the blood of our Passover lamb, Jesus, makes a trade for our own lives. We are redeemed by His blood. We have been 'bought back' from death as our Heavenly Father paid the price for our redemption, not with silver shekels, but with more costly blood. Because He made this sacrifice for us, we can choose to take back this special blessing and birthright through the blood of Jesus.

> For He made Him who knew no sin to be sin for us, that we might become the righteousness of God in Him. 2 Corinthians 5:21

If you are a firstborn child, pray the following prayer aloud. If you have a firstborn child, you can pray the prayer on behalf of that child. Everyone can pray through the first paragraph and repent for the sins of the fathers:

Father in heaven, I come before Your courts in the name of Jesus the Messiah. I repent for the sins of my ancestors for not choosing to dedicate their firstborn children to You and bring them up to fear, love, and obey You. I also repent where they instead dedicated their children to false gods in trade for power, wealth, or fame. I repent for my ancestors neglecting or rejecting Your teachings and Your Word when raising their children. I also repent for any ways that I have rebelled against You and any authority figures You have put in my life. I repent for pride, arrogance, worldliness, selfishness, and seeking my own path apart from You. I renounce these things for myself and my family line. Please forgive us and cleanse us with the blood of Jesus.

I renounce all false gods that have held a claim to me as a firstborn or to my firstborn child. I reject and evict all demons that have taken advantage of me through the firstborn title. I also renounce any counterfeit gifts that came from darkness. I dedicate myself (and my children) to the God of Abraham, Isaac, and Jacob, the Creator God of Israel, Yahweh Elohim. I declare that I have been redeemed, or bought back, by the blood of the sacrifice lamb, Yeshua haMaschiach, Jesus the Messiah. I petition that all plans of darkness over my life and destiny would be revoked in the name of Messiah Jesus. I petition that every part of my life and destiny that has been hijacked, stolen, hidden, rendered ineffective, or taken captive by satan's kingdom be collected, cleansed, and returned to me, including my God-given birthright, blessing, and inheritance. I ask that any representation of myself that is on any evil alter be removed and the altar be destroyed in Jesus' name.

I petition that my book in heaven be opened and read aloud to release the destiny that Yahweh God has purposed for me from the foundation of the world. I choose to walk in that destiny. I ask that every birthright, blessing, talent, ability, and gift needed to complete that destiny be released to me. I also ask that every Godly relationship be redeemed that has been severed, hindered, blocked, or destroyed by the enemy. May my life shine bright for the kingdom of heaven.

I make the same petition for my firstborn child. (You may go back through this prayer for your firstborn child.)

Appointed times and Life-Cycle Events

We talked about Yahweh's appointed times in chapter 4 and how the enemy also had his own appointed times. Besides his own 'holy days', satan also wants to take advantage of life cycle events that are special to Yahweh's kingdom. Marriages, births, and coming of age are all important dates on both God's calendar and satan's. God has a plan to move us forward in our spiritual journey at those time, but the enemy will try to obtain legal rights to bring destruction on us instead. You may recall some tragic events or spiritual shifts that have happened in your life during a life-cycle event or on your birthday.

There are special years in our lives that are important. The coming-of-age time around the age of 12-13 is a time when a child becomes more accountable before Yahweh God. In Jewish culture, it is referred to as a bar mitzvah (boys) or bat mitzvah (girls), which means son or daughter of commandment. This special milestone honors the privilege and responsibility of Jewish adulthood. The family and the child prepare for this special time for about six months prior to the celebration. The young man works with a tutor studying the Torah and preparing to read aloud from it in the synagogue for the first time. He will study the Torah portion that was read on the week he was born. This area of scripture speaks prophetically into the life of the child. The young man reads through this portion and chooses a section that speaks to him. He will read it in Hebrew from the actual Torah scroll and share how it connects with his life. He will also study the Shabbat prayers for a better understanding of God and his relationship with God.

The young man will also choose a mitzvah project. This project will be something he does for the community to make it a better place. It should be something in which he can use his talents and gifts to bring 'tikkun olam', or help repair the world. He may volunteer his time somewhere or do a fundraising project. He will also do a personal project to help him draw closer to God.

At the ceremony, the young man will also be blessed by those men who are spiritual leaders in his life and will receive his own tallit and tefillin. After the ceremony, he will no longer walk in the childishness of his past, but will now sit with the adults and begin to walk more focused on his faith.

In our culture, there has not been much concern about becoming responsible adults. Our culture has chosen the age of 18 as the age of entering adulthood. This age was established to allow recruitment of younger men for the war. Most kids see the age of 18 as a time to break away from their parents' rule and have independence. It is not focused on accountability to God and our place in society. What would our community look like if we chose to celebrate a child's coming of age with a renewed focus on God and using his talents and gifts to benefit the community or the world?

Because the true coming-of-age time is 12-13, the boys and girls in our culture come into this shift without any preparation. The spirit realm recognizes the shift whether we do or not. At this time, the enemy is given more access to the children. You may see new temptations coming over them and some bloodline curses beginning to operate. These are the years many children begin to rebel against the authority of the parents instead of move into a new stage of learning. We have begun to accept this rebellion and treat it as normal, but that is not God's way.

Before this time, the child was held completely under the authority of their parents. This new accountability is to help prepare the child for adulthood. It is a season where children can begin to be led by their parents while learning to have greater responsibility in the family. The child begins to take care of himself and make some of his own decisions. It is important for the child to understand that he is still under his parent's God-given authority and is required by Yahweh to obey them. Our sons and daughters need to be shepherded into their God-given purposes and a deeper relationship with Yahweh God.

Marriage and childbirth are other appointed times where bloodline curses may be released into the life of a person. Significant shifts in the spirit realm happen at these times. You may have noticed this in your life where attitudes changed or heaviness came at a time that should be joyful. Many people talk about how their spouse changed after they were married or had a baby. In our culture, we tend to focus more on honoring the people who are celebrating the life-change and their preferences rather than honoring Yahweh. What shifts would we see in the spiritual realm if we decided to honor Yahweh God in all of our life-cycle events?

Somewhere in a person's 30's is usually a time for spiritual maturity. This was the age that people in Bible times would set out in their own business or ministry. Jesus began His ministry at 30. Like many life-cycle events, this special appointed time was usually started with a 'tevilah'. A special immersion in living water was performed at life changes signifying a change from profane to holy. The experience is likened to being 'born anew.' The tevilah represented ritual purification and spiritual cleansing. It was experienced before holy days, marriage, before starting ministry, or becoming a Jewish convert. When coming out of the living water, one would be said to have a new identity. Jesus was immersed or baptized this way when He started His ministry.

> It came to pass in those days that Jesus came from Nazareth of Galilee, and was baptized by John in the Jordan. And immediately, coming up from the water, He saw the heavens parting and the Spirit descending upon Him like a dove. Then a voice came from heaven, "You are My beloved Son, in whom I am well pleased." Mark 1:9-11

The enemy may again try to sabotage this time. There seem to be special set-times for all the other years that end in '0', like 40, 50, 60, and so on. The year 50 is a "jubilee" on Yahweh's calendar. A jubilee is a time when all debts are cancelled and slaves are set free. It should be a time of freedom, rest, and a new beginning. The enemy tries to sabotage it with "over the hill" parties and early aging.

If you would like to renounce any set-times of the enemy pray the following prayer:

Father in heaven, I come before Your courts in the name of Jesus the Messiah. I repent for the sins of my ancestors and myself that would allow the enemy's appointed times to manifest in my life and my bloodline. I repent for any covenants that were made with darkness that opened the door to the enemy, even those made in ignorance. I repent for any rebellion against my parents or other authority in my own life and any ways I have agreed with the enemy's plans. I repent for any rebellion I have had against You, Yahweh God, and Your plans for me. I repent for self-centeredness, selfishness, and making my own plans apart from You. I repent for focusing my life-cycle events on myself and selfish desires instead of You and my part in Your kingdom. I ask You to forgive these sins and cleanse me and my bloodline.

I choose to renounce and detach myself and my bloodline from death, accidents, disease, misfortune, failure, rejection, tragedy, insanity, division, divorce, abuse, torment, fear, anger, and any other demon gods that have had access to our lives and life-cycle events through these sins or agreement. I command all spirits associated with these sins to release me and my bloodline now in Jesus' name.

I choose to forgive my ancestors for opening the door to bloodline curses through their actions whether knowingly or unknowingly. I petition that You Yahweh sever me and my bloodline completely from the darkness that had legal rights to influence or sabotage our life-cycles, especially death. I petition that You free us from any future set-times or appointed times on the enemy's calendar. I ask that You would cancel them and erase those appointments.

I choose to place my life and my bloodline on Your calendar, Yahweh. I choose to follow You and obey Your word and dedicate all the important times of my life to You. I invite You into all of these events. Please show me how I can honor You through my life changes and those of my future generations.

Renunciations related to birth and names

There can be unholy ties in the spirit realm to your birthdate, your name, and to a namesake. You can use the following prayers to disconnect yourself from these.

Renunciation prayer for dark name meaning

Father in heaven, I petition You for freedom from the unholy prophetic meaning of my birth name. I honor my father and mother who chose the name _____ for me and forgive them for choosing a name with a dark meaning. I choose to detach myself from the dark meaning of my name which is _____. I also renounce any secret names given to me by darkness. I detach myself from any god/goddess or demonic force that is attached to my name and any gematria or destiny used by the occult. I declare that I am in covenant with the God of Abraham, Isaac, and Jacob and am His adopted child. I take upon myself His Name and the new name He has given me. I command all spirits attached to these names or meanings to loose me now in Jesus' name.

Renunciation prayer for namesake attachments

Father in heaven, I petition You for freedom from namesake attachments and unholy bonding with _____. I honor my relative _____ and my parents who chose to name me after her/him. I do not, however chose to share an ungodly connection with _____ through the namesake attachment. I detach myself from that namesake attachment, along with any inheritance of bad habits or characteristics of _____. I repent for following along in the footsteps of _____ by agreeing with _____. I now renounce this unholy bond and ask You Father to cleanse me. I ask You to free me from any unholy attachment to _____ and loose the bonding of our souls. I return any parts of _____ that have been attached to me, back to her/him. I ask You, Father, to restore to me any parts of myself that were tied to _____ through this bond. I also petition that any demonic inheritance from _____ at the time of her/his death would be forbidden to enter my life or my bloodline. I command all spirits attached to me through the namesake to loose me now in Jesus' name.

Renunciation prayer for birthdate/birthday demonic ties

Father in heaven, I petition You for freedom from any demonic ties to my date of birth, including all birth constellation signs and entities (specifically _____), birth stones, birth flowers or colors, or any other person who shares that birthdate or negative events tied to that date throughout history. I also repent for making wishes as I blew out candles on cakes which represent worship of the queen of heaven and the incense that was raised to her. I repent of any interest or agreement with these ties, as well as any selfishness that I have shown about my birthday throughout my life. I ask You to cancel all demonic assignments released over me in the womb from conception to birth, especially those that are set to be time-released on my birthday at any point in my life. I repent for any and all sins of the bloodline that allowed those assignments to manifest and operate in my life. I renounce those sins along with any dedications of my life to darkness from my ancestors. I command all spirits associated with my birthdate or these sins to loose me now in Jesus' name.

I also repent of becoming my own master and rebelling against Your plan for my life, Father. I repent for pride, disobedience, rebellion, manipulation, control, and witchcraft against my God-given destiny and Your authority over me. I repent for speaking negative words over my life, my birth, my conception, my parents, my ancestors, or my DNA. I choose to dedicate my life to You of my own free will. You are the one who breathed life into me and created me in my mother's womb. You have written in Your book all the days of my life before I even took a breath. I choose to agree with what You have written in my book. I choose to walk in Your plan and purpose created just for me. I ask You to cleanse the date of my birth and set it apart as holy for Your kingdom. I ask You to crush and destroy any time-clocks or appointed times of the enemy over my life. I ask You to reset my future days and birthdays in the setting of Your kingdom. I choose to honor You on those days and thank You for the gift of life.

Chapter 18:
Freedom for your Finances

Many believers struggle with attacks on their finances. It can be a great cause of anxiety and fear and can be a distraction from spiritual life. Many of these believers are doing their best to use their money wisely, but are still unable to prosper. When seeking freedom from a financial curse, it is good to start by studying Yahweh God's instruction to us in the Bible.

There is much to say in scripture about money and how to handle it, more than can possibly be covered in one chapter. Wealth is a blessing for obedience to Yahweh God. He is a King and owns the cattle on a thousand hills, as well as, the gold and silver of the earth. The earth and all its abundance are His. We are to steward His finances well. We are commanded to be generous and to care for widows and orphans, to provide for our families, and bless the house of God. He promises blessings when we give and are generous.

> Bring all the tithes into the storehouse, that there may be food in My house, and try Me now in this," says the Lord of hosts, "If I will not open for you the windows of heaven and pour out for you such blessing that there will not be room enough to receive it. "And I will rebuke the devourer for your sakes, so that he will not destroy the fruit of your ground, nor shall the vine fail to bear fruit for you in the field," says the Lord of hosts. Malachi 3:10-11

> Every man shall give as he is able, according to the blessing of the Lord your God which He has given you. Deuteronomy 16:17

> So let each one give as he purposes in his heart, not grudgingly or of necessity; for God loves a cheerful giver. 2 Corinthians 9:7

> Give, and it will be given to you: good measure, pressed down, shaken together, and running over will be put into your bosom. For with the same measure that you use, it will be measured back to you." Luke 6:38

As His children, we can trust that He will supply all our needs. Yahweh tells us to seek His kingdom first and He will give us all we need. It is His good pleasure to give us the kingdom. He wants us to have an abundance to bless others.

> And my God shall supply all your need according to His riches in glory by Christ Jesus. Philippians 4:19

> And do not seek what you should eat or what you should drink, nor have an anxious mind. For all these things the nations of the world seek after, and your Father knows that you need these things. But seek the kingdom of God, and all these things shall be added to you. Do not fear, little flock, for it is your Father's good pleasure to give you the kingdom. Sell what you have and give alms; provide yourselves money bags which do not grow old, a treasure in the heavens that does not fail, where no thief approaches nor moth destroys. For where your treasure is, there your heart will be also. Luke 12:29-34

> Honor the Lord with your possessions, and with the firstfruits of all your increase; so your barns will be filled with plenty, and your vats will overflow with new wine. Proverbs 3:9-10

> "And you shall remember the Lord your God, for it is He who gives you power to get wealth, that He may establish His covenant which He swore to your fathers, as it is this day. Deuteronomy 8:18

> The Lord will open to you His good treasure, the heavens, to give the rain to your land in its season, and to bless all the work of your hand. You shall lend to many nations, but you shall not borrow. Deuteronomy 28:12

Wow! Those words are amazing! If we are cheerful in giving, tithe, bring offerings to Yahweh, and remember that He is the one who gives us power to get wealth; then blessings and plenty will overflow to us. He will open the good treasure from His heavens! This is our heritage, but oftentimes we do not see this blessing in our homes and lives. Instead, it may seem more like the picture in Haggai 1:6:

> "You have sown much, and bring in little; You eat, but do not have enough; You drink, but you are not filled with drink; You clothe yourselves, but no one is warm; And he who earns wages, earns wages to put into a bag with holes."

Why was this curse upon Yahweh's people? Why was their hard work being drained away by a pocket with holes? We see in the same chapter that the people had built up their own houses while the house of God was in ruins.

> "Thus speaks the LORD of hosts, saying: 'This people says, "The time has not come, the time that the LORD's house should be built." ' " Then the word of the LORD came by Haggai the prophet, saying, "*Is it* time for you yourselves to dwell in your paneled

houses, and this temple *to lie* in ruins?" Now therefore, thus says the LORD of hosts: "Consider your ways! Go up to the mountains and bring wood and build the temple, that I may take pleasure in it and be glorified," says the Lord. Haggai 1:2-5, 8

"Because of My house that is in ruins, while every one of you runs to his own house. Therefore the heavens above you withhold the dew, and the earth withholds its fruit. For I called for a drought on the land and the mountains, on the grain and the new wine and the oil, on whatever the ground brings forth, on men and livestock, and on all the labor of your hands." Haggai 1:9-11

You may be trying to honor God, working hard for a living, just to put your money in a "bag with holes." You may feel like you can never get ahead. You may be fearful to be generous because you are living paycheck to paycheck. Others may fall upon hard financial times every now and then, but it seems like a weekly occurrence for you: your appliance breaks down right after the warranty runs out, your teenager's car needs new tires, your husband didn't get the raise he deserved, all the bills have increased, and you still have to pay for the monthly medications from the pharmacy. You may have also noticed a pattern of financial hardship in your family line. This sounds like a curse on your finances.

Sometimes the curse flows from the iniquities of our ancestors. Many times, with a curse, the punishment fits the crime. You may have had an ancestor who was involved with a secret society like the Freemasons or who was a cruel slave owner or a tight-fisted businessman. There are many warnings in scripture about mishandling money or using it for evil purposes. The love of money can also become an idol. So many evil things have been done for the love of money. It is a path to destruction.

Now godliness with contentment is great gain. For we brought nothing into this world, and it is certain we can carry nothing out. And having food and clothing, with these we shall be content. But those who desire to be rich fall into temptation and a snare, and into many foolish and harmful lusts which drown men in destruction and perdition. For the love of money is a root of all kinds of evil, for which some have strayed from the faith in their greediness, and pierced themselves through with many sorrows. 1 Timothy 6:6-10

"No one can serve two masters; for either he will hate the one and love the other, or else he will be loyal to the one and despise the other. You cannot serve God and mammon. Matthew 6:24

He who loves silver will not be satisfied with silver; nor he who loves abundance, with increase. This also is vanity. Ecclesiastes 5:10

Now listen, you rich people, weep and wail because of the misery that is coming on you. Your wealth has rotted, and moths have eaten your clothes. Your gold and silver are corroded. Their corrosion will testify against you and eat your flesh like fire. You have hoarded wealth in the last days. Look! The wages you failed to pay the workers who mowed your fields are crying out against you. The cries of the harvesters have reached the ears of the Lord Almighty. You have lived on earth in luxury and self-indulgence. You have fattened yourselves in the day of slaughter. You have condemned and murdered the innocent one, who was not opposing you. James 5:1-6

But if anyone does not provide for his own, and especially for those of his household, he has denied the faith and is worse than an unbeliever. 1 Timothy 5:8

He who oppresses the poor to increase his riches, and he who gives to the rich, will surely come to poverty. Proverbs 22:16

In Zechariah 5:1-4, Zechariah had a vision about a curse going out against thieves.

Then I turned and raised my eyes, and saw there a flying scroll. And he said to me, "What do you see?" So I answered, "I see a flying scroll. Its length is twenty cubits and its width ten cubits." Then he said to me, "This is the curse that goes out over the face of the whole earth: 'Every thief shall be expelled,' according to this side of the scroll; and, 'Every perjurer shall be expelled,' according to that side of it."

"I will send out the curse," says the Lord of hosts; "It shall enter the house of the thief and the house of the one who swears falsely by My name. It shall remain in the midst of his house and consume it, with its timber and stones."

Ask the Holy Spirit to remind you of times in your life when you have mishandled money or did not put your trust in God to provide for you. Ask Him to expose any generational sin that could have brought about a financial curse that could be blocking Your inheritance as a child of Yahweh God. Most of us have had ancestors who have made covenants with demon gods for financial gain or who have oppressed or taken advantage of others out of greed. Most of us have also had ancestors who went through fearful times such as the great depression or a communist take-over. This can open the door to financial fear and agreement with poverty. Whatever the root cause, we can repent for and renounce these iniquities to remove the legal rights of darkness and cleanse our bloodlines.

Pray the following prayer aloud:

Father in heaven, I come before Your courts in the name of Jesus the Messiah. Your word speaks of an amazing inheritance for Your children. I know that Jesus' paid the price for me to receive that inheritance. I come today to ask You to expose and forgive the sins and iniquities in my bloodline that have been hindering those blessings in my life and to cancel any financial curse.

In Jesus' name, I repent for and renounce all of my sins and the sins of my ancestors including the known sins of _____. I renounce the love of money, theft, moving boundary stones, gambling, bribery, fraud, greed, avarice, stinginess, hoarding, cheating, false balances, laziness, idleness, foolishness, selfishness, withholding wages, withholding support of widows and orphans; withholding firstfruits, tithes, and offerings, not coming to the aid of a brother in need, not repaying a loan, charging interest to a brother, trusting in riches, owing debts, pillaging, coveting, slavery, forced labor, drug trafficking, human trafficking, hunting for souls, catering to the rich, betrayals, murders, wickedness, and in any way investing into the kingdom of darkness or stealing from the kingdom of God. I renounce all covenants, worship, dedications, sacrifices, and trades made with demon gods to gain wealth, even to the point of trading children, seed, or the fruit of the womb. I renounce agreement with Freemasonry and other secret societies, Illuminati, New World Order and the world bank, anti-Christ, ba'al, mammon, lady luck, fortune and fame. I detach myself from all these demonic forces and command them to release me and my bloodline in Jesus' name.

Please show me, Father, how I can repay any outstanding debts that I owe, anyone I have cheated, or anything I have stolen.

I repent for building my own house or kingdom while Your house lies in ruins. I repent where my ancestors have also ignored Your house. Please remove the financial drought on the land and the labor of our hands.

I repent for cursing or speaking against my own finances or the finances of others in a negative way. I cancel those curses and negative words and bless my finances and anyone I have spoken against. I choose to forgive any ancestor that made dark covenants or bad decisions that opened a door to a financial curse. I choose to forgive anyone who has stolen from me, cheated me, or treated me unfairly where money is concerned. I will not hold these sins against them any longer. I ask You to heal any wounds I have sustained from these transactions.

I repent for being envious or jealous of others who were financially prosperous.

I repent for trusting in finances instead of You. I repent for giving fear of poverty a place in my life. I choose to place my finances under Your control in Your kingdom. I ask for wisdom as a steward of all with which You will bless me. I ask You to open the windows of heaven over me and my bloodline and pour out Your blessing. I know that all the earth is Yours and You own the cattle on a thousand hills.

I petition that You will break the curse these sins have brought upon us and loose our finances and inheritance from all places, spaces, and realms where they have been locked up or hidden. I ask You to send Your heavenly host to retrieve them and cleanse them with the blood of Jesus. I ask for freedom from poverty and a poverty mindset, setbacks, disappointments, despair, shortages, bankruptcy, a pocket with holes, barrenness, drought, and lack. I ask that You would rebuke the devourer on our behalf. I ask that all land and property that has been stolen from me or my ancestors be returned to my bloodline and the thief be forced to pay back double what he has stolen. I choose to store up my treasure in heaven, where it can't be stolen or destroyed.

> Do not store up for yourselves treasures on earth, where moths and vermin destroy, and where thieves break in and steal. But store up for yourselves treasures in heaven, where

moths and vermin do not destroy, and where thieves do not break in and steal. For where your treasure is, there your heart will be also. Matthew 6:19-21

Chapter 19:
Closing Prayer and Declaration

As you prepare to make your closing statement and declarations in the heavenly courts, read them below before speaking them out loud. You do not want to make a vow or oath without sincerity and a dedication to keep it.

Prayer and Petition for a Final Ruling

In closing my case, I bow before the Great Judge of All the Earth bringing forth the evidence of my repentance and renunciations, and all the other actions I have performed to remove the legal rights of darkness in my life and my bloodline. I also bring forth the evidence of the blood of Jesus the Messiah, my covenant partner, that speaks on my behalf. I have not only repented and renounced the sins and iniquities and dark covenants of myself and my ancestors, but I have been born again, baptized into the death of Messiah and risen up a new creation. I have received the seal of the Holy Spirit and the baptism of power (or, and seek to be baptized in His power). I ask You to rule on my behalf today and enforce Your judgments on the earth.

In the name of Jesus the Messiah, I formally ask you to purge my records of transgression and iniquity following my repentance, to wipe away all legal rights the enemy has to torment me. I ask You to release me and my bloodline from all covenants, contracts, vows, oaths, trades, sacrifices, and offerings made with and to the kingdom of darkness. I ask You to revoke all curses and release any blessings that have been held up legally. I ask You to render a verdict of freedom on my behalf and let it be executed on the earth. I also ask for a permanent restraining order (order to cease and desist) to be put on satan's kingdom regarding these expunged sins, transgressions, iniquities, and covenants.

I ask You to disconnect me and my bloodline from all earthly darkness and powers from the celestial heavens and the second heavens that have gained access to us through these traumatic sins. I ask You to evict and remove every demonic spirit or entity that has lost its legal rights to me and my bloodline from my being (body, soul, and spirit), my life, my bloodline, and my destiny.

I ask You to close forever any portals or any means of access or communication in my life and bloodline to any members of satan's kingdom. I ask You to break open and destroy every demonic seal on my being, as You have the power to open the seals. I ask You to smash all of satan's timeclocks over my life and destiny and bring me fully into Your time and destiny. I ask You to redeem every second of my life and destiny stolen by the enemy, and to place them under Your authority and kingdom plan.

I ask You to fully sever all unholy soul-ties between me and any creatures, objects, places, and people, living or dead. I also petition to commit to You any human spirits or their fragments that have been attached to me, my DNA, my silver cord, or any part of my life. You are the righteous judge. I ask that You would recover any parts of my shattered soul that were held captive in soul-ties or held in other places, spaces, times, or dimensions. Please cleanse them, and restore me to wholeness.

I petition You to remove every mark of darkness on or in my body and soul, those seen and unseen. I ask that you would mark me as Your own with Your name on my forehead and with the seal of your Holy Spirit. I ask for Your anointing on my life to walk in the plan and purpose You have written in my book.

I petition You for my complete healing: body, soul and spirit. I ask You to reset my body systems to Your perfect order of life, health, and youth and revoke death's power over me. I ask You to refresh and restore my soul, healing all wounds and leaving no traces of trauma or darkness. I ask that You would strengthen my spirit man.

I petition that the water of Your Word would make me new, and Your Spirit would go before me into my home and life restoring and preparing the way for Your kingdom purpose in my life. Please release all the gifts and blessings You have set aside for me and my bloodline. I surrender them all to You.

I open every door of my life to You. Please come in and fill me fully. Please reset all of my desires to Yours. Make me a spotless bride, without any blemish. Let my mind be sound, the mind of Messiah. Let my sleep be sweet with the restoration of dreams and visions from You. May You be a wall of fire around me and the Glory within me. Thank You that You will never forsake or abandon Your covenant to me and my future generations. Nothing can separate me from Your love.

I choose today to fully commit my life to Jesus, my covenant partner, and dedicate all areas of my life to Him. I claim the blessings made available to me because of His death on the cross: forgiveness of sin and iniquity, peace with God, and healing. I also receive all the trades he has made on my behalf. I claim the protection of the blood of Jesus over my mind, body, and spirit. I submit my body as the temple of Yahweh God.

Death to the old man

The Word of Yahweh God says that you become a new creation when you die with Messiah Jesus in baptism and are raised in His resurrection power.

> What shall we say then? Shall we continue in sin that grace may abound? Certainly not! How shall we who died to sin live any longer in it? Or do you not know that as many of us as were baptized into Christ Jesus were baptized into His death? Therefore, we were buried with Him through baptism into death, that just as Christ was raised from the dead by the glory of the Father, even so we also should walk in newness of life. For if we have been united together in the likeness of His death, certainly we also shall be in the likeness of His resurrection, knowing this, that our old man was crucified with Him, that the body of sin might be done away with, that we should no longer be slaves of sin. For he who has died has been freed from sin. Now if we died with Christ, we believe that we shall also live with Him, knowing that Christ, having been raised from the dead, dies no more. Death no longer has dominion over Him. For the death that He died, He died to sin once for all; but the life that He lives, He lives to God. Likewise, you also, reckon yourselves to be dead indeed to sin, but alive to God in Christ Jesus our Lord. Romans 6:1-11

> Therefore, if anyone is in Christ, he is a new creation; old things have passed away; behold, all things have become new. 2 Corinthians 5:17

The scriptures also tell us that death is the end of a covenant:

> Or do you not know, brethren (for I speak to those who know the law), that the law has dominion over a man as long as he lives? For the woman who has a husband is bound by the law to her husband as long as he lives. But if the husband dies, she is released from the law of her husband. So then if, while her husband lives, she marries another man, she will be called an adulteress; but if her husband dies, she is free from that law, so that she is no adulteress, though she has married another man. Therefore, my brethren, you also have become dead to the law through the body of Christ, that you may be married to another—to Him who was raised from the dead, that we should bear fruit to God. For when we were in the flesh, the sinful passions which were aroused by the law were at work in our members to bear fruit to death. But now we have been delivered from the law, having died to what we were held by, so that we should serve in the newness of the Spirit and not in the oldness of the letter. Romans 7:1-6

Because the old man has died, you are no longer bound to dark covenants made by your ancestors on your behalf or by the old man you were before you made covenant with Yahweh God. As the new man who is joined with Messiah Jesus and empowered by His Spirit, you are in covenant with Him and given the privilege to use His name and authority. Using this authority, in agreement with your petitions, you can speak the following declarations and commands for both heaven and earth to witness:

Declaration

I declare that I am a new creation in Messiah Jesus, therefore, any covenants made by me or on behalf of my old man are cancelled by the death of the old man. Death is the end of a covenant. I am no longer the old man that was in covenant with darkness. I have been made new and am in union with Messiah Jesus. I am the holy temple of Yahweh God and no demonic intruders are welcome here.

As all covenants with darkness, idols and evil altars are revoked in Jesus' name; I command every representation of my bloodline, name, image, or DNA be removed from these altars and the altars be destroyed in Jesus' name.

In Jesus' name, I declare that all legal rights and claims of the kingdom of darkness to both me and my bloodline are revoked. I release and detach myself and my family from any hold which any of these demonic forces have, or have had, on our lives. You will loose your grip on us. Your assignments are cancelled. I use the sword of the spirit, the living Word of God that divides between soul and spirit, bone and marrow, and discerns the thoughts and intents of the heart to cut myself and my bloodline free. I bind all you demons together including strongmen and kingdoms and command you to leave me now and take all your dark deposits, disease, and hindrances with you. This is your immediate eviction notice! In Jesus' name, I call upon the host of heaven to assist and remove you from my being, life, bloodline, and future generations and take all of you to the place you are assigned by Jesus to await your judgment. You will all bow the knee at the mighty name of Jesus the Messiah, Name above every name! You are powerless at His feet. Your time is up in my life and my bloodline. This is a complete severing. I command you never to return to us.

In Jesus' name, I declare cancelled every curse against me or against any member of my family and command all those curses to be lifted now. I command any and all touchpoints or connections or portals provided by any marks of darkness to be destroyed now. No longer will I or my bloodline be tracked by darkness through these marks. I petition the blood of the Lamb to seal shut those doors forever, in Jesus' name."

In Jesus' name, I declare severed all unholy soul-ties to any entities or humans involved with darkness. I cancel all their claims on me and my bloodline. I command all of our DNA, destinies, and parts that were attached to these soul-ties to be released from any humans, entities, or holding areas in any realm and be returned to me and all my living relatives, children, and future generations.

I declare that I have been rescued from the kingdom of darkness and brought into the kingdom of the Son who has forgiven and redeemed me. I have been adopted into the family of Yahweh God as a son and I submit freely to Him. Nothing can separate me from His love. I am sealed for the kingdom of God with the Holy Spirit of Yahweh God. I have not been given a spirit of fear, but of power, love, and a sound mind. I declare I am free today in Jesus' name.

From this day forth, I dedicate myself and my bloodline including my children and all my future generations to the God of Abraham, Isaac, and Jacob; the One true God, King of the universe, Creator of heaven and earth. I choose to bless my children and future generations with freedom, favor, truth, health, life, strength, good stewardship, financial prosperity, Godly marriages and relationships, good communication, honor, loyalty, a good work ethic, leadership, faithfulness, peace, joy, love, kindness, compassion, humility, generosity, gratefulness, purity, protection, provision, spiritual discernment, gifts of the Spirit, wisdom, understanding, heavenly knowledge, boldness for the kingdom, and talents and abilities to be used for God's kingdom. May this bloodline be fruitful and multiply abundantly for the kingdom of Yahweh God.

Chapter 20:
Living a Life of Holiness

Now that you have completed the prayers of repentance and renunciation and presented your case in the heavenly courts, it is important to choose to follow Yahweh God in holiness and obedience in the land of promise. After Jesus forgave the sins of the woman caught in adultery and saved her from being stoned as punishment for her sin, He said, "Go and sin no more." John 8:11

It is also recommended that you find a deliverance ministry nearby that can follow up with you in agreement to cast out the demons who have lost their legal rights. Casting out demons is meant to be a ministry to each other in the body of Messiah Jesus. Just like the twelve tribes of Israel fought alongside each other until all possessed their lands, we must fight alongside each other in the battle for victory! If you cannot find a deliverance ministry nearby, there are many that can effectively use "zoom" face-timing online for ministry. It is also a good idea to seek some inner healing, as well.

As you walk out your deliverance, you will need to commit to a life of discipline. Yahweh God has given us His holy way of living to set us apart for His kingdom and to keep us from opening doors to darkness. In John 14:15, Jesus said: "If you love Me, keep My commandments." He followed that in verses 23-24 by saying:

> "If anyone loves Me, he will keep My word; and My Father will love him, and We will come to him and make Our home with him. He who does not love Me does not keep My words; and the word which you hear is not Mine but the Father's who sent Me. John 14:23-24

> For this is the love of God, that we keep His commandments. And His commandments are not burdensome. 1 John 5:3

We show our love to Jesus by following His commands. Jesus and the Father are One. Jesus followed Yahweh's commands to perfection. His commands are not burdensome, for through His covenant, He has given us the Holy Spirit who will help us to walk in them. We must choose to walk in the Spirit and not in the flesh.

Remember the ancient covenant we studied in Chapter One? If a man stepped across the bloodline on the threshold, he chose to enter the covenant. There was also an option two. If he stepped upon the blood in disrespect, he rejected the covenant. We see a reference to this in Zephaniah 1:9:

> In the same day I will punish all those who leap over the threshold, who fill their masters' houses with violence and deceit.

We see a serious warning to those of us in covenant with Yahweh God in Hebrews Chapter 10 referring to disrespecting the covenant.

> For if we sin willfully after we have received the knowledge of the truth, there no longer remains a sacrifice for sins, but a certain fearful expectation of judgment, and fiery indignation which will devour the adversaries. Anyone who has rejected Moses' law dies without mercy on the testimony of two or three witnesses. Of how much worse punishment, do you suppose, will he be thought worthy who has trampled the Son of God underfoot, counted the blood of the covenant by which he was sanctified a common thing, and insulted the Spirit of grace? Hebrews 10:26-29

When we willfully sin, we trample the blood of the covenant, the blood of Jesus, in disrespect; insulting the sacrifice He has made for us and the grace the Father has shown us. Let us therefore choose to keep the covenant and honor the sacrifice Jesus made on our behalf.

The following practices are essential to living a life of holiness before Yahweh God. They will help you grow in your relationship with Him and other believers.

1. Set aside time daily to spend with Yahweh God through worship, prayer, and praise. Remember that He has created a special day of the week just to spend time with you! The Sabbath is that special day.
2. Read your Bible and ask the Holy Spirit to give you wisdom and understanding as you read. Yahweh will give you better understanding of His holy way of living as you read His words. They are living and powerful.
3. Seek Yahweh for the plan and purpose He has for your life. Because you were created for His purpose, it will bring you more joy than you can imagine.
4. Find a group of believers to meet with regularly, to encourage you and help you to stay accountable to your covenant. Therefore, confess your sins to each other and pray for each other so that you may be healed. The prayer of a righteous person is powerful and effective. James 5:16
5. Resist the temptations and tricks of the enemy, and repent immediately if you fall into sin. Don't fall back into slavery to sin or let it reign in your body or soul. Submit yourself to God, resist the devil, and he will flee. Romans 12:1-2
6. Take Holy Communion regularly to remember your covenant.

7. Forgive as soon as the offense occurs. Don't allow bitterness to take root. "Be angry, and do not sin": do not let the sun go down on your wrath, nor give place to the devil. Ephesians 4:26-27

8. Stay away from people and places that brought temptation in the past. Start some new hobbies and habits to use for God's glory. You are a new creation.

9. Put on your armor from Ephesians chapter 6 daily. Our God has provided us with armor and weapons to fight the battle with the enemies of heaven. Those enemies are not flesh and blood, but the powers of darkness. Be equipped for the battle.

10. Pray in the spirit to build up your inner man and release the plans of heaven on earth.

May the blessings of Yahweh God overcome you as you follow Him. You have been redeemed to the promise of Abraham and Yahweh's chosen people. You have been grafted into the tree of Israel. May the following blessings come upon you and your house:

"Now it shall come to pass, if you diligently obey the voice of the Lord your God, to observe carefully all His commandments which I command you today, that the Lord your God will set you high above all nations of the earth. And all these blessings shall come upon you and overtake you, because you obey the voice of the Lord your God:

"Blessed shall you be in the city, and blessed shall you be in the country.

"Blessed shall be the fruit of your body, the produce of your ground and the increase of your herds, the increase of your cattle and the offspring of your flocks.

"Blessed shall be your basket and your kneading bowl.

"Blessed shall you be when you come in, and blessed shall you be when you go out.

"The Lord will cause your enemies who rise against you to be defeated before your face; they shall come out against you one way and flee before you seven ways.

"The Lord will command the blessing on you in your storehouses and in all to which you set your hand, and He will bless you in the land which the Lord your God is giving you. Deuteronomy 28:1-8

May you find favor with God and man as you begin a new journey in freedom and shalom. May you fulfill everything that Yahweh God has written in your book. Fight the good fight of faith!

"The Lord bless you and keep you; The Lord make His face shine upon you, and be gracious to you; The Lord lift up His countenance upon you, and give you peace."' Numbers 6:24-26

Chapter 21:
Prayer Partners and Deliverance Ministers

This chapter is for those of you who have been through your own deliverance or who have been set free through the Biblical principles in this book and want to help your friends find freedom. It is very powerful to come into agreement with someone as they choose to repent and renounce to remove the legal rights the enemy has had to keep them in bondage. It is also helpful to have someone come alongside of you to cast out the demons who have lost their legal rights. It is a ministry we have to each other in the body of Messiah, just like the Israelites fought alongside each other to possess the land of promise.

When Messiah Jesus was resurrected from the dead, He was given all authority.

> And Jesus came and spoke to them, saying, "All authority has been given to Me in heaven and on earth. Go therefore and make disciples of all the nations, baptizing them in the name of the Father and of the Son and of the Holy Spirit, teaching them to observe all things that I have commanded you; and lo, I am with you always, even to the end of the age." Amen. Matthew 28:18-20

Messiah Jesus gave His disciples authority in His name. They could cast out demons or unclean spirits.

> And when He had called His twelve disciples to Him, He gave them power over unclean spirits, to cast them out, and to heal all kinds of sickness and all kinds of disease. Matthew 10:1

> And as you go, preach, saying, 'The kingdom of heaven is at hand.' Heal the sick, cleanse the lepers, raise the dead, cast out demons. Freely you have received, freely give. Matthew 10:7-8

They would also be protected as they did this.

> And He said to them, "I saw Satan fall like lightning from heaven. Behold, I give you the authority to trample on serpents and scorpions, and over all the power of the enemy, and nothing shall by any means hurt you. Nevertheless do not rejoice in this, that the

spirits are subject to you, but rather rejoice because your names are written in heaven." Luke 10:18-20

We read in the scriptures that spirit-filled believers in Messiah Jesus who have been born again can use His name and authority to cast out demons.

And He said to them, "Go into all the world and preach the gospel to every creature. He who believes and is baptized will be saved; but he who does not believe will be condemned. And these signs will follow those who believe: In My name they will cast out demons; they will speak with new tongues; they will take up serpents; and if they drink anything deadly, it will by no means hurt them; they will lay hands on the sick, and they will recover." Mark 16:15-18

It is important for you as the deliverance minister to be baptized in the Holy Spirit and to be living a holy life. Fasting and prayer before the deliverance time is a good way to defeat unbelief and help prepare you to minister deliverance. Before you begin the deliverance, it's a good idea to spend time with the Holy Spirit and ask if there is anything you, as the deliverance minister, need to release to Him or anything that needs repentance. Checking your own inventory is wise before assisting others.

The person you are assisting should complete this manual and compile a list of demons that have been revealed to them through the Holy Spirit in the process of self-deliverance. They can be specific names or can be named by their actions ex: anger, rage, murder, fear, etc. Make sure the demons worshiped by ancestors are on the list. You can pray together for the Holy Spirit to reveal anything else before you begin to cast them out. Strongmen may surface during the actual deliverance. They may have common names or uncommon names. Just add them to the list at the time.

It is wonderful to minister in twos just like Jesus' disciples did, but if you are alone, the Holy Spirit can be your witness and partner. You can declare the following before starting and prophetically act it out:

With a strand of three cords, I bind the hands and feet of all demonic forces in and with _____ and command you not to harm me or _____. I place the blood of Jesus between us as we proceed. You are forbidden to torment _____ during these proceedings.

You will be coming before the throne of mercy and grace in agreement with the one who needs deliverance. Although we can come boldly before this throne in the name of Jesus, we also humbly show all respect before the Almighty One Who was and is and is to come. Remember that you are standing in the spirit realm in the heavenly courts before the Great Judge of All. This is a place where you will testify, bring evidence, agree in word and declaration, and then cast out the demons who have lost their legal rights. You will be an ambassador of Jesus' mighty name.

Please speak the following declaration and agreement out loud with the person receiving deliverance:

Yahweh God, Creator of Heaven and Earth, Ruler and Judge of All, we come into Your courts today with thanksgiving and praise. We thank You for ruling on behalf of _____ and the prayers and petitions she (he) has brought before You. We thank You that Messiah Jesus led captivity captive and defeated death and hell. He wiped out the charges against _____ by nailing them to the cross. He disarmed the principalities and powers, made them a public spectacle, and triumphed over them.

Today, as we stand before the throne of mercy and grace, I stand as a witness to _____ prayers of petition, repentance, renunciation, and declaration and am in agreement with them. As a part of the body of Messiah Jesus, I come as an ambassador of the name of Jesus the Messiah to cast out demons as He has commanded me.

All you demons who have been harassing and tormenting _____ have been served a subpoena to trial to receive your sentence and eviction notice from the life and bloodline of the defendant. You have been called before the throne of the Ancient of Days, Yahweh Elohim, the God of Abraham, Isaac, and Jacob. You will surrender all your weapons to the heavenly host right now and release your afflictions over _____. You will bow the knee and submit to the Name above every name, Jesus the Messiah. You will only speak upon request and will not lie before the Great Judge of All.

You and your plans have been exposed by the Light of the world. Everything is laid bare before Yahweh God and His government. All the evidence has been presented against you. You will not lie or delay. There is no plea bargaining. This is your final day in this woman (man). You cannot be forgiven or redeemed. You will never return to this woman (man) or her (his) bloodline. Your assignments and curses have been revoked and your evil reign is over.

As an ambassador of the mighty name of Jesus the Messiah, I cut you off from any help from the second heavens, and I call upon the heavenly host to assist with this eviction and enforce the ruling made in the courts today on behalf of _____ and all her (his) generations. I use the sword of the Spirt that is living and powerful, sharper than any two-edged sword, to divide _____ soul from any and all evil spirits and entities that have lost legal rights through these declarations. (Prophetically use the sword now to detach the person from the evil spirits.)

I declare _____ has made covenant with Yahweh God through the blood of Jesus the Messiah and has trusted in the sacrifice made by Him to bring her (his) salvation and entrance to the kingdom of God. She (he) has been born again and made a new creation. All covenants connected to the old man who died are null and void. _____ belongs to Yahweh and her (his) body is a temple of His Holy Spirit. Through her (his) confession and renunciation today and in the past, all your legal rights to her (him) have been removed. If any of you claim any legal rights to _____, you must speak now or forever hold your peace.

(Demons may now speak through the person's mouth or into the person's mind. If you do not hear an audible answer, ask the person if she (he) hears anything. If it is "Yes", continue with the questioning.)

Today you will obey my commands as a woman (man) of God, and ambassador of the name of Jesus. I command you to answer all questions truthfully and without delay. What is your legal right?

(If the spirit gives a legal right, you must deal with it accordingly. If the legal right has been dealt with already, say so. If it is a true legal right that has not been dealt with, go back to the prayers and deal with it before continuing. Ask again until the answer is "no" or silence.)

As you evil spirits are evicted today, I command you to return everything you have stolen from _____ and remove all your deposits from her (his) body and soul, including jewelry, clothing, weapons, seals, programming, triggering, nets, webs, grids, hooks, pulleys, snares, shackles, chains, radars, targets, marks, brands, evil cycles or time clocks, bonds, defilement, bounties, satellites, chips, evil technologies, trackers, tattoos, bondage, captivity, death, destruction, torment, torture, sickness, disease, symptoms, guards, blinders, scramblers, confusion, distraction, stumbling blocks, masks, duct tape, superglue, stitches, gags, hindrances, ties, and any other deposit of darkness or points of contact. You will release her (him) and her (his) bloodline immediately from all curses, hexes, vexes, spells, attachments, and assignments and will leave today with all your kingdom, gatekeepers, and door openers. You will take no traces or parts of _____ or her (his) bloodline with you. You will cause no harm to her (him) as you leave.

(Look into the eyes of the person you are ministering to over the next few steps as you speak to the demons and cast them out. Let the person know, you are not addressing her (him). You are speaking to the demons.)

In the mighty name of Jesus, I bind the strongmen in _____ life now and command you to speak your names.

(Write down the names of the strongmen as they are spoken. There are usually at least three or more. You may ask questions like "Who else is there?" "Who is next?" "I command you to speak in the name of Jesus." "Is anyone left?" "You must obey and bow the knee at the mighty name of Jesus!" When you have all the names, add them to the list from the previous chapters.)

As I call out your names, you will all be bound together as one. (Call out all the names on the list.)

I call upon the host of heaven to assist with the removal of the spirits and to take them to the feet of Jesus to be dealt with as He commands. I command all of the spirits named and all other evil spirits who have lost their legal rights to _____ and her (his) bloodline to leave now in the name of Jesus! Go! Come out in Jesus' name! Out now! Freedom in the name of Jesus the Messiah! Out of her (his) body, soul, spirit, being, life, and bloodline, NOW! Your time is up!

You will continue to command them out until the person feels complete release and freedom. This may take several minutes. You will need to ask the person if all of the demons are gone. Assess if she (he) is still feeling discomfort or can still feel the battle going on. Demons frequently come out on the breath. Some may cry or scream. Some people cough or gag but seldom vomit from the stomach. You may need a garbage can in rare instances.

If nothing is happening, you can encourage the person to blow or cough to release the demons. Sometimes they leave through certain body parts or other manifestation like burping or passing gas. Sometimes the spirits try to get stuck somewhere or move throughout the body hoping to hide. Just continue to command them out in Jesus' name. They must obey if their legal rights have been removed.

Looking back at taking ground in the promised land in Deuteronomy, we find two mighty weapons of Yahweh God used against the inhabitants of the land. The first one is hornets. These are sent against the people who are hiding to keep from being removed.

> Moreover the Lord your God will send the hornet among them until those who are left, who hide themselves from you, are destroyed. Deuteronomy 7:20

You can send these hornets of God in to find any demon squatters that are hiding or resisting deliverance. You can also send the fire of God into those areas to drive them out. Both these weapons are powerful!

> Therefore understand today that the Lord your God is He who goes over before you as a consuming fire. He will destroy them and bring them down before you; so you shall drive them out and destroy them quickly, as the Lord has said to you. Deuteronomy 9:3

When the person is free, use the anointing oil and pray a prayer of healing over her (him). Ask for the Holy Spirit to seal all doors that were opened to the demonic realm and place His own seal on the person. Ask Him to fill all the spaces vacated by the demons and to build His kingdom in the person. Pray that her (his) spiritual eyes be opened into Yahweh's kingdom. Release the fire of the Holy Spirit into her (his) body to cleanse and restore. Finally, pray a blessing over her (him).

Chapter 22:
Power Verses

Over the next few months, don't be surprised if the enemy tries to convince you that you are not free. It is very common to have those thoughts or to think that it will not work for you. Although this strategy is coming from the outside, it can still be convincing. Our adversary will try to take ground in our lives as long as we have breath, but, now that you are free, it will be easier to resist him. You can speak out loud and rebuke him. *"I take authority over the darkness that is telling me lies. I rebuke you and command you to leave my presence, in Jesus' name."*

You will also need some power verses to fight him.

> For the word of God is living and powerful, and sharper than any two-edged sword, piercing even to the division of soul and spirit, and of joints and marrow, and is a discerner of the thoughts and intents of the heart. Hebrews 4:12

> "Is not My word like a fire?" says the Lord, "and like a hammer that breaks the rock in pieces?" Jeremiah 23:29

> For though we walk in the flesh, we do not war according to the flesh. For the weapons of our warfare are not carnal but mighty in God for pulling down strongholds, casting down arguments and every high thing that exalts itself against the knowledge of God, bringing every thought into captivity to the obedience of Christ, and being ready to punish all disobedience when your obedience is fulfilled. 2 Corinthians 10:3-5

The Word of God is a powerful weapon! It is a sword that can divide soul from spirit. It is fire and a hammer that shatters rock. As you memorize scripture that is relevant to your battle, you will be building an arsenal against the forces of darkness.

There are many power verses sprinkled throughout this manual. You may find some in the chapters that were greatly relevant to you personally. I will list some others here, but it is very easy to find topical scriptures through a quick search online. You may need to make these verses personal to use them as weapons (use "me" instead of "you"). Remember to speak them out loud. You may also want to prophetically swordfight in the air as you speak them!

No weapon formed against you shall prosper, and every tongue which rises against you in judgment you shall condemn. This is the heritage of the servants of the Lord, and their righteousness is from Me," says the Lord. Isaiah 54:17

But the Lord is faithful, who will establish you and guard you from the evil one. 2 Thessalonians 3:3

You are of God, little children, and have overcome them, because He who is in you is greater than he who is in the world. 1 John 4:4

"Assuredly, I say to you, whatever you bind on earth will be bound in heaven, and whatever you loose on earth will be loosed in heaven. "Again, I say to you that if two of you agree on earth concerning anything that they ask, it will be done for them by My Father in heaven. For where two or three are gathered together in My name, I am there in the midst of them." Matthew 18:18-20

Behold, I give you the authority to trample on serpents and scorpions, and over all the power of the enemy, and nothing shall by any means hurt you. Luke 10:19

And they overcame him by the blood of the Lamb and by the word of their testimony, and they did not love their lives to the death. Revelation 12:11

And the Lord will deliver me from every evil work and preserve me for His heavenly kingdom. To Him be glory forever and ever. Amen! 2 Timothy 4:8

It shall come to pass in that day that his burden will be taken away from your shoulder, and his yoke from your neck, and the yoke will be destroyed because of the anointing oil. Isaiah 10:27

So shall they fear the name of the Lord from the west, and His glory from the rising of the sun; when the enemy comes in like a flood, the Spirit of the Lord will lift up a standard against him. Isaiah 59:19

There are so many warfare verses in the book of Psalms! Because they are written as prayers, you can just speak them straight out.

The Lord is my light and my salvation; whom shall I fear? The Lord is the strength of my life; of whom shall I be afraid? When the wicked came against me to eat up my flesh, my enemies and foes, they stumbled and fell. Psalm 27:1-2

Let God arise, let His enemies be scattered; let those also who hate Him flee before Him. As smoke is driven away, so drive them away; as wax melts before the fire, so let the wicked perish at the presence of God. But let the righteous be glad; let them rejoice before God; yes, let them rejoice exceedingly. Psalm 68:1-3

I shall not die, but live, and declare the works of the Lord. Psalm 118:17

I will both lie down in peace, and sleep; for You alone, O Lord, make me dwell in safety. Psalm 4:8

I called on the Lord in distress; the Lord answered me and set me in a broad place. The Lord is on my side; I will not fear. What can man do to me? Psalm 118:6

I sought the Lord, and He heard me, and delivered me from all my fears. They looked to Him and were radiant, and their faces were not ashamed. This poor man cried out, and the Lord heard him, and saved him out of all his troubles. The angel of the Lord encamps all around those who fear Him, and delivers them. Psalm 34:4-7

Whenever I am afraid, I will trust in You. Psalm 56:3

Because you have made the Lord, who is my refuge, even the Most High, your dwelling place, no evil shall befall you, nor shall any plague come near your dwelling; for He shall give His angels charge over you, to keep you in all your ways. In their hands they shall bear you up, lest you dash your foot against a stone. You shall tread upon the lion and the cobra, the young lion and the serpent you shall trample underfoot. "Because he has set his love upon Me, therefore I will deliver him; I will set him on high, because he has known My name. He shall call upon Me, and I will answer him; I will be with him in trouble; I will deliver him and honor him. With long life I will satisfy him, and show him My salvation." Psalm 91:9-16

I have compiled a special weapon from the Psalms. This one is very powerful. As you speak it, the battle manifests literally in the spirit realm against your enemies.

I will love You, O Lord, my strength. The Lord is my rock and my fortress and my deliverer; my God, my strength, in whom I will trust; my shield and the horn of my salvation, my stronghold. I will call upon the Lord, who is worthy to be praised; so, shall I be saved from my enemies. (1-3) He sent out His arrows and scattered the foe, lightnings in abundance, and He vanquished them. (14) He delivered me from my strong enemy, (17) He is a shield to all who trust in Him. (30) It is God who arms me with strength, and makes my way perfect. He makes my feet like the feet of deer, and sets me on my high places. He teaches my hands to make war, so that my arms can bend a bow of bronze. (32-34) You have also given me the shield of Your salvation; (35) You enlarged my path under me, so my feet did not slip. (36) He delivers me from my enemies. You also lift me up above those who rise against me; You have delivered me from the violent man. (48) (Psalm 18)

Depart from me, all you workers of iniquity; for the Lord has heard the voice of my weeping. Let all my enemies be ashamed and greatly troubled; let them turn back and be ashamed suddenly. (Psalm 6:8,10)

Upon the wicked He will rain coals; fire and brimstone and a burning wind shall be the portion of their cup. (Psalm 11:6)

Arise, O Lord, confront him, cast him down; deliver my life from the wicked with Your sword, (Psalm 17:13)

Be exalted, O Lord, in Your own strength! We will sing and praise Your power. (Psalm 21:13)

Prayer of Release for Freemasons & their Descendants

& PETITION FOR WITHDRAWING (Demit)

from Unmasking Freemasonry Removing the Hoodwink

by Selwyn R. Stevens, Ph.D

If you were once a member of a Masonic organization or are a descendant of someone who was, we recommend that you pray through this prayer from your heart. Please don't be like the Freemasons who are given their obligations and oaths one line at a time and without prior knowledge of the requirements. Please read it through first so you know what is involved. It is best to pray this aloud with a mature Christian present. We suggest a brief pause following each paragraph to allow the Holy Spirit to show any related issues which may require attention.

A significant number of people also reported having experienced physical and spiritual healings as diverse as long-term headaches, bad backs, nightmares, heart conditions and epilepsy as the result of praying through this prayer. Christian counselors and pastors in many countries have been using this prayer in ministry and counselling situations for over two decades, with real and significant results.

Some language could be described as 'quaint Old English' and are the real terms used in the Masonic ritual. The legal renunciation opens the way for spiritual, emotional and physical healing to take place.

There are differences between British Commonwealth Masonry and American & Prince Hall Masonry in the higher degrees. Degrees unique to Americans are marked with this sign "*" at the commencement of each paragraph. Those of British Commonwealth decent shouldn't need to pray through those paragraphs.

"Father God, creator of heaven and earth, I come to you in the name of Jesus Christ your Son. I come as a sinner seeking forgiveness and cleansing from all sins committed against you, and others made in your image. I honor my earthly father and mother and all of my ancestors of flesh and blood, and of the spirit by adoption and godparents, but I utterly turn away from and renounce all their sins. I forgive all my ancestors for the effects of their sins on me and my children. I confess and renounce all of my own sins, known or unknown. I renounce and rebuke Satan and every spiritual power of his affecting me and my family, in the name of Jesus Christ.

True Holy Creator God, in the name of the True Lord Jesus Christ, in accordance with Jude 8-10; Psalm 82:1 and 2 Chronicles 18, I request you to move aside all Celestial Beings, including Principalities, Powers and Rulers, and to forbid them to harass, intimidate or retaliate against me and all participants in this ministry today.

I also ask that you prevent these beings of whatever rank, to not be permitted to send any level of spiritual evil as retaliation against any of those here, or our families, our ministries, or possessions.

I renounce and annul every covenant made with Death by my ancestors or myself, including every agreement made with Sheol, and I renounce the refuge of lies and falsehoods which have been hidden behind.

In the name of the Lord Jesus Christ I renounce and forsake all involvement in Freemasonry or any other lodge, craft or occultism by my ancestors and myself. I also renounce and break the code of silence enforced by Freemasonry and the Occult on my family and me. I renounce and repent of all pride and arrogance which opened the door for the slavery and bondage of Freemasonry to afflict my family and me. I now shut every door of witchcraft and deception operating in my life and seal it closed with the blood of the Lord Jesus Christ. I renounce every covenant, every blood covenant and every alliance with Freemasonry or the spiritual powers behind it made by my family or me. In the name of Jesus Christ, I rebuke, renounce and bind Witchcraft, the principal spirit behind Freemasonry, and I renounce and rebuke Baphomet, the Spirit of Antichrist and also the spirits of Death, and Deception.

I renounce and rebuke the Spirit of Fides, the Roman goddess of Fidelity that seeks to hold all Masonic and occultic participants and their descendants in bondage, and I ask the One True Holy Creator God to give me the gift of Faith to believe in the True Lord Jesus Christ as described in the Word of God.

I also renounce and rebuke the Spirit of Prostitution which the Word of God says has led members of Masonic and other Occultic organizations astray, and caused them to become unfaithful to the One True and Holy God. I now choose to return and become faithful to the God of the Bible, the God of Abraham, Isaac and Jacob, the Father of Jesus Christ, who I now declare is my Lord and Savior.

I renounce the insecurity, the love of position and power, the love of money, avarice or greed, and the pride which would have led my ancestors into Freemasonry. I renounce all the fears which held them in Freemasonry, especially the fears of death, fears of men, and fears of trusting, in the name of Jesus Christ.

I renounce every position held in the lodge by any of my ancestors or myself, including "Grand Master," "Worshipful Master," or any other occultic title. I renounce the calling of any man "Master," for Jesus Christ is my only master and Lord, and He forbids anyone else having that title. I renounce the entrapping of others into Freemasonry, and observing the helplessness of others during the rituals. I renounce the effects of Masonry passed on to me through any female ancestor who felt distrusted and rejected by her husband as he entered and attended any lodge and refused to tell her of his secret activities. I also renounce all obligations, oaths, curses and iniquities enacted by every female member of my family through any direct membership of all Women's Orders of Freemasonry, the Order of the Eastern Star, or any other Masonic or occultic organisation.

Removing the Unholy Garments

(All participants should now be invited to sincerely carry out in faith the following actions:

(1) Symbolically remove the blindfold (hoodwink) and give it to the Lord for disposal;

(2) In the same way, symbolically remove the veil of mourning, to make way to receive the Joy of the Lord;

(3) Symbolically cut and remove the noose from around the neck, gather it up with the cabletow running down the body and give it all to the Lord for His disposal;

(4) Renounce the false Freemasonry marriage covenant, removing from the 4th finger of the right hand the ring of this false marriage covenant, giving it to the Lord to dispose of it;

(5) Symbolically remove the chains and bondages of Freemasonry from your body;

(6) Symbolically remove all Freemasonry regalia, including collars, gauntlets and armor, especially the Apron with its snake clasp, to make way for the Belt of Truth;

(7) Remove the slipshod slippers to make way for the shoes of the Gospel of Peace;

(8) Symbolically remove t he ball and chain from the ankles;

(9) Invite participants to repent of and seek forgiveness for having walked on all unholy ground, including Freemasonry lodges and temples, including any Mormon or any other occultic and Masonic organizations;

(10) Proclaim that Satan and his demons no longer have any legal rights to mislead and manipulate the person seeking help.)

33rd & Supreme Degree

In the name of Jesus Christ, I renounce the oaths taken and the curses and iniquities involved in the supreme Thirty-Third Degree of Freemasonry, the Grand Sovereign Inspector General. I renounce the secret passwords, DEMOLAY-HIRUM ABIFF, FREDERICK OF PRUSSIA, MICHA, MACHA, BEALIM, and ADONAI and all their occult and Masonic meaning. I renounce all of the obligations of every Freemasonry degree, and all penalties invoked. I renounce and utterly forsake The Great Architect Of The Universe, who is revealed in the this degree as Lucifer, and his false claim to be the universal fatherhood of God. I reject the Masonic view of deity because it does not square with the revelation of the One True and Holy Creator God of the Bible. I renounce the cabletow around the neck. I renounce the death wish that the wine drunk from a human skull should turn to poison and the skeleton whose cold arms are invited if the oath of this degree is violated. I renounce the three infamous assassins of their grand master, law, property and religion, and the greed and witchcraft involved in the attempt to manipulate and control the rest of mankind. In the name of God the Father, Jesus Christ the Son, and the Holy Spirit, I renounce and break the curses and iniquities involved in the idolatry, blasphemy, secrecy and deception of Freemasonry at every level. I renounce the Pantheism of the Ancient and Accepted Rite of English and American Freemasonry, and the Atheism of Grand Orient Freemasonry. I appropriate the Blood of Jesus Christ to cleanse all the consequences of these from my life. I now revoke all previous consent given by any of my ancestors or myself to be deceived.

Blue Lodge

In the name of Jesus Christ, I renounce the oaths taken and the curses and iniquities involved in the First or Entered Apprentice Degree, especially their effects on the throat and tongue. I renounce the Hoodwink blindfold and its effects on spirit, emotions and eyes, including all confusion, fear of the dark, fear of the light, and fear of sudden noises. I renounce the blinding of spiritual truth, the darkness of the soul, the false imagination, condescension and the spirit of poverty caused by the ritual of this degree. I also renounce the usurping of the marriage covenant by the removal of the wedding ring. I renounce the secret word, BOAZ, and it's Masonic meaning. I renounce the serpent clasp on the apron, and the spirit of Python which it brought to squeeze the spiritual life out of me. I renounce the ancient pagan teaching from Babylon and Egypt and the symbolism of the First Tracing Board. I renounce the mixing and mingling of truth and error, the mythology, fabrications and lies taught as truth, and the dishonesty by leaders as to the true understanding of the ritual, and the blasphemy of this degree of Freemasonry. I renounce the breaking of five of God's Ten Commandments during participation in the rituals of the Blue Lodge degrees. I renounce the presentation to every compass direction, for all the Earth is the Lord's, and everything in it. I renounce the cabletow noose around the neck, the fear of choking and also every spirit causing asthma, hayfever, emphysema or any other breathing difficulty. I renounce the ritual dagger, or the compass point, sword or spear held against the breast, the fear of death by stabbing pain, and the fear of heart attack from this degree, and the absolute secrecy demanded under a witchcraft oath and sealed by kissing the Volume of the Sacred Law. I also renounce kneeling to the false deity known as the Great Architect of the Universe, and humbly ask the One True God to forgive me for this idolatry, in the name of Jesus Christ. I renounce the pride of proven character and good standing required prior to joining Freemasonry, and the resulting self-righteousness of being good enough to stand before God without the need of a saviour. In the name of Jesus Christ, I now command healing of my throat, vocal cords, nasal passages, sinus and bronchial tubes, for healing of the speech area, and the release of the Word of God to me and through me and my family.

In the name of Jesus Christ, I renounce the oaths taken and the curses and iniquities involved in the Second or Fellow Craft Degree of Masonry, especially the curses on the heart and chest. I renounce the secret words SHIBBOLETH and JACHIN, and all their Masonic meaning. I renounce the ancient pagan teaching and symbolism of the Second Tracing Board. I renounce the Sign of Reverence to the Generative Principle. I cut off emotional hardness, apathy, indifference, unbelief, and deep anger from me and my family. In the name of Jesus' Christ, I now command healing of the chest/lung/heart area, and also for the healing of my emotions, and ask to be made sensitive to the Holy Spirit of God.

In the name of Jesus Christ, I renounce the oaths taken and the curses and iniquities involved in the Third or Master Mason Degree, especially the curses on the stomach and womb area. I renounce the secret words TUBAL CAIN and MAHA BONE, and all that their Masonic meaning. I renounce the ancient pagan teaching and symbolism of the Third Tracing Board used in the ritual. I renounce the Spirit of Death from the blows to the head enacted as ritual murder, the fear of death, false martyrdom, fear of violent gang attack, assault, or rape, and the helplessness of this degree. I renounce the falling into the coffin or stretcher involved in the ritual of murder. In the name of Jesus Christ, I renounce Hiram Abiff, the false saviour of Freemasons revealed in this degree. I renounce the false resurrection of this degree, because only Jesus Christ is the Resurrection and the Life! I also reject the false and pagan view of immortality presented in this degree. I renounce the pagan ritual of the "Point within a Circle" with all its bondages and phallus worship. I renounce the symbol "G" and its veiled pagan symbolism and bondages. I renounce the occultic mysticism of the black and white mosaic chequered floor with the tessellated boarder and five-pointed blazing star from ancient witchcraft. I renounce the All-Seeing Third Eye of Freemasonry or Horus in the forehead and its pagan and occult symbolism. I rebuke and reject every spirit of divination which allowed this occult ability to operate. (Action: put hand over forehead) I now close that Third eye and all occult ability to see into the spiritual realm, in the name of the Lord Jesus Christ, and put my trust in the Holy Spirit sent by Jesus Christ for all I need to know on spiritual matters. I renounce all false communions taken, all mockery of the redemptive work of Jesus Christ on the cross of Calvary, all unbelief, confusion and depression. I renounce and forsake the lie of Freemasonry that man is not sinful, but merely imperfect, and so can redeem himself through good works. I rejoice that the Bible states that I cannot do a single thing to earn my salvation, but that I can only be saved by grace through faith in Jesus Christ and what He accomplished on the Cross of Calvary. I renounce all fear of insanity, anguish, death wishes, suicide and death in the name of Jesus Christ. Death was conquered by Jesus Christ, and He alone holds the keys of death and hell, and I rejoice that He holds my life in His hands now. He came to give me life abundantly and eternally, and I believe His promises. I renounce all anger, hatred, murderous thoughts, revenge, retaliation, spiritual apathy, false religion, all unbelief, especially unbelief in the Holy Bible as God's Word, and all compromise of God's Word. I renounce all spiritual searching into false religions, and all striving to please God. I rest in the knowledge that I have found my Lord and Savior Jesus Christ, and that He has found me. In the name of Jesus Christ, I now command healing of my stomach, gall bladder, womb, liver, and any other organs of my body affected by Masonry, and I ask for a release of compassion and understanding for me and my family.

York Rite

I renounce and forsake the oaths taken and the curses and iniquities involved in the York Rite Degrees of Masonry. I renounce the Mark Lodge, and the mark in the form of squares and angles which marks the person for life. I also reject the jewel or occult talisman which may have been made from this mark sign and worn at lodge meetings; I renounce and forsake the oaths taken and the curses and iniquities involved in the Mark Master Degree with its secret word JOPPA, and its penalty of having the right ear smote or cut off and the curse of permanent deafness, as well as the right hand being chopped off for being an imposter. I also renounce and forsake the oaths taken and the curses and iniquities involved in the other York Rite Degrees, including Past Master, with the penalty of having my tongue split from tip to root; and of the Most Excellent Master Degree, in which the penalty is to have my breast torn open and my heart and vital organs removed and exposed to rot on the dung hill.

Holy Royal Arch Degree

In the name of Jesus Christ, I renounce and forsake the oaths taken and the curses and iniquities involved in the Holy Royal Arch Degree especially the oath regarding the removal of the head from the body and the exposing of the brains to the hot sun. I renounce the false secret name of God, JAHBULON, and declare total rejection of all worship of the false pagan gods, Bul or Baal, and On or Osiris. I also renounce the password, AMMI RUHAMAH and its occultic meaning. I renounce the false communion or Eucharist taken in this degree, and all the mockery, scepticism and unbelief about the redemptive work of Jesus Christ on the cross of Calvary. I cut off all these curses and their effects on me and my family in the name of Jesus Christ, and I command healing of the brain and the mind.

I renounce and forsake the oaths taken and the curses and iniquities involved in the Royal Master Degree of the York Rite; the Select Master Degree with its penalty to have my hands chopped off to the stumps, to have my eyes plucked out from their sockets, and to have my body quartered and thrown among the rubbish of the Temple. I renounce and forsake the oaths taken and the curses and iniquities involved in the Super Excellent Master Degree along with the penalty of having my thumbs cut off, my eyes put out, my body bound in fetters or shackles and brass, and conveyed captive to a strange land; and also of the Knights or Illustrious Order of the Red Cross, along with the penalty of having my house torn down and my being hanged on the exposed timbers. I renounce the Knights Templar Degree and the secret words of KEB RAIOTH, and also Knights of Malta Degree and the secret words MAHER-SHALAL-HASH-BAZ. I renounce the vows taken on a human skull, the crossed swords, and the curse and death wish of Judas of having the head cut off and placed on top of a church spire. I also renounce the unholy communion.

Ancient & Accepted or Scottish Rite

(NOTE: in this rite, only the 18th, 30th, 31st 32nd & 33rd degree are operated in British Commonwealth countries.)

* I renounce the oaths taken and the curses, iniquities and penalties involved in the American and Grand Orient Lodges, including of the Secret Master Degree, its secret passwords of ADONAI and ZIZA, and their occult meanings. I reject and renounce the worship of the pagan sun god as the Great Source of Light, and the crowning with laurel - sacred to Apollo, and the sign of secrecy in obedience to Horus;

* of the Perfect Master Degree, its secret password of MAH-HAH-BONE, and its penalty of being struck to the Earth with a setting maul;

* of the Intimate Secretary Degree, its secret passwords of YEVA and JOABERT, and its penalties of having my body dissected, and of having my vital organs cut into pieces and thrown to the beasts of the field, and of the use of the nine-pointed star from the Kabbala and the worship of Phallic energy;

* of the Provost and Judge Degree, its secret password of HIRUM-TITO-CIVI-KY, and the penalty of having my nose cut off;

* of the Intendant of the Building Degree, of its secret password AKAR-JAI-JAH, and the penalty of having my eyes put out, my body cut in two and exposing my bowels;

 * of the Elected Knights of the Nine Degree, its secret password NEKAM NAKAH, and its penalty of having my head cut off and stuck on the highest pole in the East;

* of the Illustrious Elect of Fifteen Degree, with its secret password ELIGNAM, and its penalties of having my body opened perpendicularly and horizontally, the entrails exposed to the air for eight hours so that flies may prey on them, and for my head to be cut off and placed on a high pinnacle;

* of the Sublime Knights elect of the Twelve Degree, its secret password STOLKIN-ADONAI, and its penalty of having my hand cut in two;

* of the Grand Master Architect Degree, its secret password RABBANAIM, and its penalties;

* of the Knight of the Ninth Arch of Solomon or Enoch Degree, its secret password JEHOVAH, it's blasphemous use, its penalty of having my body given to the beasts of the forest as prey, and I also renounce the revelations from the Kabbala in this and subsequent degrees;

* of the Grand Elect, Perfect and Sublime Mason or Elu Degree, its secret password MARAH-MAUR-ABREK and IHUH, the penalty of having my body cut open and my bowels given to vultures for food, and I reject the Great Unknowable deity of this degree;

Council of Princes of Jerusalem

* of the Knights of the East Degree, its secret password RAPH-ODOM, and its penalties; * of the Prince of Jerusalem Degree, its secret password TEBETADAR, and its penalty of being stripped naked and having my heart pierced with a ritual dagger;

Chapter of the Rose Croix

* of the Knight of the East and West Degree, its secret password ABADDON, and its penalty of incurring the severe wrath of the Almighty Creator of Heaven and Earth. I also reject the Tetractys and its representation of the Sephiroth from the Kabbala and its false tree of life. I also reject the false anointing with oil and the proclamation that anyone so anointed is now worthy to open the Book of Seven Seals, because only the Lord Jesus Christ is worthy;

18th Degree

I renounce the oaths taken and the curses, iniquities and penalties involved in the Eighteenth Degree of Freemasonry, the Most Wise Sovereign Knight of the Pelican and the Eagle and Sovereign Prince Rose Croix of Heredom. I renounce and reject the false Jesus revealed in this degree because He doesn't point to the light or the truth since the True Lord Jesus Christ is the Light of the World and the Truth. I renounce and reject the Pelican witchcraft spirit, as well as the occultic influence of the Rosicrucians and the Kabbala in this degree. I renounce the claim that the death of Jesus Christ was a "dire calamity," and also the deliberate mockery and twisting of the Christian doctrine of the Atonement. I renounce the blasphemy and rejection of the deity of Jesus Christ, and the secret words IGNE NATURA RENOVATUR INTEGRA and its burning. I renounce the mockery of the communion taken in this degree, including a biscuit, salt and white wine.

Council of Kadosh

I renounce the inappropriate use of the title "Kadosh" used in these council degrees because it means "Holy" and it is here used in a unholy way.

* I renounce the oaths taken and the curses, iniquities and penalties involved in the Grand Pontiff Degree, its secret password EMMANUEL, and its penalties;

* of the Grand Master of Symbolic Lodges or Ad Vitum Degree, its secret passwords JEKSON and STOLKIN, and the penalties invoked, and I also reject the pagan Phoenician and Hindu deities revealed in this degree;

* of the Patriarch Noachite or Prussian Knight Degree, its secret password PELEG, and its penalties;

* of the Knight of the Royal Axe or Prince of Libanus Degree, its secret password NOAH-BEZALEEL-SODONIAS, and its penalties;

* of the Chief of the Tabernacle Degree, its secret password URIELJEHOVAH, and its penalty that I agree the Earth should open up and engulf me up to my neck so I perish, and I also reject the false title of becoming a "Son of Light" in this degree;

* of the Prince of the Tabernacle Degree, and its penalty to be stoned to death and have my body left above ground to rot. I also reject the claimed revelation of the mysteries of the Hebrew faith from the Kabbala, and the occultic and pagan Egyptian, Hindu, Mithraic, Dionysian and Orphic mysteries revealed and worshipped in this degree;

* of the Knight of the Brazen Serpent Degree, its secret password MOSES-JOHANNES, and its penalty to have my heart eaten by venomous serpents. I also reject the claimed revelation of the mysteries of the Islamic faith, I reject the insulting misquotations from the Koran, and the gift of a white turban in this degree;

* of the Prince of Mercy Degree, its secret password GOMEL, JEHOVAH- JACHIN, and its penalty of condemnation and spite by the entire universe. I also reject the claimed revelation of the mysteries of the Christian religion because there are no such mysteries. I reject the Druid trinity of Odin, Frea and Thor revealed in this degree. I also reject the false baptism claimed for the purification of my soul to allow my soul to rejoin the universal soul of Buddhism, as taught in this degree;

* of the Knight Commander of the Temple Degree, its secret password SOLOMON, and its penalty of receiving the severest wrath of Almighty God inflicted upon me. I also reject the claimed revelation of the mysteries of Numerology, Astrology and Alchemy and other occult sciences taught in this degree;

* of the Knight Commander of the Sun, or Prince Adept Degree, its secret password STIBIUM, and its penalties of having my tongue thrust through with a red-hot iron, of my eyes being plucked out, of my senses of smelling and hearing being removed, of having my hands cut off and in that condition to be left for voracious animals to devour me, or executed by lightning from heaven;

* of the Grand Scottish Knight of Saint Andrew or Patriarch of the Crusades Degree, its secret password NEKAMAH-FURLAC, and its penalties; I renounce the oaths taken and the curses and iniquities involved in the Thirtieth Degree of Masonry, the Grand Knight Kadosh and Knight of

the Black and White Eagle. I renounce the secret passwords, STIBIUM ALKABAR, PHARASH-KOH and all their occult meaning.

Sublime Princes of the Royal Secret

I renounce the oaths taken and the curses and iniquities involved in the Thirty-First Degree of Masonry, the Grand Inspector Inquisitor Commander. I renounce all the gods and goddesses of Egypt which are honoured in this degree, including Anubis with the jackal's head, Osiris the Sun god, Isis the sister and wife of Osiris and also the moon goddess. I renounce the Soul of Cheres, the false symbol of immortality, the Chamber of the dead, the false teaching of reincarnation, and the false god, RA, in the name of Jesus Christ. I renounce the oaths taken and the curses and iniquities involved in the Thirty-Second Degree of Masonry, the Sublime Prince of the Royal Secret. I renounce the secret passwords, PHAAL/PHARASH-KOL and all their occultic meaning. I renounce Freemasonry's false trinitarian deity AUM taken from Hinduism, as well as its parts; Brahma the creator, Vishnu the preserver and Shiva the destroyer. I also renounce all the other Hindu deities and beliefs involved in Freemasonry, in the name of Jesus Christ. I renounce the Zoroastrian deity of AHURA-MAZDA, the claimed spirit or source of all light, and the worship with fire, which is an abomination to God, and also the drinking from a human skull in many rites.

Shriners (Applies only in North America)

* I renounce the oaths taken and the curses, iniquities and penalties involved in the Ancient Arabic Order of the Nobles of the Mystic Shrine. I renounce the piercing of the eyeballs with a three-edged blade, the flaying or scouring of the feet, the madness, and the worship of the false god Allah as the god of our fathers. I renounce the hoodwink, the mock hanging, the mock beheading, the mock drinking of the blood of the victim, the mock dog urinating on the initiate, and the offering of urine as a commemoration.

All other degrees

I renounce all the other oaths taken, the rituals of every other degree and the curses and iniquities invoked. These include the Acacia, Allied Degrees, The Red Cross of Constantine, the Order of the Secret Monitor, and the Masonic Royal Order of Scotland. I renounce all other lodges and secret societies including Prince Hall Freemasonry, Grand Orient Lodges, Mormonism, the Ancient Toltec Rite, The Order of Amaranth, the Royal Order of Jesters, the Manchester Unity Order of Oddfellows and its womens' Order of Rebekah lodges, the Royal Antediluvian Order of Buffaloes, Druids, Foresters, the Loyal Order of Orange, including the Purple and Black Lodges within it, Elks, Moose and Eagles Lodges, the Ku Klux Klan, The Grange, the Woodmen of the World, Riders of the Red Robe, the Knights of Pythias, the Order of the Builders, The Rite of Memphiz and Mitzraim, Ordo Templi Orientis (OTO), Aleister Crowley's Palladium Masonry, the Order of the Golden Key, the Order of Desoms, the Mystic Order of the Veiled Prophets of the Enchanted Realm, the women's Orders of the Eastern Star, of the Ladies Oriental Shrine, and of the White Shrine of Jerusalem, the girls' order of the Daughters of the

Eastern Star, the International Orders of Job's Daughters, and of the Rainbow, the boys' Order of De Molay, and the Order of the Constellation of Junior Stars, and every university or college Fraternity or Sorority with Greek and Masonic connections, and their effects on me and all my family.

Lord Jesus, because you want me to be totally free from all occult bondages, I will burn all objects in my possession which connect me with all lodges and occultic organisations, including Masonry, Witchcraft, the Occult and Mormonism, and all regalia, aprons, books of rituals, rings and other jewellery. I renounce the effects these or other objects of Freemasonry, including the compass and the square, have had on me or my family, and I break all forms of slavery originating from Freemasonry in the name of Jesus Christ.

In the name and authority of Jesus Christ, I break every curse of Freemasonry in my life, including the curses of barrenness, sickness, Arthritic and other muscular and joint infirmities, mind-blinding and poverty, and I rebuke every evil spirit which empowered these curses.

I also renounce, cut off and dissolve in the blood of Jesus Christ every ungodly Soul-Tie I or my ancestors have created with other lodge members or participants in occultic groups and actions, and I ask you to send out ministering angels to gather together all portions of my fragmented soul, to free them from all bondages and to wash them clean in the Blood of Jesus Christ, and then to restore them to wholeness to their rightful place within me. I also ask that You remove from me any parts of any other person's soul which has been deposited within my humanity. Thank you Lord for restoring my soul and sanctifying my spirit.

I renounce and rebuke every evil spirit associated with Freemasonry, Witchcraft, the Occult and all other sins and iniquities. Lord Jesus, I ask you to now set me free from all spiritual and other bondages, in accordance with the many promises of the Bible. In the name of the Lord Jesus Christ, I now take the delegated authority given to me and bind every spirit of sickness, infirmity, curse, affliction, addiction, disease or allergy associated with these sins I have confessed and renounced, including every spirit empowering all iniquities inherited from my family.

I exercise the delegated authority from the Risen Lord Jesus Christ over all lower levels of evil spirits and demons which have been assigned to me, and I command that all such demonic beings are to be bound up into one, to be separated from every part of my humanity, whether perceived to be in the body or trapped in the dimensions, and they are not permitted to transfer power to any other spirits or to call for reinforcements.

I command, in the name of Jesus Christ, for every evil spirit to leave me now, touching or harming no-one, and go to the dry place appointed for you by the Lord Jesus Christ, never to return to me or my family, and I command that you now take all your memories, roots, scars, works, nests and habits with you. I surrender to God's Holy Spirit and to no other spirit all the places in my life where these sins and iniquities have been.

Holy Spirit, I ask that you show me anything else which I need to do or to pray so that I and my family may be totally free from the consequences of the sins of Freemasonry, Witchcraft, Mormonism and all related Paganism and Occultism.

(Pause, while listening to God, and pray as the Holy Spirit leads you.)

Now, dear Father God, I ask humbly for the blood of Jesus Christ, your Son and my Savior, to cleanse me from all these sins I have confessed and renounced, to cleanse my spirit, my soul, my mind, my emotions and every part of my body which has been affected by these sins, in the name of Jesus Christ. I also command every cell in my body to come into divine order now, and to be healed and made whole as they were designed to by my loving Creator, including restoring all chemical balances and neurological functions, controlling all cancerous cells, reversing all degenerative diseases, and I sever the DNA and RNA of any mental or physical diseases or afflictions that came down through my family blood lines. I also ask to receive the perfect love of God which casts out all fear, in the name of the Lord Jesus Christ.

I ask you, Lord, to fill me with your Holy Spirit now according to the promises in your Word. I take to myself the whole armor of God in accordance with Ephesians Chapter Six, and rejoice in its protection as Jesus surrounds me and fills me with His Holy Spirit. I enthrone you, Lord Jesus, in my heart, for you are my Lord and my Savior, the source of eternal life. Thank you, Father God, for your mercy, your forgiveness and your love, in the name of Jesus Christ, Amen."

Since the above is what needs to be renounced, why would anyone want to join? Copying of this prayer and the Petition are both permitted and encouraged provided reference is made to Book title, Author, Publisher & web address - www.jubileeresources.org.

PETITION FOR WITHDRAWING (Demit)

Lodge No...

Town/City...

Gentlemen:

When initiated into the Entered Apprentice degree, I was induced to swear that, "I will always hele, ever conceal and never reveal any of the secret arts, parts or points of the hidden mysteries of ancient Freemasonry, which have heretofore, may at this time or shall at any future period be communicated to me as such." In my ignorance, and being led line by line, I indulged in the blood oath you required of me.

Now, gentlemen, after having examined the highest documents of the institution of Freemasonry, I have found that the god of Masonry is positively not the God of the Bible. Freemasonry is in no way compatible with the Christian Faith. Being a Christian as I now am, and confessing the Lordship of Jesus Christ as I do, and having learned of the true nature of Freemasonry, I present to you my Petition of Withdrawal.

I renounce my association with and my obligations to the craft of Masonry, without the least equivocation, mental reservation, or self-evasion of mind. For the Word of God says: "Do not be unequally yoked together with unbelievers. For what fellowship has righteousness with lawlessness? And what communion has light with darkness?" (2 Corinthians 6:14).

I have no animosity towards you gentlemen, nor any other man in the Lodge. I trust you did not seek to deceive me deliberately, but the teachings of Freemasonry had deceived us both. I no longer desire any Masonic ritual at my funeral. I request that you formally acknowledge this petition in writing as soon as possible.

Respectfully,

Name...

Address...

Date...